MOUNT
ON THE
COSTA BLANCA

The Pinos Valley with the Bernia Ridge in the background. (Route 7)
Photo: Bob Stansfield

MOUNTAIN WALKS ON THE COSTA BLANCA

by

BOB STANSFIELD

CICERONE PRESS
MILNTHORPE, CUMBRIA

ISBN 1 85284 165 6
A catalogue card for this book is available from the British Library.

ACKNOWLEDGEMENTS AND DEDICATION

These walks represent a selection of the results of six years' exploratory work by the Leaders of the Costa Blanca Mountain Walkers, and I readily acknowledge their help and generosity in allowing me to chronicle their discoveries. I would particularly like to thank the following for their work on the routes enumerated: Bill Assheton (Routes 1,10,11,29), Ted Forrest (5,30), Maurice and Eunice Gibbs (5), George and Betty Goddard (13,27), Roy Hancliff (11), Don Helliwell (23), Peter Reason (9,15,18,20), Eric Taylor (21). For the Costa Blanca Way my thanks are due to Bill Assheton, Chris Batnick, Gladys Brettell, Vicky Carter, Betty and George Goddard, Jim Johnson, Roger Massingham and Bruno, Peter and Joanna Reason, Vincent and Elena Schultz, Roy Sharman and Eric Taylor. Other members of the Group, who have assisted me are far too legion to mention individually here, but may rest assured that their contribution is greatly appreciated.

Roger Massingham, local mountaineer, journalist and author, has been of inestimable help, using his skills and fluent Spanish to gain information, when my limited linguistic skills proved inadequate.

My dear wife Kathy, for more years than we both care to remember, has been my most constant mountain companion. She held the rope firm when I slipped on soft summer snow, whilst descending the Brévent above Chamonix, in mist and rain. I was, of course, grateful to her then, and I am no less grateful now for her unstinted collaboration at every stage of the preparation of this guide. Without her help the book would not have been possible.

I take the greatest of pleasure in dedicating this modest volume to her, with love and thanks.

Front Cover: Puig Campana from the start of Route 30. Photo: B.Evans

CONTENTS

ADVICE TO READERS

Readers are advised that whilst every effort is taken by the author to ensure the accuracy of this guidebook, changes can occur which may affect the contents. A book of this nature with detailed descriptions and detailed maps is more prone to change than a more general guide. New fences appear, waymarking alters, there may be new buildings or eradication of old buildings. It is advisable to check locally on transport, accommodation, shops etc. but even rights of way can be altered, paths can be eradicated by landslip, forest clearances or changes of ownership. The publisher would welcome notes of any such changes.

PART 1:

Introduction

When I commenced my exploration of these mountains of Las Marinas, I started a new mountain log-book which I called *The Fragrant Fells*. I hope that readers will agree that the title of this book is both literal and apt. Wherever you walk in these beautiful mountains of the Levant, you will brush aside, or crush beneath your boots, a great variety of fragrant herbs, the like of which you would normally be buying in small packets, at Sainsbury's or Tesco's. How often has a soft warm breeze wafted a new, tantalising scent across my track, the source of which I have often had difficulty in tracing.

These are truly the mountains of my old age. In my more youthful years, only the Alps seemed to matter, except, of course, for my beloved Lake District, and other British hills. Spain never called, mainly because it didn't seem to have any Alpine tradition, or famous mountain guides to inspire the young climber with their memoirs, nor was there anyone like Gaston Rébuffat to fire the imagination with magnificent photographs.

When, in later years, I did eventually discover the mountains of Las Marinas, it was love at first sight, and they have filled my declining years with a joy which equals, if not surpasses, the fading memories of those heady days on the Aonach Eagach, the Black Cuillin, Striding Edge, Crib Coch, Dow Crag and the Milestone Buttress, and even our modest Alpine tours.

If I can inspire and help others to share and appreciate these wonderful and neglected mountains of Las Marinas, I shall be more than content. To all who use this Guide, I wish many happy mountain days, which I hope they will treasure always, as I do.

Bob Stansfield
Calpe, January 1995

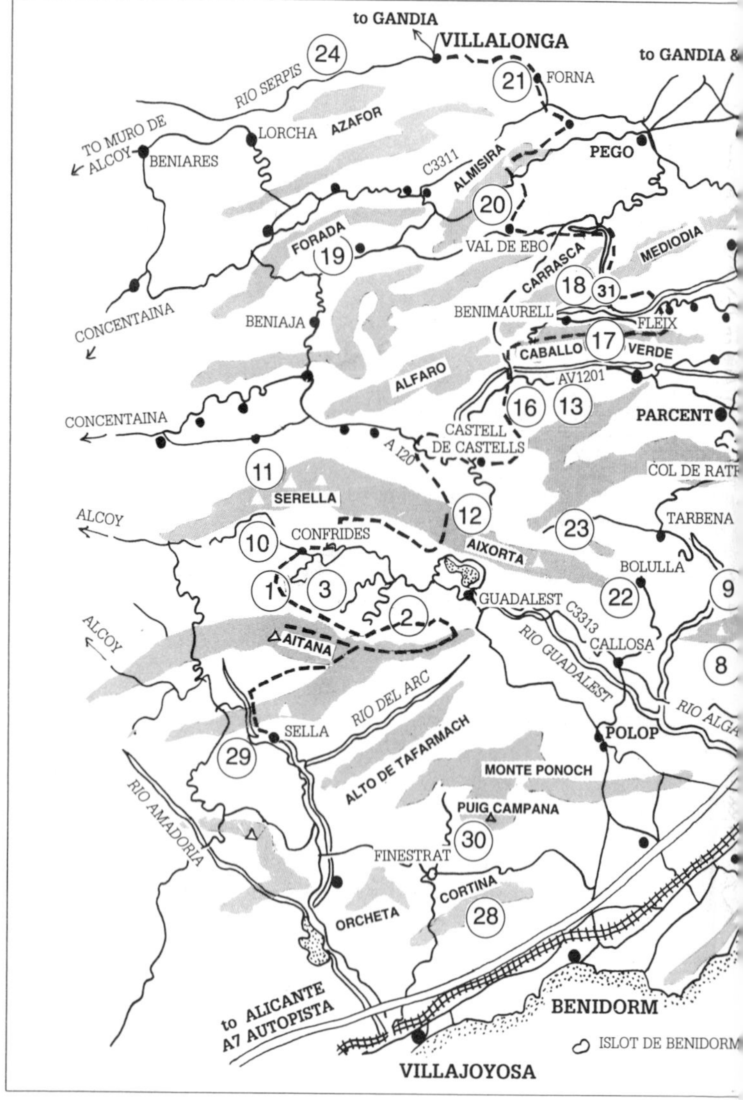
to GANDIA
VILLALONGA
to GANDIA &
FORNA
RIO SERPIS
TO MURO DE ALCOY
BENIARES
LORCHA
AZAFOR
C3311
ALMISIRA
PEGO
FORADA
VAL DE EBO
CARRASCA
MEDIODIA
CONCENTAINA
BENIAJA
BENIMAURELL
FLEIX
CABALLO VERDE
ALFARO
AV1201
PARCENT
CONCENTAINA
CASTELL DE CASTELLS
A 120
COL DE RAT
SERELLA
ALCOY
TARBENA
CONFRIDES
AIXORTA
BOLULLA
GUADALEST
C3313
ALCOY
AITANA
CALLOSA
RIO GUADALEST
RIO DEL ARC
RIO ALGA
SELLA
POLOP
ALTO DE TAFARMACH
MONTE PONOCH
RIO AMADORIA
PUIG CAMPANA
FINESTRAT
CORTINA
ORCHETA
to ALICANTE
A7 AUTOPISTA
BENIDORM
ISLOT DE BENIDORM
VILLAJOYOSA

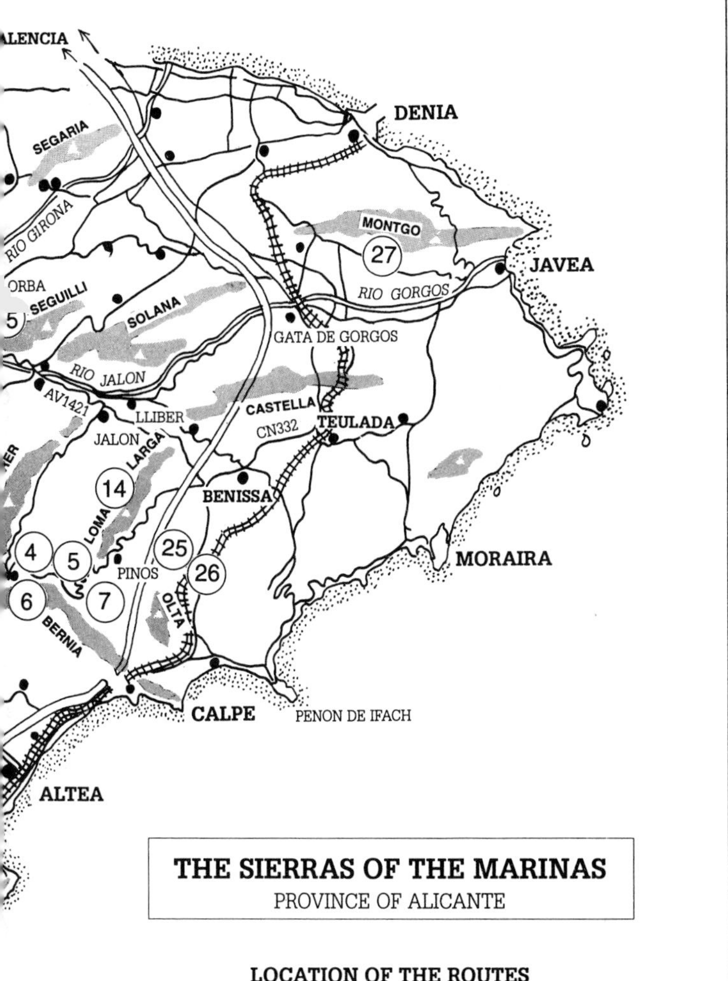

THE SIERRAS OF THE MARINAS

PROVINCE OF ALICANTE

LOCATION OF THE ROUTES

– – – COSTA BLANCA MOUNTAIN WAY

SOME FIRST THOUGHTS

The objective of this book is to provide a simple, easily understood Guide, in order that both visiting and resident mountain walkers can share the delights of ascending and traversing this most satisfying and picturesque mountain area. There can be nothing more frustrating than to visit a new mountain range bereft of good reliable maps, waymarkings, or local information, or even any interest in walking routes. I defy anyone to extract details about mountain walking from either the Provincial or local Tourist Offices. One of the main reasons for the popularity of the Costa Blanca Mountain Walkers, whose log-books regularly contain the names of over 2000 walkers each season, is the lack of any local information.

This Guide is not offered in any way as a manual for mountain walking. Readers are assumed to have acquired these skills elsewhere. I have, however, included some modest strolls, which are suitable for walkers of any age or ability. I feel that it is also necessary to include such advice as seems appropriate to highlight the differences between walking in these mountains and those of Britain. I have also indicated briefly some of the main differences which a newcomer will find in living, even temporarily, in Spain and I hope that those readers who know Spain well will bear with me in this.

I have, I hope, resisted the temptation to clog up the text with too much general information which is readily available elsewhere and I have confined myself to matters which are relevant to mountain walkers, and which may have been omitted from other books. I include in the Appendix a reading list.

In this text I have endeavoured to keep to Castilian Spanish when recording place names etc. There is, however, a spirited revival of the use of Valenciano (similar to Catalan), the old language of this Province. The surveyors of the new editions of Mapas Militar seem to be amongst the most enthusiastic supporters of the Valencian tongue, and this could cause some confusion to those familiar with the Castilian names of mountain features. If I occasionally lapse unintentionally into Valenciano, I apologise. Appendix A contains a glossary of Valenciano terms for most mountain features, and will, I hope, be useful.

COSTA BLANCA

Alicante is one of the three provinces of Valencia, an ancient kingdom with its own language, customs and flag. Spanish kings, and more recently a dictator have tried hard to prohibit such manifestations of local pride, and until the recent restoration of the monarchy, and the move towards democracy, the language, local costumes and fiestas were prohibited by law. Now, there is a spirited revival, Valencia is a region with autonomy and its own government, and the flag proudly flies alongside the national one. Don't be at all surprised to hear country folk speaking Valenciano or a mixture of both languages, and nearly all notices, including road signs, are in Valenciano.

Spain, like France, has now designated all its coasts in the interest, no doubt, of tourism. The region known as the Levant bordering the Mediterranean includes the Costa Blanca, which includes our province of Alicante, and runs from Denia in the north to Torrevieja in the south. With the exception of Switzerland, Spain is the most mountainous country in Europe, and the Costa Blanca is no exception, with the mountains coming right down to the sea. Luckily, the development of tourism has largely been confined to the coastal strip, where vines and oranges have given way to villas, apartments and the major resort of Benidorm. Inland, however, the countryside remains with one or two exceptions, unspoilt, with the country people still making a living from agriculture. It is not many years ago that Benidorm was a poor fishing village, and women walked barefoot to Callosa de Ensarria to sell fish in the more prosperous inland town.

By far the greatest concentration of mountain scenery is to be found in the north of the Costa, in the district known as Las Marinas, and these are the mountains traversed by the Costa Blanca Mountain Way.

The Costa has excellent communications, and on the coast accommodation is lavish. Inland, there is little call for hotels, and except for the larger towns, accommodation is difficult to find.

The climate is typically Mediterranean, the rain falling mainly in spring and autumn in heavy downpours. This gives us over 300 glorious mountain days, although not everyone will want to be on the hills in the middle of a hot August day when even at 1000m, it can be 98°F (37°C).

THE AREA

The area covered by this Guide comprises mainly two Comarcas (Local Authorities), La Marina Baja and La Marina Alta (lower and higher), in the Province of Alicante, which is roughly the coastal area from Denia in the north, to Villajoyosa in the south. It is easily identifiable, even on the TV weather maps, as a large promontory between Valencia and Alicante.

The ridges and valleys of the mountains radiate roughly from the city of Alcoy, 50km from the coast, like the fingers of a hand. The most northerly valley is that of the Rio Serpis, and is actually in the Comarca of Safor. Next comes the beautiful Val de Gallinera, famous for castles and cherries. Further south, we have the remote Val d'Ebo and the Val d'Alcala, accessible only by negotiating the acute hair-pin bends on the most difficult, but most picturesque road in the area. Then there is the Val Laguart, a lovely unspoilt valley, with a road which leads right to its head, and continues across the Caballo Verde ridge at Col de Garga. The road continues, again with many a hair-pin, down into the next valley, that of the Rio Jalon, probably one of the most attractive valleys for tourists due to the picturesque situation, ringed by high mountains, with the broad lower valley ablaze with the blossom of thousands of almond trees in the spring (February here). It is the only mountain valley which has been granted appellation status for the wines it produces. Further south, another tortuous mountain road negotiates the side of the Pinos Valley, to reach the high plateau of the Bernia. The next valley, that of the Rios Guadalest and Algar, is without doubt the most popular with tourists in general, and the road has been improved to accommodate the many coaches which bring them daily from Benidorm. Despite this the valley remains unspoilt and, set amongst the highest peaks of the region, with the added attraction of the only large stretch of open water, the Embalse de Guadalest justifies its reputation as the most beautiful of valleys. The final valley is that of the Rio Sella, which leads inland from Villajoyosa to cross the Aitana ridge at Paso de Tudons.

The Mountains

It is a mistake to classify a mountain solely by its height - its form is much more important. Our mountains, though modest in height average 1000m or 3300ft. Some, however, reach 1558m or 5000ft. They all have the true characteristics of a mountain - rocky summits, sheer crags, deep gullies and ravines, exciting ridges and pinnacles, and, above all, magnificent views. In addition they have the distinct advantage of accessibility with good approaches by road to the high plateaux or passes, and can all be climbed comfortably in a day, many in a few hours. No need here for cable-cars, mountain huts, or a long walk in, before you can even set foot on the mountain.

Geology

"The Alpine structures of Southern Spain, south of the MESETA, are divided into three units of BETICS (sensu stricto), SUB-BETICS and PRE-BETICS" (C.B.Mosley, *Field Guide to the Costa Blanca).*

To an old mountaineer, ignorant of the finer points of geology, this means limestone with some nostalgic intrusions of gabbro. The limestone, a sedimentary rock, is easily eroded by the chemical action of the rain, and rivers soon disappear underground, forming a network of shafts and caverns, beloved of the potholer. There are many areas of limestone pavement, with their fissures (grykes), which make for difficult walking. Much of the rock is friable, and on some of the ridges "jug handles" are liable to come away in your hand. Despite this, there are a lot of difficult climbs put up on great walls of solid rock, particularly on Puig Campana, Peñon d'Ifach, Toix and Altea Hills, the Sella area and Monte Ponoch.

ACCOMMODATION

On the coast there is plenty of accommodation to be found of every description. Hotels, hostels and apartments abound. There are also casas de Huespedes (boarding houses), pensiones (guest houses), fondas (inns) and casas de labranzas (farm houses) to be had, and the Provincial Tourist Board (Patronata Provincial de Turismo), Esplanada de Espana, 2 Alicante, will supply a list of accommodation. However, much of the known inland accommodation is not included, even some well-known hostales. It could be that this is the countryman's distrust of authority, but you must take this into account when planning the walk. Details of reliable (commercial) accommodation is given in this Guide, but hospitality can be found, however rudimentary, even in the remote villages.

Package Holidays

These are very good value, especially if you take a "special offer", which allows the tour operator to choose your hotel and resort within the Costa Blanca.

Hotels

Benidorm has more hotel beds than any other resort in Europe, so it is more than likely to be offered by your travel agent. There are also good hotels at all other resorts, and an excellent parador (state-run luxury hotel) in Javea. Alongside the CN332, at Gata le Gorgos, Oliva, Vergel, and Calpe are motels.

Apartments

There are hundreds of these at the main resorts, and are extremely popular with the Spaniards as well as other nationalities. Self-catering is not a problem, due to the relatively cheap menus available in bars and restaurants.

Villas

Most agents can supply a list of villas for rent, to suit individual needs, and most include the use of a private swimming pool. These are very good value, especially for a large party.

Youth Hostels

Youth Hostel Aubergue La Marina, next to La Comita Campsite, first turning right leaving Moraira towards Calpe. Director Amparo Franqueza, accommodation for 130 in 2, 4, 6 bedrooms. Usual activities including mountaineering (opened September 1994).

Accommodation Inland

Benimantell Pension El Tresellador, at Font Moli, 12 beds (no tel.)

Castell de Castells Pension Castells, Calle San Vincente 18 (551 82 54). Acc. for 8 (English)

Cocentaina Hotel Oden **, Av. Pio XII (main road) (559 12 12). Lots of good accommodation but can be monopolised mid-week by business customers

Cuatroretondeta Fonda Els Fraires, Calle Valencia (551 12 34) Acc. for 8 (English)

Confrides Fonda El Pirineo (main road), newly extended and improved. (558 58 58) 7+ rooms

Fachega Bar Avenida (main road) 5 rooms (551 80 07)

Lliber Hostal Sendas, on Gata road (no tel.) 6 rooms (English)

Mura de Alcoy Pension Copacabana. Av. de Alcoy (96) (553 09 02) 20 rooms

Orba Hostal Quixote, Main Sqr 4 rooms

Pego Hostal Reig, Calle St. Miguel 107-9, (96) (55 15 40) 8 rooms

Relliu (nr Sella) Sandra O'Donaghue (English), Carrer Alcoi 48 (685 61 11) 2 rooms

Where To Stay

This is very much an individual choice depending on the area in which you intend to walk, but Calpe is considered to be the central point on the coast.

From Calpe, in 15min, you can be across the Pass of the Windmills, ready to start your exploration of the beautiful Jalon Valley.

In 30min, you can enter the Val Laguart, which will take you high into the mountains, or explore the Pinos Valley, which will take you to the high plateau of the Sierre Bernia, or go south to the thriving inland town of Callosa d'Ensarria, through extensive groves of citrus fruits. From Callosa d'Ensarria, you have to decide whether to visit the Algar Valley with its attractive waterfalls, or to head into the Guadalest Valley, without doubt the most beautiful and picturesque valley of them all.

In 45min, you can be in the interesting town of Pego, ready to explore the unspoilt valley of the Gallinera, with its four castles, six typical Spanish villages, all with Moorish names and, at the head of the valley, lies the beautiful Barranca Encantada (Enchanted Valley).

Just a kilometre before you reach Pego, you might be tempted to turn off with the signs for Val d'Ebo, and climb, for 9km on the steepest, most dramatic, but definitely the most scenic road on the Costa (count the alpine bends, if you can drag your eyes away from the views).

Going south, in one hour you can be in Finestrat, a beautiful village, built on top of high cliffs, with casas colgadas (hanging houses) on the south side, pretty Hermita, set in beautiful gardens, on the highest point, and an eccentric old pianist, who has painted musical scores all over the front of his house, and plays requests in seven languages! From here, you get fantastic views of Alicante's second-highest mountain. Puig Campana. In a further 15min, you can be in the mountain village of Sella.

All these times refer to leisurely driving on provincial roads. For those in a hurry, and with unlimited funds, the A7 autopista will reduce the times given considerably.

This itinerary from Calpe may be of some use in deciding where to stay on the Costa Blanca, but wherever you stay on the coast, you will have easy access to the mountains.

COMMUNICATIONS

By Air

There is an international airport at Valencia, which is sometime used by those visiting the north of the Costa Blanca, but by far the most popular is the one at Alicante, El Altet, which is much used by package tour operators. There are taxis (rather expensive) and a bus service to Alicante Bus Station from the airport. All tour operators provide coach transport from the airport, and hire cars are available here, but it is better to hire your car in advance.

By Road

The main trunk road, CN332, runs down the coast, giving access to all the resorts. Only Benidorm, however, is so far by-passed, so at peak times there can be delays in passing through the towns.

The A7 autopista (motorway) is superb except for the fact that you have to pay rather dearly for this service and, as a result of this toll charge, you will find it uncrowded, even in the height of summer.

Minor roads may be narrow by British standards, but have an excellent surface. Caminos rural, even narrower, will take you high into the mountains, and usually have a good surface. Forestry roads give access, even to the summit of some mountains, make excellent footpaths, but are only really suitable for four-wheel drive vehicles, due to the variable surface, steep gradients and the tendency to disappear after a storm.

Bus Services

The service from Alicante city is extensive, and operated by Alcoyana.

Ubesa (Union Benissa) operate a service from Alicante to Valencia, with links to other towns along the route. Benidorm has a municipal service, including a service in the tourist season to Algar and Guadalest. Other resorts along the coast have a limited service solely to satisfy local needs.

The bus service to mountain villages is either non-existent or extremely poor, and this means of transport is virtually useless for those who wish to engage in mountain walking.

Information from Central Bus Station, Plaza de Seneca, Alicante (522 0700).

Trains

Alicante has main-line connections with the rest of Spain and Europe. The main line runs inland to Valencia via Alcoy.

El Trenet, a narrow-gauge, single-track railway owned by the Provincial Government of Alicante runs daily services from Alicante to Denia. This line is extremely picturesque, especially between Benidorm and Benissa, where the track runs close to the Corniche. This is not a speedy service, as the train stops at every station, and some trains do not run from Altea to Denia, turning back at Altea del Olla.

With the exception possibly of Calpe, and the halt of Ferrandet, the line is of little use to mountain walkers. From Calpe station, there is a bus service to the base of the Penon d'Ifach, and from Ferrandet, you can step out on to the Olta route. The railway company has commissioned a local mountaineer to survey a number of walks from stations along the route.

Information

R.E.N.F.E. (Main Line), Avenida de Salamanca, Alicante.
F.G.V. (Coastal), Ferrocarriles de la Generalitat, Avenida de Villajoyosa, 2 Alicante.

Taxis

They have a green light fitted to their roof, and operate in the same manner as taxis the world over. Costa Blanca taxis are far more expensive than those in Madrid and Barcelona. They are certainly not an option for the walker wanting a day out in the mountains.

Car Hire

By far the best option for the visiting mountain walker. The smaller cars are very reasonable to hire, sturdy and reliable. They can be booked in Britain, as part of a package, available at the airport or at your hotel. A recommended firm, which has proved reliable and gives good value for money is Premier Car Hire (01279 641040). A current British (EEC) driving licence is generally acceptable. There are even small four-wheel drive vehicles available for hire, but be sure to book in advance for this type of vehicle.

Telephones

Telephone kiosks are not always the best bet. Although they look modern and efficient they can gobble up your small change, and still not connect you. Many a time, you will find that the machine will not operate because the cash container is full. A much more sensible idea is to use the facilities of a Locutorio, a manned kiosk, where the operator will connect your call for you, more expensive but efficient. Most bars have pay phones which always seem to work but the problem here is the noise of the TV. Using the phone in your hotel bedroom may be efficient but the charge can be excessive.

Fax

There are facilities in most hotels, and public facilities (commercial) at all the resorts.

WHEN TO WALK?

The Weather

Residents on the Costa do not, generally, walk in the mountains when it is raining, nor do they do so until the tracks have dried out. This may have British walkers rolling on the floor, but we have 300 plus dry days in our idyllic climate, and to cancel a walk now and again because of the weather is no great loss. I too was brought up to believe that I actually enjoyed getting wet and cold, and that you could not call yourself a true mountaineer until you had had your share of cold British rain down your neck, but I have come to face the reality of life. Walking is better, healthier and more pleasant, not to say safer, in dry weather!

The climate on the mountains closest to the sea is much the same as on the coast, with two exceptions. The coast, under the maritime influence of the Mediterranean, does not suffer from frost at all, whereas inland, and over 300m, you will get regular frosts in winter, and even some snow higher up on Aitana and Serrella. The dry conditions on the coast are not reflected on the mountains, which get a slightly higher rainfall and much mist in winter, when the coast is clear. Note how roses flourish in the mountain gardens. Probably, the only safe prediction as to the weather is that from mid-June to mid-September you will be extremely unlucky if you get a wet day, as drought is the general rule throughout this period. Some time during September/October, the "Gota Fria" arrives. This consists of tempests and torrential rain which occur when the cold moist air stream from the north meets the overheated Mediterranean at the end of the summer. There is very heavy rain for many continuous days, resulting in landslides, floods and general devastation, much to the "surprise" of the local authorities - it has only been happening since the Carthaginians were here! In 1990, I did not notice it happening - we had a lot of rain, but no real "Gota Fria" that year.

Obviously, our 16ins of annual rain has to fall some time, and generally the spring and autumn months can include short periods of wet, unsettled weather. The end of the year, Christmas, then New Year are normally settled and sunny, but generally the unsettled periods are short and clear up quickly (residents complain bitterly if they don't see the sun for three days, and fear that the end of the world is near). The Costa Blanca Mountain Walkers have their season from the beginning of October to the end of May. It is not normal to have to cancel our weekly walks on more than a couple of occasions, but in 1990/1991 we had to cancel four out of fifty-two meets.

Conclusion

The only conditions really to be avoided are torrential rain during the "Gota Fria". For the rest of the year, as long as you avoid unsettled conditions, and are well equipped, walks can be attempted in comfort. All village bars have TV, and a copy of the local paper, *Informacion*, on whose penultimate page is a detailed weather forecast for the day. Be prepared for snow on the ridge tops of Serrella and Aitana (it lay deep for three weeks in January 1991 but the Puerto del Castillo was still open). The Costa does not have the same variation in daylight hours as Britain. At the Summer Solstice (June 22nd), there are sixteen hours of daylight, and at the Winter Solstice (Dec 22nd) ten hours. There is a slightly shorter twilight period than in Britain. Obviously, May-July give the greatest flexibility in planning your walks in daylight; a winter crossing needs very careful planning.

Temperatures

Winter temperatures are not to be compared with those encountered when hill-walking in Britain, but here, on the highest mountains, you do need windproof clothing, as on exposed ridges the wind can bite deeply. The generally sunny conditions give moderate temperatures during the day even in winter but, when the sun goes in the drop in temperature, added to the wind-chill factor, can be dramatic.

From mid-June to early September, the sun is very high in the sky, and temperatures often rise to over 90°F (plus 35°C). On the very few occasions when I have walked at over 1000m in mid-summer, I have not noticed an appreciable drop in temperature due to altitude. Precautions against sunstroke, sunburn, heat exhaustion, and cramps (this last is due to lack of salts) should be taken seriously. Over five seasons of walking, we have found that some of our members suffer from cramps during the first meets in hot conditions during October, after a lazy summer reclining by the swimming pool.

TEMPERATURE AND RAINFALL CHARTS

Temperature (C°)	Max	Min	Average
Jan	16	7	12
Feb	17	6	10
March	20	8	14
April	22	10	15
May	26	13	18
June	29	15	23
July	32	19	26
Aug	32	20	28
Sept	30	18	22
Oct	25	15	18
Nov	21	10	14
Dec	17	7	11

Rainfall

Listed below is the actual rainfall for a year at Calpe. To the north of Denia rain is a lot more reliable and when you reach the Costa Brava even more rain falls. Further south of Alicante is a virtual desert.

1993			
Jan	0mm	July	4mm
Feb	182mm	Aug	2.5mm
March	33mm	Sept	28mm
April	9mm	Oct	60mm
May	16mm	Nov	150mm
June	0mm	Dec	5mm
		Total	489.5mm (19in)

Other Considerations

There are floral treats in store during the whole year in this limestone area (see section on Flora) but probably spring is the most colourful time, from February to late May.

FLORA

The botanist calls our dry, rocky terrain Maquis or Garigue, and the plants which prosper through the long hot summer are tough and spiky. Cross-country walking is, therefore, quite painful, and can be dangerous as the undergrowth can hide fissures.

The vast variety of wild flowers, however, add to the enjoyment of walking, and tends to make botanists of us all. Of course, only those species tolerant of lime flourish, but throughout the year there is always some joy to be discovered by the wayside or clothing the slopes of the mountains. The most impressive display is in the early spring, when the valleys are filled with almond and orange blossom. The slopes become clothed in the pink and white of the Mediterranean heath mixed with the yellow of anthyllis, and later, the broom and gorse. Giant asphodels and fennels, and verbascums, add to the display. Many cultivated species such as phlomis (yellow and purple), antirrhinum and gladioli grow wild here, and underfoot are grape hyacinth, miniature iris, crocus, and an orange tulip (*Tulipa Australis*), and blue flax makes the slopes of Montgo look like a garden. Flora unique to this area include the rusty foxglove (*Digitalis Obscura*), and usually on some of the scree, the tiny rush-leaved daffodil (*Narcissus Requienii*). In the woods the orchids flourish: venus, bee, spider and purple pyramid. On the tops the unusual hedgehog broom (*Erinacea Anthyllis*) is to be admired. Even in July, the beautiful pink centaury (*Centaurium Erythraea*) still blooms along with the red valerian (*Centranthus Ruber*), and on the shady side of a crag or a bridge, blue throatwort (*Trachelium Caeruleum*) flourishes. Rock roses, cistus and potentilla still bloom on the high ground.

Summer heat and lack of water reduces the display, but those plants that have adapted to these conditions continue to bloom. Be prepared to walk on a carpet of herbs, lavender, sages, thyme, rue, curry plant and cotton lavender, which succeed in the high places. In autumn, once the "Gota Fria" is over, there is another surge of bloom, but not as dramatic as in the spring, and shade and moisture-loving plants take advantage of the autumn season to bloom, pennywort, hart's-tongue fern, and violets, for example, which cannot tolerate the rest of the year's harsh conditions. Wild roses and blackthorn bloom again on the high slopes.

FAUNA

The wild flowers are a joy, but the wildlife of this area is a disappointment, due to over-hunting. Spaniards are inveterate hunters, but do not restrict themselves to game. Any wild bird (except the hoopoe, whose killing is said to bring bad luck) is a prime target, and it is said that in certain areas even large dragon-flies are not safe! Birds are still indiscriminately shot for food, netted, using water as a bait or by employing a bird-lime made of boiled wine. The more colourful specimens are trapped, using a captive bird as a lure, then sold in small cages as song birds to end their days on some old lady's town balcony. By feeding and supplying water, I have enticed about 18 species of birds to my garden, but it has taken five years to win their confidence.

The ornithologist needs luck and patience, but there are eagles to be seen, most harriers, many warblers, and, on the crags, choughs, but, quite naturally, they avoid man like the plague. The most colourful birds, hoopoe, roller and bee-eater, are not mountain birds, but may be seen in the valleys. Such pheasant and partridge which have escaped the gun may also be seen. There is, however, compensation for the keen twitcher in the wetlands of La Albufera and the Marjal Mayor near the coast.

Wild boar, foxes, hares and rabbits still roam the high places, but are rarely seen. A friend, alone on Caballo Verde Ridge, swears that he was visited by a lynx (a protected species), but we all annoy him by insisting that it was only a civet. Lizards and snakes are common in summer, and the dear little geckos come out at night to hunt mosquitoes, moths, etc. Toads (*Bufo Bufo Sapo Comun*) the size of your hand frequent the damp places of the Fuentes and wash-houses.

Flocks of sheep and goats are to be seen grazing, under the watchful eye of the pastor (shepherd), with his motley collection of dogs, and in some valleys, where there is reliable water (like the Val de Infierno) bulls are grazed, always, thankfully, supervised by a herdsman.

The ancient, abandoned Salinas (salt pans) under Penon d'Ifach at Calpe are to be designated a Natural Park. The Salinas attract a great variety of waders and water birds including the greater flamingo, which now winters here in flocks exceeding 100 birds.

NASTIES

The only poisonous snakes found in Spain are the vipers, and of the three species, only one, Vipera La Tast (*Vibora Hocicuda*), is found in our region. It is very easy to recognise, with a triangular head, yellow-coloured, with a wavy line down the spine, and dots on each flank. It can grow to 73cm, but more normally measures 60cm. It avoids man, but, as in Britain, it may be found basking on a rock. The bite of a viper needs urgent medical attention. I have never seen a scorpion on the mountains, but then I do not disturb their habitat by poking in crevices or lifting stones. Again, their sting needs prompt medical aid.

During the last six years Costa Blanca Mountain Walkers have taken over 9000 walkers into the mountains without meeting any snakes. Towards the end of our sixth season, a member, sitting on a wall enjoying his lunch, was bitten by a viper which had mistaken his trouser leg for a suitable hiding place. The snake escaped but our member was very ill for over a week. He offers the following advice.

1. Remember that snakes are very active in warm weather especially the middle of the day.
2. Be careful where you sit down. Do not move rocks (scorpions like the shade too) and remember that snakes live in walls.
3. Wear breeches, gaiters or just tuck your pants into your socks. You cannot blame a snake for mistaking your trouser leg for a suitable bolt hole.
4. Treat all snake bites as poisonous and get medical aid as soon as possible. Even non-poisonous snake bites could cause problems.

Bees

These creatures are not, of course, nasties, until one stings you. You will find that the farmers move their small, wooden hives about the mountains to take advantage of the nectar which is available all the year round. The only time I have been stung was when I crossed the bee's "flight path" which no doubt led to a bountiful supply of goodies. The only reason I was stung was because I stopped to try to extricate one which had got tangled in the few hairs I still possess. The best advice is, of course, to leave them well alone, to continue making their delicious honey, keep moving and carry some hydrocortisone.

The processional caterpillar (*Thaumet Opea Pitycampa*) is a menace in pine forests. This creature spins its nest in the pine trees, which defoliates the tree, and can kill small saplings. In the spring they form a chain to find a hole in the ground in which to pupate. Processions 2m long are not unusual. Every part of this creature is poisonous, especially the hairs which disintegrate to form a noxious powder, which causes severe skin rashes. Having unintentionally slept with two of these creatures, I cannot advocate too strongly that you shake out clothing and bedding. The most effective antidote for the rash is vinegar, although olive oil and lemon juice are also recommended. Hydrocortisone simply did not work in my case.

WAYMARKINGS

Where there could be confusion on a route, I have always preferred to build a cairn; only where it cannot be avoided do I desecrate the countryside with a paint marker. But do not confuse these markers with the boundary marks made by surveyors, which generally include a number and ⊙. When I first explored these mountains, I discovered lots of small metal crosses, and was much impressed by the religious devotion of the local people. I now know that they originally marked private hunting areas, and the notices on them had been blasted off by poachers!

Further north, in Valencia, the Centro Excursionistas de Valencia is at present producing Guides, and waymarking long-distance footpaths (Senders de Gran Recorregut) and marking them in the alpine fashion (red and white). I fear that it may be many years before they extend their activities to this area.

A local climbing group (Grupo de Montana Altea) has signposted and marked mountain routes on the Bernia, using the same system, but in yellow and white.

CAMPING

There are plenty of campsites on the coast, but none in the mountains so far. In 1994 EEC money will be available to improve employment and facilities in mountain villages and at least one, Val de Gallinera, has started work on a campsite in anticipation of a grant. A list of campsites will be provided by the Provincial Tourist Board, and general information is available from

Agrupacion Nacional de Camping de Espana,
Duque de Medinaceli 2,
Madrid.

Oficina de Turismo Tourist - Info
Explanada de España 2
03002 Alicante (Tel: 521 22 85 & 520 00 00

Oficinas Municipales de InformacionTuristica
Avda. Europa,
03500 Benidorm (Tel: 586 00 95)

Oficinas Municipales de InformacionTuristica
Avda Ejércitos Españoies 66
03710 Calpe

In England a list of camp sites and information is available from

Spanish National Tourist Office,
57-58 St James's Court,
London SW1 (Tel: 0171 499 0901)

There is no need for a Camping Carnet in Spain. Camping Libre, or camping off-site, is popular with the Spaniards. The advice of the Tourist Board is to ask the Ayuntamiento (Town Hall) in the villages for permission and advice. Camping Libre may be restricted in certain areas which are vulnerable to forest fires.

There is to be a municipal camping site in the Val de Gallinera near to the Sports Centre and swimming pool.

Water

In this area, all public water supplies are reliable and drinkable. In the mountains, there is normally no surface water, and the streams, running underground, are not subject to pollution. There is hardly any use of chemical fertilisers. Wherever there is an old finca, there will be a well, but unless there is evidence of recent use, I would treat it with caution. If in doubt, use sterilising tablets as a safeguard.

RIGHTS OF WAY

The Spanish Law of Trespass would seem to be basically the reverse of the English Common Law, where there is no general right of access to land, even common land, without Statutory or Common Law rights. I am advised that in Spain you may wander at will, providing that you obey a few sensible rules. You should not commit damage, hunt, light fires, etc. and you should not enter private land by climbing walls or fences and, where land is plainly private or the owner has given notice of privacy, you should respect his wishes. Many unsurfaced roads can be chained with a notice "Camino Privato or Particular", but these notices, are to restrict access by motor vehicles and do not normally affect walkers. In addition the Spanish Civil Codes give many absolute rights of access which can only be removed by Statute. These include all riverbanks, lakes and the coast, to the top of mountains and to historical sites, castles, ermitas, sanctuaries and springs and wells. In all my wanderings I have never encountered any problems from landowners, only help, advice and, sometimes, refreshment. How unlike my experience working for the R.A. in Suffolk. Long may this happy state of affairs continue.

CLOTHING AND EQUIPMENT

It is assumed that people walking the Way are experienced in mountain walking, hence this section can be kept short. Thankfully, we do not need very heavy clothing but do make sure that especially in winter you have reserves of warm clothing, including a windproof anorak and trousers. I do not advocate shorts in our mountains as they do not protect you from the spiky vegetation, nor do they conserve core heat in an emergency. If walking in summer, always have a long-sleeved shirt and a hat, and carry barrier cream to protect you from the sun. You also need lots of water and some salt tablets. Any comfortable ankle boot with a good cleated sole will suffice.

EMERGENCIES AND MEDICAL CARE

It is assumed that at least one member of the party has basic first aid training, and that each member has a small simple first aid kit for their own use.

There is no volunteer mountain rescue organisation in Valencia; each incident is dealt with on an "ad hoc" basis by the Guardia Civil (522 11 00), who will organise the rescue in conjunction with the Cruz Roja (Red Cross) which is organised on a local basis, and manned by young conscientious objectors, as an alternative to doing Military Service. There is no official ambulance service either, and private ambulances are expensive. In addition, the Guardia Civil or the Cruz Roja will probably make a charge for their services, especially if a helicopter has to be brought in. It is, therefore, essential that adequate medical insurance cover is taken out.

Most large towns now have Insalud (National Health) Medical Centres, which are staffed 24 hours a day. At Denia and Villajoyosa there are excellent hospitals with full facilities. Denia hospital is on the southern edge of the town (under Montgo mountain), and the one at Villajoyosa is on the northern outskirts on the CN332. Both are well signposted.

Membership of the Federacion Espanola De Deportes De Montana y Escalada, Calle Alberto Aguilers, 3-4 o, izda, 2815, Madrid, confers the usual services of other mountain organisations, including full medical, recovery, etc. in case of a mountain accident or illness. Annual subscription is 5000pts.

Farmacias (Chemists)
I am told that many pharmacists are doctors who did not pass their finals. Whether this is true or not, I have the highest regard for the Spanish pharmacists, who are most reliable people. Many Spaniards seek their advice, and in the villages they often carry out first aid treatment. Remember however, that in the villages their opening hours are restricted, and even in the towns they close for the "siesta".

At night, on Fiestas and Sundays, there is always a Farmacia Guardia open, but you may have to go to the nearest large town. Information may be obtained from the local police or posted on the pharmacy shops.

FOOD AND DRINK

These days there is not a lot of difference in shopping in Spain, compared to the UK, as even the smaller shops have adopted self-service, and those who are self-catering need only make a shopping list of the Spanish names, and be able to convert pesetas to their sterling equivalent. I only seek to highlight some of the things that are not available, or difficult to obtain.

Bread
The standard white "barra" is regulated as to size and price by government decree. It is absolutely scrumptious when fresh, but within a short time becomes a lethal weapon. There is a vast variety of other bread, all of which are more expensive.

Pies and Pasties
These are not what they seem, using peas, peppers, and other vegetables, in addition to tuna fish, as a filling.

Fish
The Costa Blanca is awash with every conceivable variety of fish, from

squid to lobsters, to sea bream, swordfish, fresh tuna and salmon. The Spaniards are addicted to the salted and dried cod, always traditionally brought here from Galicia in the north. Today, however, fresh or frozen cod is available at most supermarkets, but fish fingers and frozen packet steaks are hake.

Meat
Everyone says that the Spaniards do not hang their best beef long enough, and there are a lot of amateur butchers, so watch out for bone splinters. Mutton is extremely difficult to locate, and the lamb is slaughtered far too early, with the result that you do not get fine lamb chops or fillets here. Many restaurants, however, will, to order, roast a succulent leg of lamb with rosemary for you.

Pork, on the other hand, in any form, is absolutely delicious, as is the veal.

Poultry
Chicken, turkey, and even quail are of exceptionally high quality. Most are corn-fed, and are of a reasonable price.

Bacon
Available in a number of varieties, and of excellent quality.

Eggs
Including quail eggs, they are graded and packed as in the UK, but watch out for those that have already been hard-boiled (cocido). They are of excellent quality.

Sausages, Black Puddings and Tripe
These are all specialities of the region (Jalon has 14 butchers who all specialise in this local produce) but beware, they bear no comparison to the delicacies beloved of north-country folk. With perseverance, I am sure that you will find one of them to your taste, once you have experimented with the red sobrasada sauce, used in some sausages, and the rice, onions, and some unidentified ingredients used in the puddings, many of which are delicious.

Cheese
Whilst Dutch and French cheeses are imported in variety, I have only found one English cheese - good old reliable Cheddar. Spanish cheeses from the north, especially La Mancha (Manchego), a mixture of goat and sheep cheese, are first class.

Fruit and Vegetables
There is a bewildering variety available in the markets and shops, all of excellent quality. The season extends well beyond that in Britain (e.g.,

strawberries from February to July), oranges are available all the year round, and ridiculously cheap. There are many exotic varieties readily available: melons, artichokes, asparagus, avocados, kiwi fruit, figs, dates, and lots of almonds.

For The Homesick Brit

Many large supermarkets are now trying to cater for their foreign customers, at a price. Bisto, Marmite, HP and Lea and Perrins sauce, baked beans, and Argentinian corned beef are normally easily obtainable. In each tourist resort, there is usually one small shop favoured by the British community, where many other British foods are available, including Robertson's marmalades in variety (vastly superior to the Spanish product), pies, sausages, pasties, crumpets and scones, and even, sometimes, Terry's chocolate oranges. British butchers are much appreciated by the ex-pat community, as they do not massacre the beef, and there are quite a few here.

Markets

Spanish markets are an institution to which you can soon become addicted. Whilst village markets are small, intimate affairs, the ones on the coast attract the tourist (bus loads are brought in from Benidorm and other resorts), and have become gigantic affairs. They are a wonderful way to absorb local colour, buy gifts and souvenirs. You are expected to bargain with gypsies and Moroccans, but the Spanish trader will usually stick to his price, whilst being agreeable, sometimes, to give you a discount (descuenta) or round the figure down to the nearest 100 pesetas.

A list of market days and of car boot sales and rastros (flea markets) appears below.

Monday

Callosa d'Ensarria; Denia (general); Elche (in the Plaza de la Fruta, Plaza de Barcelona, and Plaza de San Josep); Santa Pola; La Nucia.

Tuesday

Alicante (fruit and veg); Altea (fruit, veg and general); Benidorm (fruit and veg), Jalon (fruit, veg and general).

Wednesday

Benidorm: Campello; Guadamar del Segura; Ondara; Petrer; Teulada; Polop de la Marina (fruit and veg); Benitachell.

Thursday

Alicante; Jávea; Villajoyosa.

Friday
Alfaz del Pi; Denia (fruit and veg); Finestrat; Gata de Gorgos; Moraira; La Nucia; Torrevieja.

Saturday
Alicante, Benissa; Calpe; Elche (Plaza de Fruta, Plaza de Barcelona and Plaza San Josep); Jalon (mini rastro); Pedreguer; Santa Pola.

Sunday
Benidorm; Elche (craft market) Plaza de Raval; La Nucia; Lliber and Teulada (mini rastro).

Wine

In this bounteous land it is a tradition to make your own wine, and most farmers do so, but mostly only for their own use. Whilst the main wine-growing areas are to the south, near Alicante, which has its own "Denominacion", our area still grows a lot of vines, and there are bodegas (wineries) at Gata le Gorgos, Teulada, Benissa, Denia, Javea and Jalon, the only mountain valley to produce wine commercially.

The land, climate and quality of the vines has meant that from early times this land has been a prolific producer of extremely drinkable wine, which has kept a great many people happy, despite lack of pedigree. The wine is so strong that it has always been in demand to boost other more anaemic brews. Unfortunately many bars and restaurants take little care of their wines, and this affects those whites, and even reds, which have been kept beyond their time. Insist on tasting the wine first as a precaution against being served an old white which has gone off. If in doubt, drink red.

There is now the "Cosejo Regulador de la Denominacion de Origen" which grants "Appelacion" status each year to those wines which reach a certain standard, and there are many excellent wines, of diverse variety, granted this status.

Sherry, Montilla (poor man's sherry) and Cava (not a champagne but most people are fooled), and the local Moscatel, a lovely sweet desert wine, are surely well known outside Spain already.

The "Appelacion" is produced by the Bodega de la Pobre Virgin at Jalon (capacity 1,700,000 litres) where you can join the coachloads of tourists in tasting the wine (degustacion) and purchase some, from the vat, or in the bottle. For the expert, the whites are from Moscatel grapes and the reds and rosados from Gironet. Teulada holds a wine festival in October when you can join in the fun and sample the new vintage.

Most restaurants will supply a very drinkable wine with the menu. Valencian, Alicante, Jumilla and the wines of Murcia are the most popular. More select wines are available on the wine list. In the mountains you often receive a generous jug of home brew, but seldom a good white, due to the fact that there is little call for anything but red by the locals. If Tio Paco's brew proves a little daunting, mix a spritzer by adding a little soda water or lemonade.

Viniculture Made Easy

In a remote valley, leading south from Jalon towards the Bernia Plateau, at Maserof, an Englishman has restored an old finca and derelict vineyards. He will offer you a package of ten vines, which he undertakes to tend, harvest, and make into wine by traditional methods. All you have to do is pay up, and collect your ten bottles, of your own personal wine, each year.

Purchase of the vines also confers membership of The Maserof Club which meets most Sundays for tastings and a paella. You are also welcome at the vendimia where the grapes are trod by the feet of "village maidens".

RESTAURANTS

As might be expected, the restaurants in the towns and on the coast are more sophisticated and expensive, but, even here, there are good inexpensive small restaurants. In addition, there are the ubiquitous Oriental restaurants which are always excellent value. There is even a McDonalds in Benidorm, and take-aways are now quite common (por llevar).

In the mountains, you must generally accept more spartan fare, provided mainly to the taste of the locals, not the tourists. Nevertheless, it is possible to dine cheaply and well in the most unlikely localities. In the mountain bars and restaurants, you can nearly always get salad and pork chops with wine and bread, accompanied by the ever-present "patatas fritas" (chips). *The Marling Menu Master*, published by William and Clare Marling has proved invaluable.

It is useful to know that Gazpacho Andaluz is a cold soup, whilst Gazpacho Manchego is a steaming thick meaty broth, that Paella Valenciano is the one without the sea-food, whilst Paella Alicantino is the one full of the stuff, shells and all, and that Serrano Ham is the one to sole your boots with, and York is the ham which most of us enjoy.

Menu del Dia (Menu of the Day)

One of the good things that Franco decreed was that all restaurants should provide a simple menu consisting of starter, main course, sweet, and bread and wine, for a fixed price. This law has now lapsed, but a great many restaurants still offer a good meal at an attractive price. There are, however, some restaurateurs who cheat. Wine is interpreted to mean a small glass, sweet, simply an orange, and IVA (VAT) not mentioned until you get your bill. These people are in the minority, and are usually non-Spanish.

The Jalon Valley has 30+ excellent restaurants, which cater for tourists' tastes and pockets, and are justifiably popular. Recommended is the Restaurant Los Almendros a short way along the road to Murla and Pego, from Alcalali. The restaurant offers a three-choice menu, changed daily, with gargantuan helpings. They are also generous with the jumilla (house wine), and the waiter will just count the number of people on your table, divide by two, rounding UP in the case of odd numbers. You will get a formidable menu here, no matter how much of a trencherman you are. The bill is surprisingly modest, and the patron and his staff are very pleasant.

A few metres along the Pedreguer road on the by-road to the Ermita is La Solana. This restaurant is a little more up-market, and is run on exactly the same principles, but with a more extensive menu. It is a little more expensive, but is certainly value for money. As you drive from the car park note the signs which indicate the presence of a totally different type of restaurant, Beniarrosa, which is distinguished by being a French restaurant, but identical with the others in its approach to its clients. Here, however, are dishes undreamed of by Spanish chefs, mammoth chicken or beef pies, sizzling fresh from the oven, and the vegetables are out of this world. Price are similar to La Solana.

Weekends and Fiestas

Spaniards seldom entertain at home, even the family, preferring to celebrate special occasions at a favourite restaurant especially one in the country. At weekends and fiestas you will be lucky to get a table unless you book well in advance and sometimes they take over one of the small restaurants for a wedding or first communion. Coach trips from Alicante and Valencia are also common and if you add to this the foreign residents who love taking Sunday lunch out, the weekends and fiestas are best spent at home. When the almond blossom is in bloom, the Jalon restaurants are full every day.

Tipping

Spaniards seldom tip anyone. Foreigners, it seems, are expected to do so according to most guidebooks, and no-one refuses a tip do they?

Only give a very modest one after a good meal with good attentive service.

COUNTRY CODE

(a) Respect all property - if you shelter in an abandoned finca, do no damage and leave no litter
(b) Prevent fires - do not leave glass around, and make sure cigarettes are extinguished.
(c) Leave no litter in the countryside - take it home with you
(d) Do not pick growing fruit - remember it is the farmer's livelihood
(e) Do not uproot or pick wild flowers - take seeds only

Forest Fires

Every summer, many hectares of forest are destroyed by forest fires as it only takes a spark to ignite the tinder-dry scrub. There is no doubt that some fires are caused deliberately, either by arsonists or by the owners in order to gain permission to develop the land. Most, however, are due to carelessness, either by the farmers themselves, a cigarette end thrown from a vehicle, or by the townspeople having a traditional Sunday paella in the country. Campers, probably the most careful people, can suffer when the local government imposes a ban on camping during high fire-risk periods. The mountain behind my house was set on fire in 1988 by a pot-holer who placed his hot lantern on a rosemary bush as he emerged from the entrance to his subterranean exploration.

La Conselleria de Medio Ambiente (Council for the Environment) has laid down new procedures for dealing with forest fires. Especially when the dreaded Poniente wind blows, like a gale, from the west, the Met. Office will update the following gradings for seven areas within Valencia every 48 hours. During alarms traffic will be checked, and restricted in the mountain areas affected. Walking and camping may be banned or restricted by police and Guardia.

Gradings

PREALERTA - All services on stand-by

ALARMA - Mobilisation of all forces at disposal of the Conselleria, the Civil Governor and the Forestry Brigades

ALARMA EXTREMA - Notification of all police, fire, Guardia Civil and Mayors of all towns and villages in area

---

Approach to Confrides Castle from Benifato (Route 3) Photo: Maurice Gibbs

Descending the Aitana ridge looking east to Peña Roc with Val de Taguinaon right and Toix and Peñon Ifach in the far distance (Route 1) *Llona Martin*

Almond blossom in January. Bernia Ridge behind (Routes 4, 6 & 7) *Brian Evans*

DOGS (Notes for Spanish residents)

Dogs merit this special note because of the many problems encountered in Spain. All residents know, of course, that a current inoculation certificate is necessary against rabies, and a colour coded tag must be worn by the dog. Generally, for dogs over 30kg in weight, the owner needs to carry a muzzle. During the hunting season, only licensed hunting dogs can roam at will; others need to be on a lead in the mountains. This makes good sense, as I would hate my dog to be shot in mistake for a fat fox. By the way, the hunting dogs are usually very friendly. They are the descendants of the long-legged creatures depicted on the walls of ancient Egyptian temples. Letting your dog roam is not a very good idea anyway, because of other hazards. The undergrowth hides fissures, pot-holes and abandoned wells, which could prove fatal if a dog falls down them. During the spring, hunters put down poisoned bait to try to get rid of foxes, wild cats, etc., and so protect the game. The law requires that the poison be put out only at dusk, and removed at dawn, but like many Spanish laws it is hardly ever able to be enforced.

In 1991, we had two cases of dogs being poisoned on our walks and the dogs had to be carried off the mountain, as they were paralysed. Thankfully, we managed to get them to a vet in time to save their lives.

There are natural hazards, too, for an inquisitive hound. Both viper and scorpion wounds can cause the death of a dog unless promptly treated by a vet, and the processional caterpillar can also poison a dog. If eaten or taken in the mouth, the swelling can cause asphyxiation. Finally, there is the sand fly, which comes out at night, and whose bite can carry Leishmaniosis, a very dangerous disease. So, if camping, take a pup tent as well!

THE COUNTRYSIDE

One of the main differences between the countryside and that of Britain is the almost total absence of manor houses and stately homes, set in parkland. Throughout its history, Valencia has never been a particularly wealthy province, and the Senorios (feudal landlords, tenants of the king), were usually absentees, preferring to live in their palacios in the cities. There were, however, one or two exceptions: at Alcalali, Penaguilla, Calpe, for example, the remains of fortified palacios can still be seen. Most mountain villages seem to have been left to themselves to scratch a meagre living from a poor soil and a harsh climate. It is remarkable how little the life of the campesino has changed whilst his children go on to become computer analysts, bankers, and public relations advisers, leaving most villages solely occupied by the very young and the very old.

You will find that, many of the villages have strange sounding names, a reminder of the long centuries of Moorish occupation.

Fuentes (Springs)
In ancient times, a good and reliable water supply was essential for survival in this arid region, and the site of a farm or a village depended on the springs issuing from subterranean reservoirs. These village fuentes were well maintained, and usually included a lavadero (wash-house) for the housewives. Surprisingly, many are still in use, and not only by the older ladies. Nearby can sometimes be found the remains of old watermills, especially where a reliable flow of water existed (Bolulla). At Font Moli, above the village of Benimantell, however, the fuente feeds a reservoir which once provided a head of water for the mill. Today, many villages have refurbished their fuentes, embellishing them with ceramics, and providing shade trees, barbecues and picnic sites, much loved by the Spaniards at week-ends and fiestas for holding paella parties. Don't be surprised if you find people filling the boots of their cars with plastic bottles of the spring water. Spaniards and others seem to have a distinct distrust of the public water supply, despite the fact that most coastal resorts have a reliable supply of excellent water.

Irrigation
The regulation and allocation of water to those landowners whose deeds give them the right to irrigation is vested in a committee of landowners in each village. Each farmer is annually allocated a time when he may open the sluice gates, and allow the precious water to flow on to his land. This, if he is unlucky, could be in the middle of the night, nevertheless, at the exact time when his allotted period expires, you may rest assured that his neighbour will be waiting to ensure that the sluice gates are closed, ready for him to get his share of the water. Serious disputes concerning water rights are settled by ancient court, which sits on the steps of the cathedral in Valencia.

When the A150 between Altea la Vieja and Callosa d'Ensarria was widened, it was necessary to reconstruct the water conduits alongside it, and this is a good place for those who wish to study these irrigation systems, which nourish the extensive crops of nispero and citrus fruits. The Moors seem to be credited with the introduction of irrigation during their occupation of the area.

The Huerta
This means, literally, irrigated land, used for vegetables. Huerto means

an orchard of citrus fruit, and, where the land levels out on the coastal plain, vast areas of rich soil have been irrigated all along the coast of Valencia, diverting the water of the rivers by means of pumps and irrigation channels since Moorish times. The huerta inland from Denia is particularly interesting. Rising from the vast sea of orange and lemon trees the tall chimneys of the old steam pumping stations can still be seen. Further north, near Sagra, can be found an old Moorish water mill, still in reasonable condition.

Fincas And Casitas

The ruins of these farms and cottages are to be found high in the mountains, and show how hard these farmers had to work to wrest a living from this harsh land. You will hardly find any dressed wood, except perhaps, the door. All beams and lintels are rough-hewn. Windows are usually small and unglazed, and generally only on the north side. Roofs were lined with bamboo from the river, and then tiled. The space was then filled with almond shells to provide insulation; sometimes the traditional Valencian arches between the beams are plastered. Not far from the back door you will find the housewife's beehive-shaped oven, which was heated with brushwood until a sufficient temperature had been reached then sealed with a stone. The nearby well, with its lavadero, and troughs for the animals, completed the facilities available.

Not all these remote fincas were occupied the whole year. Some, like the old village under the crags of Bolulla Castle, were used as shelters when the herdsmen and shepherds took their animals to summer pasture. Others were used by the family when it was necessary to work on the land. Today, with the advantage of motor transport, the land is cultivated on a daily basis, with the farmer living in his village house.

Riu-Raus

This is a distinctive type of architecture, to be found only where the Muscatel grape is cultivated for the manufacture of raisins. They are long, arched porches along the wall of a single-storey building, and are so attractive that they have been incorporated in many modern villas. Their purpose, however, is strictly practical, in that the long loggia provides shelter from the weather for the trays of ripening raisins.

Village Bars

Most villages have at least one bar, and it serves as a social centre. Opening hours vary with the demands of customers. .

There is usually a corner reserved for the pensioners of the village, where they can talk and play cards and dominos. The bar will always have some food available, although it may only be an omelette or tapas (snacks), and there are TV, local papers and a telephone. Once open, the bar remains so until the last customer leaves at night. The bar may be the headquarters of the local Hunting Club, or the Palomeros who fly pigeons with coloured markings in competition. The object is for the competing cocks to entice a hen back to the loft, and often a lot of money changes hands in side bets.

Dogs are generally not allowed in the bars.

Village bars help to make a perfect mountain day for me. They are a handy place to rendezvous with your friends, and a pleasant and interesting location to take refreshments, reminisce, and make plans for future expeditions.

One cannot really complain about the inflated prices for refreshment on the coast. Even in some Spanish bars just inland from the coast, there is a sliding scale of charges for drinks, despite the law that charges must be prominently displayed. The lowest price is for family, friends, and favoured customers, the middle price is for normal customers, and those foreigners who are regulars, the highest price is for foreigners, tourists, and anyone the patron takes a dislike to! Normally, country and mountain village bars will give you a friendly welcome, even though they may be curious about you, and like to know what you are doing in their village.

Sadly I have recently noticed a change in attitude amongst a small minority of bar owners, no doubt inspired by tales of a quick fortune to be made by adopting the inflated prices of the coast. They seem to treat all foreigners as eccentric millionaires, who do not know the value of Spanish money, and don't care if they don't get any change. It is not my intention to suggest that you spoil your holiday by haggling over every drink, but it might be prudent to learn a few Spanish phrases to use in the situations outlined above, such as:

Cuanto es?	How much is it?
Es muy caro	It's very expensive
A donde es mi cambio?	Where is my change?
Madre mia, caramba	(shrug shoulders, beat forehead, stamp feet) My goodness, tut-tut, general displeasure
Yo no estoy contento	I am not happy
Vamonos	We are leaving

Village Houses

As might be expected, these are a little grander, with tiled balconies and rejas (grilles) over the windows, a left-over from the Moorish preoccupation of protecting the female members of the family. Note the large double doors, which allowed horses, mules and carts, to be taken through the house to the courtyard at the rear. Even today, in the villages and larger towns, you can still see the ruts in some of the doorsteps, worn by the cartwheels, and the small stone pillars placed on each side of the door arch, to protect the masonry from damage from the cartwheels. The stone used in town and village houses is a coloured limestone called "tosca", and very attractive it is, when carved to form arches and doorways.

Churches

Mountain villages are usually poor, without benefactors, and on the surface, the outside of the churches sometimes seem sadly neglected. There are, however, exceptions, and the beautiful domed church of Jalon has a Grandee of Spain for its benefactress, who, amongst her other titles, is Baroness of Jalon and Lliber. The insides of churches are usually particularly beautiful, but you will, except on Sundays and fiestas, have to seek out the guardian to obtain the key. They are all kept locked, due, no doubt, to the Spanish propensity for burning down churches in time of revolt. The tower of the church at Murla was built on the base of the old Moorish castle. It fell down during a recent storm, killing two elderly ladies.

In addition to the village church, there is usually a sanctuario, or a hermita, dramatically situated on the mountainside above the village.

Spanish village cemeteries are easily identified by an avenue of the tall Mediterranean cypress trees, and normally include a calvary (Stations of the Cross). Some are beautifully decorated with ceramics. The cemeteries are interesting places to study the history of the village, especially the names of the main families. It is traditional to place the dead in brick cubicles built into walls around the cemetery, rather than bury them in the earth. Only the very important families have vaults.

Crops

On the dry land, olives, vines, carobs and almonds prosper, often with a spring catch crop of vegetables sown between the lines of trees. The olives, almonds and carobs are harvested, as they were centuries ago, by spreading a net on the ground, and knocking the fruit down with a long bamboo pole. Green olives are picked first, then cured, a long and tedious process. Most of the olives sold in the shops are the produce of Andalucia, but in mountain restaurants, you will probably be served with a local product.

Ripe purple olives are crushed in an almazara (olive press). The oil extracted is usually for home consumption, or sold in village shops.

Almonds, for which the Jalon valley is rightly famous, are grown in a great number of varieties. The blossom ranges in colour from white to deep purple, and this indicates whether the almond is sweet or bitter, and used either for eating, making turron (nougat), or for extracting oil. There are a number of cooperatives where the farmers can take their crops, and there are crushing plants in Altea, Fleix and Tormos, identified by the great mounds of almond shells in the factory yard. In remote villages, the mobile shelling machine is set up in the village square. You cannot miss it, the noise is ear-shattering.

The carob (locust bean) makes good animal fodder, and is useful for making chocolate. Wherever the Muscatel grape is grown, eg., Calpe, Teulada and the Jalon valley, some of the crop was made into raisins, by scalding with caustic soda, and leaving in the sun on wicker mats to dry. This practice is now only carried on in a few villages, eg., Lliber. The production of raisins gave rise to the distinctive architecture of Riu-Raus (see Fincas and Casitas).

Nature's Bounty

Mountain villagers have always been adept at living off the land. After rainfall, you may see groups of women and children foraging in the ditches by the roadside, seeking wild asparagus and snails. On the high mountains, the men will probably be collecting mushrooms, especially the large brown ones, a much sought-after delicacy.

Livestock

The further inland you go from the coast, the more chance there is that you will see long-legged mules, donkeys, and the lovely miniature shire horses, used by the farmers in cultivating their land. Although most farmers have turned to tractors, the mule and donkey have a distinct advantage when it comes to cultivating narrow terraces, or using the Mozarabic trails.

Cattle, including bulls, are often grazed in some valley bottoms, where there is a reliable water supply, eg., Maserof, Almadich and the Val de Infierno near Isbert's dam. Thankfully, they are always supervised by the vaquero (herdsman).

The mixed flocks of sheep and goats can still be seen grazing under the care of the pastor (shepherd), and his motley collection of dogs, whose purpose is to protect the flock against wolves! The shepherd guides his flock by throwing stones and shouting, but the lead ewe seems to decide where the flock will go, whilst the dogs mill about showing off. The flocks are corralled at night.

Other livestock, pigs, chicken, ducks, rabbits etc. are, it seems, raised in secret by the little old ladies you see returning home with baskets of grass and herbs.

FIESTAS

Be prepared to find the village shop and even the bakery closed on fiesta days. The more local the fiesta, the less likely you are to find supplies, although the village bar will remain open as usual. The Patronal Festival is the most important. Village fiestas are modest, intimate affairs, unlike the more affluent towns where impressive processions, concerts, bull-running and extensive sports pro-grammes are the norm. Valencia was the last province to be reconquered by the Christian kings, so the fiestas of Moors and Christians are impressive sights. The most famous one is in Alcoy, an industrial town some 40km inland, where in 1276 St George is alleged to have appeared to inspire the Christian troops, who then overcame the beseiging Moors led by Al Azraq. Since then they have celebrated their victory over the Moors. The museum has costumes and photographs dating from the nineteenth century. In recent times, the developing coastal resorts have followed this example, and there are spectacular celebrations in Villajoyosa, Benidorm, Altea, Callosa Ensarria, Calpe, Javea, Denia and Pego.

Volta En Carro

In Las Marinas in July each year, there is an unusual expedition through the mountains of old "covered wagons" pulled by teams of mules or horses. Their owners are farmers or businessmen determined to keep up the old traditions, and each night they camp and accept the hospitality of a mountain village for a paella and a fiesta.

Tira Y Arrastre

This is a most unusual sport, a trial of strength, practised by Valencians. Each team of horses and men together pull a weighted cart along the shingle bed of a river in competition with each other. It is reported that it is only the men who need reviving after their exertions; apparently the horses take it in their stride!

El Bous

Bull-running is now not confined to Pamplona, but has been adopted as part of most fiestas. It seems, on the face of it, a harmless sport and an opportunity for the young to show their mettle. Whilst accepting that the Spaniards are not as sensitive as others about animals, this activity often gets out of hand with young people, sometimes the worse for drink, goading the frightened animals with sharp instruments, letting off fireworks and throwing bottles and cans at them. The Civil Governor has regularly threatened local mayors that if his local inspectors (retired matadors!) report any cruelty, he will ban the event in future (but he never does).

Bous a Carre

A street is closed off, stands erected for spectators, and boards behind which a hard-pressed "torero" can hide.

Bous a Mar

The same, except that the event is held on the harbour wall, and refuge taken in the sea.

Bous Embolat

This is often the end of the event, with all lights being extinguished, and the poor animal, with flaming torches fixed to its horns, chased down the street.

Hogueras and Fallas

In Valencia, since the middle ages, carpenters have celebrated the day of St Joseph (19th March), their patron, by spring cleaning their workshops, and burning all the old wood and shavings, including the rough racks on which they hung their outdoor clothes. In later years crude effigies of local personalities were added, and today it has developed into a major art form. A huge industry exists in Valencia to produce giant displays of papier maché sculptures on wooden frames, often with a humorous or political message, as local personalities are mercilessly caricatured. All year round the Filas (clubs) of the various districts of the city work to raise funds so that they can commission the many artisans who will make the giant tableaux. With great festivity, a display of fireworks, and the many bands competing with each other, the whole lot goes up in flames at midnight, as the poor fireman try to prevent the nearby buildings from catching fire. Only one Falla, the one judged to be the best, is saved for display in the museum.

In Alicante, they celebrate the day of their patron St Juan (June) in a similar manner but the displays are called Hogueras, and many of the resorts along the Costa have added the Fallas to their lists of fiestas.

La Pilota Valenciana

This is a Valencian version of the Basque game of handball, but not using a basket, strapped to the hand to give velocity to the ball. There are two versions, Raspat, where the ball is skimmed over the surface of a street, and Llarges, where it is bounded off a high wall. The game is still played in Calle Garcia Ortiz at Calpe every Sunday afternoon, but even small mountain villages have their purpose-built court, recognised by its high, green painted walls set at 90 degrees.

Tourist offices will supply full details of local fiestas, and publish a monthly leaflet for the whole of the province. Details of all local events appear in the three English-language newspapers.

Religious Fiestas

Spaniards observe many more religious holidays than we do in the UK. In addition to the Patronal fiestas of villages and towns the main ones are:

6th January	Epiphany. Known as the Three Kings, when children receive their presents. Normally lasts for a whole week.
March	San Jose, patron saint of carpenters. Burning of Hogueras in Valencia. Wooden and papier maché effigies burned are sometimes 15m high.
March/April	Semana Santa (Holy week). Very important in Spain.
May	Ascension, Pentecost and Corpus Christi.
June	St Juan - burning of Fallas - Alicante and Costa
25th July	San Santiago.
August	Assumption of the Virgin Mary.
November	All Saints.
8th December	Immaculate Conception.
25th December	Christmas Day (one day only).

In addition, the following secular fiestas are held:

1st January	New Year's Day. Traditional to eat one grape for each chime as midnight sounds.
1st May	Labour Day.
9th October	Valencian Day.
12th October	Columbus Day (Dia de la Hispanidad).
6th December	Spanish Constitutional Day.

RELICS OF THE PAST

Castles

Valencia is rich in castles, and there are many ruins in the mountains, not all of them marked on maps. "Castle" is rather a grand name, as some of them were only fortified lookouts. All date from the Moorish occupation and Reconquest in the seventeenth century, and whilst some of them are in reasonable repair (ie. Forna), others are just a few dressed stones or a single wall. Serrella has a cistern which still holds water, and in which mountain toads breed each year.

Eras

Where there is an extensive farmhouse, you will always find a well, an oven, and an era. This last is a flat surface for threshing and crushing cereals, by means of a metre-long tapered stone with a metal rod running through it. The stone was pulled over the grain by man or mule. When I first started walking in the area, most eras had at least one stone, left after the last harvest some hundred years ago. Sadly, most of them have now been taken away as souvenirs.

There is a gigantic era stone at the entrance to the village of Guadalest, and the Ponsoda restaurant on the road from Benimantell to Polop has lined the edge of the car park with them. At the Jami restaurant in Confrides, there is another good specimen, and you will park on what was once the era of an old finca (now the restaurant).

Almazeras

These are the old presses, normally used for crushing olives, but occasionally used for grapes. One or sometimes two conical stones ran in a circular stone trough, and were powered by mule or donkey. The stones were supported by a metal frame and cogwheel, and a good example can be seen at Km 169.7 next to the old venta (inn) on the CN332 at Calpe. The old inn is now a disco. There was another one in working order in the Val de Gallinera, in the remote village of Lombay, but this year, the roof fell in and buried it. The stones, along with millstones and old wine presses, are much sought after to decorate fuentes and glorietas in the villages, eg. Lorcha and Cuatretondeta.

Mozarabic Trails

"Mozarabic" is a term reserved for those Moors who stayed on after the Reconquest, and accepted the Christian religion. (The word "Mudejar" refers to those Christians who were allowed to follow their religion during the Moorish occupation - the Church in Calpe was built during this period.)

The Spaniards use the term "Mozarabic" to describe the narrow stepped trails which cross our mountains, zig-zagging down into the depths of the deepest ravines, and up the other side. They are truly marvels of engineering, with revetments used to support the trail in desperate places. Surprisingly, many of them have withstood the ravages of time, nature, and lack of maintenance. They are best seen in the Val de Laguart, where the Camino de Juvias first descends the sheer sides of the Barranco del Infierno, and then climbs out of the valley on the other side, towards the Val d'Ebo.

Neveras

These are deep cylindrical ice-pits, usually constructed on the northern slopes of the high mountains, for the purpose of making ice from snow. They are normally about 15m deep, and 10m in diameter. The larger ones had supporting stone beams, and a wooden roof which was tiled. Smaller ones were corbelled, built up in steps from bricks and stones, to make a dome. They were mainly used during the seventeenth and eighteenth centuries, and fell into decay with the introduction of refrigeration by electricity.

In winter, the pits were filled with snow, sometimes in sacks, and sometimes layered in straw. During the summer men with mules spent the night at the nevera cutting the ice into blocks, insulating it with straw, and transporting it by mule down the hazardous trails to the villages before the sun rose. Whether it is true or not I do not know, but an old villager in Fachega told me that his father remembered seeing the fires lit by the ice-cutters on the mountain Pla de la Casa, and could describe to me the route taken back to the village down the Barranco del Moro.

There is an excellent example of an arched nevera above Agres on the Moro del Contador, near the Refugio Santiago Reig del Mural, on the way to climb Monte Cabre. Next to the Refugio is a small corbelled nevera, with the roof intact. There are also good examples on the Pena Mulero route and the biggest, deepest and highest is a few metres below the summit of Pla de la Casa.

Salinas (salt pans)

The only place in the area where salt was produced by evaporation are the salinas on the isthmus, under the Peñon d'Ifach at Calpe. Salt was last produced here in 1988, by pumping sea water from a point near the

Queen's Baths (Roman remains) on the Arenal beach. The area of the salinas has now turned into a freshwater lake, and attracts a great many water birds, including the colourful flamingos from the Camargue in France, who winter here. One day, it is hoped that plans to turn the area into a Natural Park may soon materialise. Salt is still produced commercially further south in Torrevieja and Santa Pola.

Mountain Crosses

On a prominent crag above many mountain villages can be found a stone or metal cross, which protects the village, from Moors, lightning and tempests. In 1952, the cross on top of Perereta (826m) above the tiny village of Benimaurell, was restored by the young men of the village, no doubt at the instigation of the old people, who felt they still needed the protection of the old cross, which had disintegrated.

Windmills

Water mills, mentioned in the section 'Springs', needed to be near a reliable source of water. Windmills, which were more numerous, needed the best possible position to tap their power source, the wind. You will find them on any piece of high ground near a village, on the coast (Calpe) and even the top of cliffs (Javea). They are gregarious, like the company of other mills, and on Cabo St Antonio, near Javea, there are over ten of them on the cliff edge. They were used to grind wheat and indicate the amount of cereals which were grown on the narrow terraces in ancient times. Many of the mills, date from pre-Moorish times but today only the ruined towers remain, unused for over 100 years. When in use the mill had a conical cap, which could be rotated to catch the wind, and which accommodated the sails which were sometimes of wood, but more often of canvas. Wooden shafts and gears drove the large grinding stones on the ground floor. Some mills were also used as early lookout towers.

Watch Towers

These round lookouts were built in the sixteenth century on the coast to provide an early warning of raids by pirates. Piracy had always been rife in this part of the Mediterranean, even in the fourteenth century. Raids by ships from Africa and even from the one remaining Moorish kingdom, Granada, were quite common. After the final expulsion of the Moors in 1609, the raids became more frequent and the authorities had to take steps to combat them by building the towers and by providing a fleet of defensive ships. The costal towns were, of course, the most vulnerable to attack. In 1636, the pirates, after pillaging the village of Calpe, took nearly all the population back to Algiers as slaves. They were released many years later, when a ransom had been paid. We even know the names of some of these desperados: Dragut, Barberroja (red beard) and Picelilli Pacha. Moraira has restored its tower on the beach, and one of the many windmills on Cabo St Antonio near Javea, was also used as a lookout.

MAPS AND GUIDES

The official Mapas Militar are at 1:50,000, the nearest thing to our own Ordnance Survey. The detail and printing, however, are far from OS standard, and buying a new edition does not guarantee an updated map. I find that it pays to keep old maps. They are often more reliable as the editor of the series is capricious, to say the least, in removing information from new editions. It also takes a very long time before new roads are shown on the maps and the vast network of forestry and rural roads remains unmarked. Now we have the 1:25,000 M.O.P.U. (Min. of Public Works) maps, still produced by the Institutio Georgrafico Nacional, who produce the Mapas Militar. These maps are still based on the old 1:50,000 grid system, with four sheets to the area covered. The printing is better, and new roads are shown (still not the rural and forestry), but I have on some sheets found important detail missing, which appeared on old smaller-scale maps.

Maps Required For Las Marinas

1:50,000 Mapas Militar

Jativa	29-31	(795)
Alcoy	29-32	(821)
Benisa	30-32	(822)
Villajoyosa	29-33	(847)
Altea	30-33	(848)

1:25,000 M.O.P.U.

796	I Gandia	III Oliva	IV Denia
795	Jativa	Sheet IV (Villalonga)	
822	Benisa	Sheets I, II & III (Orba, Benisa & Tarbena)	
847	Villajoyosa	Sheets II & IV (Relliu & Villajoyosa)	
821	Alcoy	Not yet published	
848	Altea	Not yet published	

Road Maps

These are quite good but are, at times, misleading to say the least. They have the annoying habit of not showing road numbers for Provincial and minor roads, which we mountaineers use an awful lot. And there are glaring mistakes on some, such as showing a dam which failed 20 years ago and the wetlands below Pego as a vast lake. Some roads, which were completed years ago and now have an official number, are shown as mule tracks. I must insist that I offer this information, not to boost the status of OS but to prepare you for using Spanish maps. Some of my friends even dispute the contours and the spot heights on some sheets of Mapas Militar.

Michelin	1:400,000	Central/Eastern Spain 445
Firestone	1:200,000	Costa Blanca T28
M.O.P.U.	1:200,000	Province of Alicante (based on Mapas Militar)

Map Suppliers

Many newsagents and bookshops now display a sign showing that they supply Mapas Militar, but don't get excited - their stock-keeping is atrocious. I list suppliers who are (more or less) reliable.

Altea	Newsagent near Supermarket Pepe Clara, Calle Ingen Munoz, in centre of town
Alicante	Librea International, Altmir 6, near Town Hall
Benidorm	Librier Atlas, Calle Valencia
Calpe	Papeleria Vasquez, Av. Gabriel Miro and 2 other shops
Jalon	The Sweetie Shop, on main road just before you reach the river (English)
Valencia	Papeleria Regolf, Mar2, side street near Cathedral and Zaragoza Gardens
In England	Stanfords 27A Floral Street, London WC2E 9LP The Map Shop, 15 High Street, Upton-upon-Severn, Worcs WR8 OHJ

stock the Military Maps plus smaller scale tourist maps of the area.

Recommended Guidebooks In English

Michelin Guide to Spain
Berlitz Guide to the Costa Blanca

Guide to Costa Blanca - Alicante Tourist Board
Alicante & Costa Blanca Guide - ANAY Touring Publications

Recommended Rock Climbing Guides
Rock climbing Guide to the Peñon d'Ifach by Juan Antonio Andres Martinez, pub. by the author in Spanish, English, French and German, lavishly illustrated in colour, but no written descriptions of the routes.
Costa Blanca Climbs by Chris Craggs, pub. Cicerone Press, excellent Guidebook in the traditional English style and gradings.
One of the most popular rock climbing locations in the area is at Sella. Topo Guides can be purchased at the bar in the village square, or up the valley at a climbers refuge below the crags.

USEFUL READING

Geology
The Geological Field Guide to the Costa Blanca by C.B.Moseley (The Geologists' Association)

Ornithology
Country Life Guide to the birds of Britain and Europe by Bertel Bruun (Country Life)

Botany
Flowers of South-West Europe by Oleg Polunin and B.G.Smythes (Oxford)
Flowers of the Mediterranean by Oleg Polunin and Anthony Huxley (Chatto and Windus)
Wild flowers of Spain (3 booklets) by Clive Innes (Cockatrice)
Wild flowers of Southern Spain by Betty Molesworth Allen (Mirador Books, Malaga, 1993). Covers Andalucia but applicable to Costa Blanca area.

Wildlife
Wildlife in Spain by John Measures (Crowood Press)

General Reading
Iberia by James Michener (Fawcett)
Spain by Jan Morris (Penguin)
As I walked out one midsummer morning by Laurie Lee (Penguin)
The Spaniards by John Hooper (Penguin)
The Spaniard and the Seven Deadly Sins by Fernando Diaz Plaja (Pan)
Culture Shock Spain by Marie L.Grafe (Kupera)
Spain by Dominique Aubler and Manuel Tunon de la Lara (Vista Books Longmans)

Marching Spain by V.S.Prichett (Hogarth Press)
The Face of Spain by Gerald Brenan (Penguin)
Lookout Magazine publishes handy books on many topics relating to living in Spain, from cooking to the law, but most of the guidebooks relate to Andalucia.
The Story of Spain by Mark Williams, however, covers the whole country.

Local English Language Newspapers
Costa Blanca News (Friday)
Weekly Post (Sunday)
The Entertainer (Fridays) available free at supermarkets and some newsagents.

All these publications give details of walks by Costa Blanca Mountain Walkers and other walking groups. The *Weekly Post* also publishes walking guides.

GLOSSARY

The Mapas Militar normally use Castellano as their language, except for some place names which are in the Valenciano language. In recent editions of the maps, however, there is an increasing tendency to replace Castellano with Valenciano, no doubt in sympathy with the revival of this ancient language. This short glossary includes those mountaineering terms which occur most often on maps and in guides.

CASTELLANO	VALENCIANO	ENGLISH
Simas	Avenc	Pot-holes & fissures
Cima/Cumbre	Cim	Summit
Funta/Pico	Punta/Punuxa/Pic	Peak
Pennaco	Penyal	Crag
Montana	Muntanya	Mountain
Collado	Col	Col
Paso/Puerta	Pass/Port	Pass
Castillo	Castell	Castle
Penn/Peñon	Penja/Penyal	Cliff, crag, or mass of rock
Finca	Finca	Country house/ Farm
Hoyo	Forat	Hole
Lomo	Llom	Shoulder
Cordillera/Sierra/ Cadena	Serra	Mountain range

CASTELLANO	VALENCIANO	ENGLISH
Fuente	Font	Fountain or spring
Pozo	Pou	Well
Rio	Riu	River
Arroyo	Rierra	Stream
Cascada	Cascada	Waterfall
Lago	Llac	Lake
Embalse	Embassament	Reservoir
Presa	Presa	Dam
Colina	Tossal	Hill
Alto/Collado	Alt	High Place
Casa	Casa	House
Casa de la Branza	-	Farmhouse
Ruinas	Ruinas	Ruins
Nevera	Nevera	Ice-pit
Bancal	Bancal	Terrace
Valle	Val	Valley
Cauce Seco	Caixer Sec	Dry river-bed
Barranco	Canal	Gully or ravine
Camino	Cami	Road
Senda	Sender	Footpath
Corral	Corral	Cattle pen/small farm or hamlet
Casa de Molino	Moli	Mill

Arc del Atanços
Tarbena Circuit
(See p141)

PART 2:
Walking Routes

INTRODUCTION

These routes originated as hastily scribbled directions to satisfy friends who were experiencing difficulty in finding routes in our mountains. By popular demand, they were produced as simple guide sheets for the use of members of the local walking group. At present there are over 100 routes available, and an additional 30 shorter 'strolls', all surveyed by a dedicated team of leaders with the Costa Blanca Mountain Walkers. Each new season this group leads over 50 day walks into the mountains, over half these being new ones. As a result of all this exploration, it was possible, in 1992, to inaugurate the first Long Distance Walk - the Costa Blanca Mountain Way - 130km from Villalonga in the north to Sella in the south, to mark the celebration of the Group's 5th Anniversary. In 1993, a second long distance route - the 60km Gallinera Way - was published, and two further Long Distance Walks - the Serrella Way and the Aitana Way - are being surveyed. There is, it seems, no limit to the number and variety of walks available, and I hope that the reader will approve this short selection, which is intended to be representative of all the types of walk available, and provide a good introduction to walking on the Costa Blanca.

Weekends And Fiestas

Spain is no different from the rest of Europe and at these times you can expect the countryside, with its narrow roads, to be crowded, especially the picnic spots. Another hazard, which needs to be taken seriously, are the hunters. Spain's hunting seasons vary according to the prey, but generally extend from October to January. Game (rabbits, hares, pheasants, partridge, thrushes etc.) can only be slaughtered on Sundays and Fiestas. Wild boar are no luckier, they may be done to death on Thursdays and Fiestas. This means that the frustrated hunters bang away at everything that moves on the few days when they can use their hunting licences and a prudent mountaineer leaves them to it, unless he wishes to have his head mounted on a hunter's wall as a trophy!

In the text I have endeavoured to keep to Castilian Spanish when recording features or place names in the mountains. The older Mapas Militar always use Castilian. Since the upsurge in the teaching and use of the Valenciano, the old language of this kingdom, based on Catalan, its keenest exponents seem to be the surveyors who produce these maps. All the new editions of Mapas Militar, and the new 1:25,000 edition, use Valenciano exclusively for place names and mountain features, which can make life a little difficult at times.

ROUTE-FINDING

Here, due to the garigue (spiky vegetation), you cannot enjoy true cross-country walking as you can in Britain and the Alps. Here, I am afraid, there is no such thing as walking from peak to peak on a carpet of heather. On the very few occasions when I have been forced to pursue a direct route, I have found it to be time-consuming, wearisome, painful, and sometimes dangerous. The relief felt on reaching a rough but reasonable path is a joy to be savoured after this type of experience, looking back over my route, I have always vowed never to do the same foolish thing again.

All the screes I have found so far will not "run", and progress down them is painful, slow, and dreary with the possible exception of the north scree on Puig Campana (see Route 30).

I wish that I could say that I always studied my maps first when looking for a new route, to find the mule tracks and country roads on the mountain of my choice. What actually happens is that the route is usually spotted from the summit of a neighbouring mountain, encouraged by a good approach on a forestry road, and then we get out the map. Sadly the salient features, so carefully noted, often do not appear on the map. If you know what you are looking for, it is surprising how many new Mozarabic trails you can spot for further exploration. It follows, of course, that however remote the casita, there had to be a mule track to it and also to the terraces so that the farmer could cultivate them, but whether they have survived is another matter. Mule tracks between villages seem to follow the easiest line, along a valley bottom or over a col, and there are still tracks to most of the castles and fuentes. If you are forced to climb terraces, try to look for the access provided for the mule at the end of a section. It may take a little more time, but it is easier. Trails made by hunters are well waymarked by empty cartridge cases and empty tins of seafood (I wonder if fishermen eat tinned rabbit). Most hunters, these days, however, do not go far from their cars, especially now that the forestry roads allow them to take them so high on the mountain.

GRADINGS

Gradings, despite all efforts to be objective, are never entirely successful, and eventually each individual grades a walk subjectively. In my grades, which are based on the capabilities of an ancient mountaineer, I have always erred on the side of caution. I hope that those younger and fitter walkers will not be too disappointed by finishing some of the walks a little earlier than the time given. There will be more time to spend in the local bar.

Timing

I have allowed for occasional short stops but not for longer breaks. Remember that the weather and temperature can considerably extend the time given if you are to enjoy the walk.

Route Categories

A = All good tracks
B = Mainly good tracks, but some rough walking
C = Mainly rough walking

Route Grades

Scramble (Sc)	Rock work below the rock climbing grades
Strenuous (S)	Steep, rough, and a need to be able to get your knee under your chin
Moderate (M)	Good general standard of walking, with reasonable gradients
Easy (E)	Exactly what it says, but remember that it is still a mountain walk
Stroll (St)	A gentle amble of 2-3h in majestic scenery, with a handy restaurant at the end

If two grades are used, the first grade takes priority over the second, ie. Mod/Stren means a moderate walk with some strenuous sections.

LIST OF WALKS

Route	Walk	Grade (Category)	Km	Walking Time (h)	Ascent (m)	Alt. (m)	Start
SIERRA AITANA							
1	Aitana Summit	M (B)	12	4	500	1558	Fuente Partagas
2	Under Peña Mulero	St	8	3	300	1000	Font Moli
3	Confrides Castle	M (B)	7	2.5	300	1100	Loma del Castellet
SIERRA BERNIA							
4	Main Summit via West Ridge	Sc (C)	7	5	480	1129	Bernia
5	East Ridge & Peak	Sc (C)	6	6	560	961	Pinos
6	Fort and Circuit	M (B)	14	4.5	300	1000	Bernia
7	Pinos Valley	M (A)	12	6	300	625	Pinos
8	Peña Severino	M (B)	9	4	330	880	Bernia
9	Paso del Bandoleros	M (C)	7	4	-250	—	Bernia
SIERRA SERRELLA							
10	Summits & Pla de la Casa	S (B)	13	7.75	600	1379	Puerto Ares (Confrides)
11	Agulles de la Serrella	Sc/S	7.5	6	759	1359	Cuatroton-deta
12	Serrella Castle	M (A)	13	3.5	650	1050	Beniarda
VAL DE JALON							
13	Cordilleras de Almadich	M/S	17	5.5	700	800	Benichembla
14	Lloma Larga	M (B)	9	4.5	586	600	Collado de Molinos
15	Orba Castle	M (B)	6	3	100	400	Puerto de Orba
16	Fig Tree Walk to El Forat Negre	E (A)	15	5	486	866	Barranco de Gallistro
VAL DE LAGUART							
17	Caballo Verde Ridge	S (C)	14	5	450	842	Benimaurell
18	Day of 5000 Steps	S (B)	18	6.5	400	750	Benimaurell

Route	Walk	Grade (Category)	Km	Walking Time (h)	Ascent (m)	Alt. (m)	Start
VAL DE GALLINERA							
19	Forada Ridge	M/S	9	6.5	600	902	Benisiva
20	Almisira via Alto de Chap	Sc (B/C)	14	5	457	757	Benirrama
21	Forna to Villalonga	M (B)	10	5	200	375	Forna
VAL DE ALGAR							
22	Bolulla Castle	E (A)	9	4	500	739	Bollulla
23	Tarbena Circuit	M (B)	18	5	600		Val de Alt
OTHER SIERRAS							
24	Lorcha to Villalonga and Rio Serpis Valley	M (A)	20	8	242	510	Lorcha
25	Sierra de Olta	M (C)	10	4.45	500	591	Calpe
26	Dorset Circuit of Sierra de Olta	M (B)	15	4.5	Neg	—	Calpe
27	Montgo from Jesus Pobre	S (B)	12	7.5	593	712	Jesus Pobre
28	Sierras de Cortina	E (A)	7	2.5	170	520	Nr Benidorm
29	Peña Divino and Alto de la Peña Sella	M (B)	13.5	5.5	360	1160	Val Tagarina
30	Puig Campana	S/Sc	14	6	1060	1410	Font Moli Finestrat

31 Barranco del Infierno (by Roger Massingham)

(See also Costa Blanca Way, Stage 2: Val d'Ebo to Fleix)

Sierra Aitana

ROUTE 1: AITANA SUMMIT M(B) 12km 4h

The highest of our province's mountains is no Matterhorn, not even a Puig Campana, but a broad ridge of high ground stretching east to west from Polop to Puerto de Tudons on the Sella to Alcoy road. If it were not for the white radar domes on the Western summit, few people would be able to identify this mountain, I'm sure.

The summit itself is occupied by the military, who also have the easiest ascent, by a road leading off east from the Puerto. Sadly, this road is out of bounds. Our route will approach from the north, by way of the Simas de Partagas - a set of giant fissures which form a line of impressive cliffs above the Guadalest Valley. Whilst this is a moderate walk, most

Summit of Aitana from the north (Route 1) Photo: Llona Martin

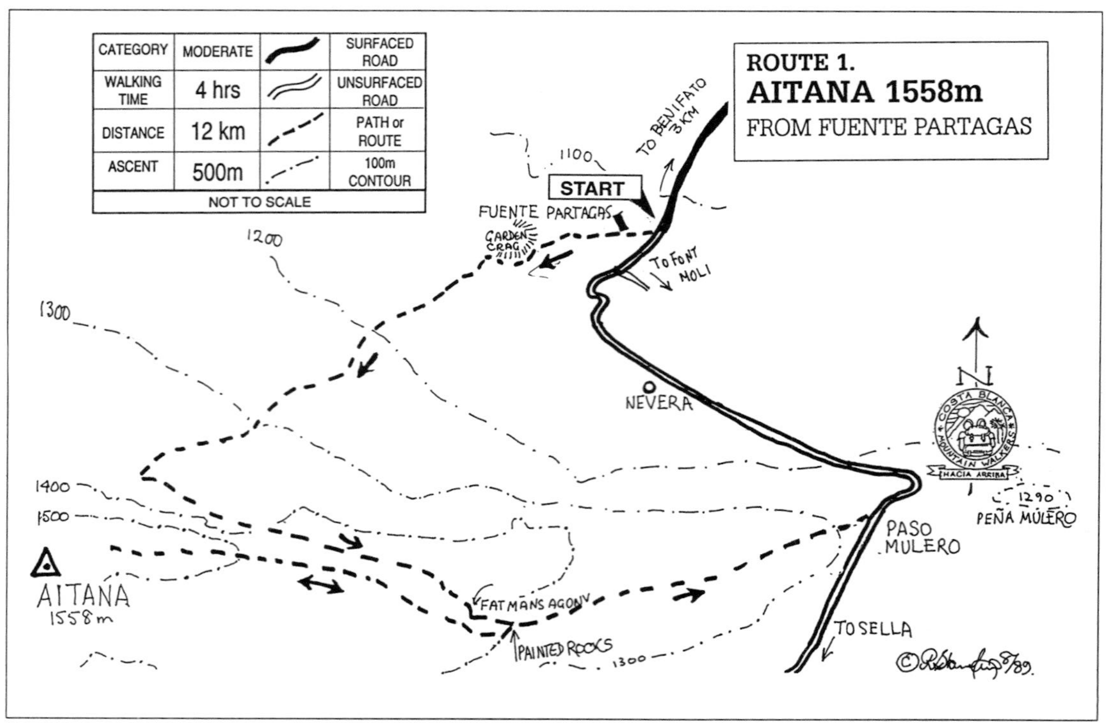
ROUTE 1.
AITANA 1558m
FROM FUENTE PARTAGAS
CATEGORY
MODERATE
SURFACED ROAD
WALKING TIME
4 hrs
UNSURFACED ROAD
DISTANCE
12 km
PATH or ROUTE
ASCENT
500m
100m CONTOUR
NOT TO SCALE
START
FUENTE PARTAGAS
GARDEN CRAG
TO BENIFATO 3KM
TO FONT MOLI
1100
1200
1300
1400
1500
NEVERA
N
COSTA BLANCA
MOUNTAIN WALKERS
HACIA ARRIBA
1290
PEÑA MULERO
PASO MULERO
TOSELLA
FAT MANS AGONY
PAINTED ROCKS
AITANA
1558m
©R.Stansfield 8/89.

of it is rough walking with few good paths, and the crossing of the Partagas is a rock scramble.

Making A Start To The Fuente de Partagas

Leave the C3313 beyond Guadalest near Km.15, and turn left with sign to Benifato (watch out for this, there is little warning), and go towards the village. Just as the houses start, turn right (south) along a narrow surfaced road next to a house named Casa la Foya. This is an access road which winds upwards for 3km until it becomes unsurfaced at a low building - the Fuente Partagas. Here you will find picnic tables, the Partagas stream running down the road. The road continues to climb left, and goes south-east to the Paso Mulero and Sella - this will be your return route.

Towards The Partagas Rocks

Behind the Fuente can be seen the solid wall of double cliffs which are the Partagas, and it is necessary to first outflank them by turning them on their western end. To do this, strike up west-south-west, keeping a prominent crag (Garden Crag) on your right, towards a small col, then seek out an indistinct path which zig-zags upwards in the same direction, until the masts, on the summit of Aitana, are visible. Look back now, and you will see that the impressive Garden Crag is, in fact, cultivated nearly up to its summit, and you have glorious views of the coast, Penon d'Ifach, the Bernia and Mala del Llop, with Confrides Castle just below the ridge. *20min*

Carry on heading for the summit masts for a while, passing a deposito and a spring, until you reach a large flat area which gives onto a broad shelf running almost parallel with the main ridge.You can now see all the summit installations. *1h 10min*

To "Fat Man's Agony"

Change direction now to south-east to follow below the Partagas cliffs away from the summit. You have now outflanked the lower cliffs, and we now have to cross another band to join the main ridge of Aitana itself. The track moves slowly upwards towards another small col, but soon has to cross some scree, and you can now actually touch the crags. Ahead is a jumble of rocks filling a gully. A prominent yew tree will be seen high up, and a gap in the rocks to the left of it. This is "Fat Man's Agony", and our route. Behind us, high up on the ridge, is a small rock window. Scramble up the rocks, pass the tree, go through the gap, and you have crossed one of the Simas de Partagas. Turn left as you leave the gap, and traverse until you meet a path near some painted rocks - souvenirs of past Speleological explorations. Look back into the fissures, they are very impressive. *1h 30min*

At these painted rocks, turn right (due west) and climb along the edge of the fissures to reach the broad summit of Aitana, the highest point (not quite 1558m but near enough) which is accessible to the public in the whole province. *2h*

Wonderful Views

From the summit can be seen the second and third highest peaks in the Province, Puig Campana (1410m) looking south-east, and Mont Cabrer (1389m) to the north-west. Further access to the west is prohibited, so views in the direction of Alcoy are limited. In all other directions, however, the vistas seem endless. It is not often that you can pick out the square tower of Cocentaina Castle (north-north west) from our walks. Confrides, Serrella and Guadalest Castles are also visible to the north-east.

The ice-pit, or nevera, was a necessity in ancient times for keeping food fresh. It was always dug on the northern slope of a hill in order to be shaded from the sun, and to be near the snow-line. The best example

Fuente de Partagas

to be seen, still with part of the roof intact, is on Mont Cabrer near Concentaina. Below you on the northern flanks, see how many of these circular pits you can spot. You will visit one on your descent.

Enjoy your time on the roof of Alicante and, if by any chance, any of you are, like me, obliged to wear a hearing-aid, do switch it off if the radar is operating - the bleeps will drive you mad!

Descents

If you have become "hooked" on "Fat Man's Agony", then, by all means, reverse the ascent route. An alternative, which I recommend, is to follow the ridge down and over Peña Alta to Paso Mulero, and the road back to the fuente. It is a very scenic route, noted for some prickly vegetation and few paths until the road is reached.

To Paso Mulero

Go south-east first down the ridge to avoid the fissures until you reach the painted rocks. Now the route will be generally east, following the edge of the cliffs wherever possible to avoid the vegetation. Look back to enjoy magnificent views of the dramatic land-slips which have occurred on Aitana, probably caused by the great earthquake in the seventeenth century. The route is rather undulating between small summits, one of which is Peña Alta (but don't ask me which) until the road to Sella can be seen below. *2h 30min*

Keep going ahead until a reasonable path appears, which leads you down to the pass, and turn left along the good forestry road, which will lead you back to your transport at Fuente Partagas. *3h 30min*

Visit To Nevera

It is easy going now, the good road taking us west towards the fuente. After about 10min, start to search the left-hand side of the road for the remains of a nevera - about 100m from the road - and try to visit it. There was once, of course, a stone and wood roof, but the pit and its access doors can still be seen.

Rejoin the road, head back to the Fuente Partagas, and the hospitality of the Venta de Benifato on the main road. *4h*

ROUTE 2: UNDER PEÑA MULERO St. 8km 3h

Getting There

Leave the C3318 just beyond Guadalest at the entrance to the village of

Font Moli and Serrella Castle

Benimantell (Km.12.9) and turn uphill with a sign to "El Trestellador", a very acceptable restaurant. After one kilometre you pass the drive to the restaurant, and in a further half kilometre the tiny hamlet of Font Moli (Molino de Ondara on the map) is reached with its tiny wash-house, fuente, and the ancient water-mill from which it takes its name.

Our stroll starts from here and is a circular route lasting about 3h at the most. The first hour is, however, all uphill and you will climb 300m to the base of the cliffs of Peña Mulero, so please take it easy and do not spoil the rest of your stroll by trying to go too fast.

Making A Start

The route is above the actual fuente with its picnic tables. You can either climb a rough track to the left of the fuente or walk along the surfaced road to find the unsurfaced forestry road which is our route upwards towards Peña Mulero. Climb steadily above the hamlet with expanding views of the Guadalest Valley. Shortly after a concreted piece of road, note a good track going right this is your return route. Keep on upwards, noting that you have red rectangular boundary markers fixed to the trees on the left-hand side of your route. In about three-quarters of an

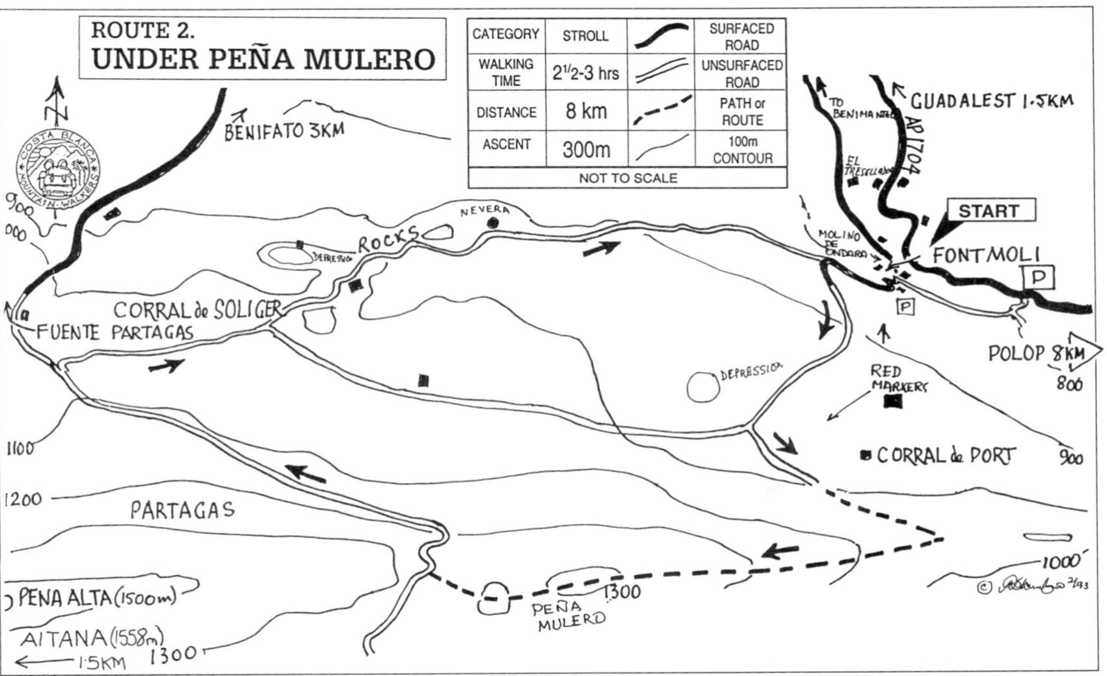
ROUTE 2.
UNDER PEÑA MULERO
CATEGORY
STROLL
SURFACED ROAD
WALKING TIME
2½-3 hrs
UNSURFACED ROAD
DISTANCE
8 km
PATH or ROUTE
ASCENT
300m
100m CONTOUR
NOT TO SCALE
GUADALEST 1·5KM
TO BENIMANTELL
AP 1704
EL TRESCULADOR
START
MOLINO DE ONDARA
FONT MOLI
P
POLOP 8KM
800
RED MARKERS
CORRAL de PORT
900
1000
DEPRESSION
NEVERA
ROCKS
BENIFATO 3KM
CORRAL de SOLIGER
FUENTE PARTAGAS
1100
1200
PARTAGAS
PEÑA MULERO
1300
PENA ALTA (1500m)
AITANA (1558m)
1·5KM
1300
COSTA BLANCA MOUNTAIN WALKERS

hour you get your first view of Peña Mulero on the Aitana Ridge ahead, and in an hour, the road to the ridge bears left and you turn off right under the cliffs in a westerly direction heading for a small col. *1h*

Climb now, gently underneath the magnificent buttresses of Peña Mulero's summit, passing through some attractive boulders and little pinnacles to gain a col with evidence of cultivation.

The Traverse

This is the highest part of your stroll, nearly 1000m, and no more climbing from now on, only a level traverse and then the gentle descent back to Font Moli. From the col descend a little and pass a small casita and a cultivated area with good views appearing of the forestry road climbing to the Paso Mulero on its way to Sella. The northern crags of Aitana, Confrides Castle artistically poised on its magnificent crag, eventually comes into view ahead. In 45min you reach a junction at which you turn down right - to continue would bring you, in 15min, to Fuente Partagas, under the crags of Aitana itself. *2h 15min*

To The Nevera And Font Moli

In 10min notice a cultivated hollow with a small shelter on the left-hand side and then a ruined finca where you turn down left to pass through a narrow cleft in some rocks. Just past the cleft watch out for a nevera, or ice-pit, on the left-hand side of the road.

The road now descends in easy stages to the east, and watch as you go to spot each of the villages of the Guadalest Valley as they appear. First is Benimantell, then Guadalest, Benifato and Beniarda. Finally Abdet, at the very head of the valley, comes into view. Confrides remains hidden behind its castle. Across the valley are views of the Sierras Serrella and Aixorta, with Bernia and Ferrer in the distance. You can pick out Serrella Castle by the forestry road which zig-zags up to Puerto del Castillo beneath its crag. Soon you reach the concrete road again. Turn left down to the start of the walk at Font Moli, ready no doubt for a picnic or a meal at one of the many restaurants in the valley. *3h*

ROUTE 3: CONFRIDES CASTLE M(B) 7km 2.5h

Confrides Castle attracts other names. Benifato claims it, and somehow, it has gained the name "El Castellet". As far as I know, it is the only castle on Aitana, and stands on an isolated turret of rock at the end of a northern spur of the mountain, with a commanding view of the whole

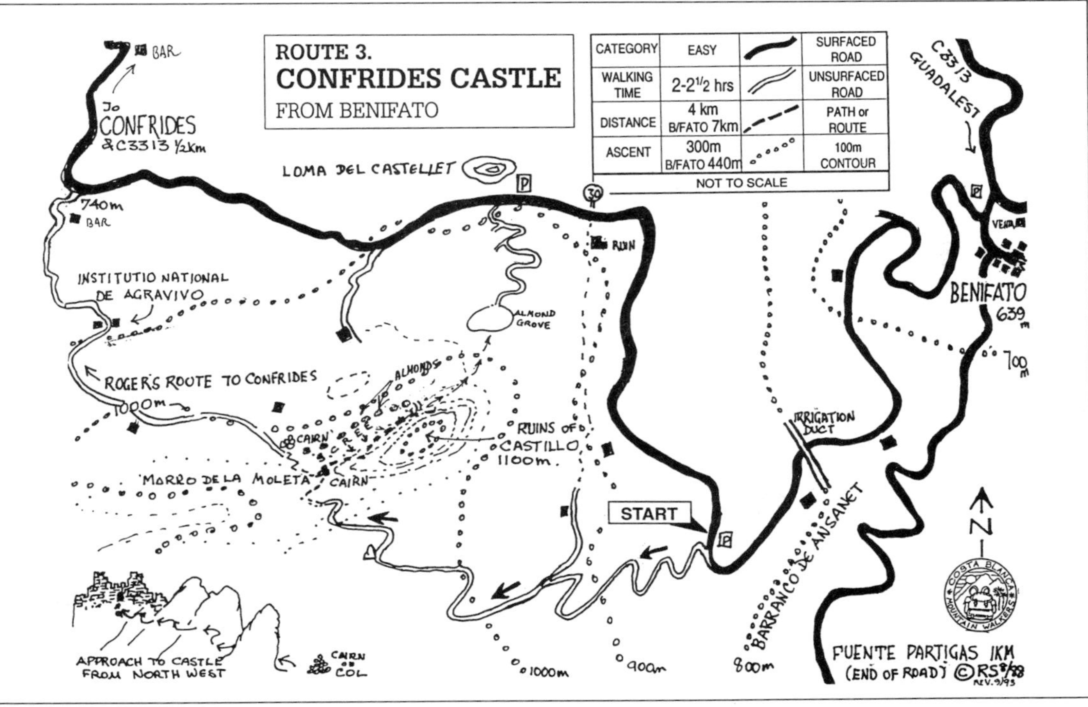
ROUTE 3.
CONFRIDES CASTLE
FROM BENIFATO
CATEGORY
EASY
WALKING TIME
2-2½ hrs
DISTANCE
4 km B/FATO 7km
ASCENT
300m B/FATO 440m
SURFACED ROAD
UNSURFACED ROAD
PATH or ROUTE
100m CONTOUR
NOT TO SCALE
BAR
To CONFRIDES & C3313 ½Km
740m
BAR
LOMA DEL CASTELLET
P
30
RUIN
C3313 GUADALEST
VEMA
BENIFATO 639m
700m
INSTITUTIO NATIONAL DE AGRAVIVO
ALMOND GROVE
ALMONDS
ROGER'S ROUTE TO CONFRIDES
1000m
CAIRN
RUINS OF CASTILLO 1100m.
MARRO DE LA MOLETA
CAIRN
IRRIGATION DUCT
START
BARRANCO DE ANSANET
N
COSTA BLANCA MOUNTAIN WALKERS
APPROACH TO CASTLE FROM NORTH WEST
CAIRN ON COL
1000m
900m
800m
FUENTE PARTIGAS 1KM (END OF ROAD)
© RS 8/88
REV. 9/93

of the Guadalest Valley. Within sight are two other castles, its sister on the other side of the valley, Serrella, and in the centre of the middle valley Guadalest Castle itself. We will approach the castle from Benifato (south-east).

A pleasant walk on good tracks, but care is required for the final ascent to the castle over rocky ground. Purists may leave their transport at Benifato, and walk a pleasant 3km on the metalled road through almond, cherry and pear orchards. Others may wish to take their transport higher up the road.

Making A Start

Leave the C3313 beyond Km.15, and turn left, signed Benifato. The sign comes on you rather suddenly around a bend in the road, and is easily missed. Almost immediately, a very tight turn is needed to join an unclassified road on the right, leading over Loma de Castellet to Confrides. No signpost, but a notice indicating Instituto Nacional de Agravivo (Research Farm Unit). Ignore a forestry road leading off to the right and after 3km, a side road on the left (red markers) is the start of your walk. A few cars can be accommodated on the roadside, but a larger party should park 2km further on at the summit of the road, and walk down the road to the starting point (allow 20min).

The red waymarks on the wall will help you throughout this route, although your first objective, the col between Aitana and the castle, is clearly visible most of the time. The unsurfaced road twists and turns to gain height, and, at first, heads towards Aitana. Pass a sign "Finca de Castillo" on the right, and now you have clear views of the summit of Aitana, with its white globular radar domes. *15min*

You now have a good view of a great gully cut into the flank of Aitana (Barranco de Alfafani). Ignore a side track going left, then pass a boulder on the left-hand side with lots of paint on it, and then two metal gateposts on the right. At this point, say goodbye to Aitana, as you pass through a few mature pines, and the track steepens for the final pull up to the col, now clearly visible. Reach the col with its prominent cairn. *35min*

The Col

You now have a view to the north-west and the upper Guadalest Valley. The best route to the castle is on the western side of the crags, and needs care, although there are a number of good paths. First, however, keep to the eastern side of the first rock pinnacle, before zig-zagging upwards,

On the Sierra Bernia (Route 5) Photo: Maurice Gibbs

Sierra Bernia - the main summit from the eastern peak (Route 5) *Maurice Gibbs*
Bernia - 'Billboard Wall' and last steps to the east summit (Route 5) *Maurice Gibbs*

heading for the "Front Doorway". Towards the top, beware of side paths leading to impressive view-points, and watch out for a shaft which leads to an underground cave system. When climbing here in winter, we were able to warm ourselves in the "warm air" from the caves. Go through the gateway and into the castle ruins. *1h 10min*

The Castle

The ruins are impressive, there is a good part of a tower, pieces of a castellated wall, and a cistern with stone pipes. The views, as might be expected, are also sensational, with the whole of the valley laid out before you, and offer a good opportunity to test your map-reading skills by identifying all the villages and summits in the area.

Descent

In addition to reversing the approach route, there are other routes on the western side which can be used.

Before leaving the castle it is a good idea to check your chosen descent route, especially the one to Lomo del Castellet. The key to the descent is a small circular grove of almonds north-east of the castle, from which a good track leads to the surfaced road.

A. Descent to Lomo Del Castellet

Leave the summit and retrace route to the col, and just before reaching the cairn, turn sharp right to find a good track leading across the screes directly under the castle crags (north-east). The track ends in a broader track leading from a single terrace of almond trees which is the route to Confrides. From here to the small almond grove, cross over the Confrides track, until you see a marker, then follow a good track, avoiding one which drops down to the left, until you can see the almond grove ahead (north-north-east). Behind you are really dramatic views of the castle, as you cross the grove to join a broad road. This leads, in a few minutes to the motor road, where you turn right to your parking place at Loma del Castellet. This route now has red waymarkings. Refreshments and meals are available at Venta de Benifato on the main road below the village. *45min*

B. Descent to Confrides

From the col a broad track can be seen to the left (west) leading from Confrides. The adventurous will strike down left finding some short stretches of path to join the track near some fire damage (15min). A better descent is to follow the Lomo Route as far as the good track (red marker) and then turn left (west) through a single terrace of almond trees on very stony ground to join the main track which leads to Confrides (35min). You will pass a restaurant on your way down to Confrides, where there are a further six restaurants.

Hoopoe

Sierra Bernia

INTRODUCTION

The Mini-Cuillin Of The Costa

The 12km gabbro rock ridge of the Black Cuillin on the Isle of Skye is considered to be the nearest thing to an alpine ridge that Britain has to offer and I never fail to remember it whenever I see the Bernia Ridge. True, the rock is different and the Cuillin much longer, but they are both about the same height, and both have a magnificent mixture of walking, plus modest and very severe rock climbing. Bernia is a 4km limestone ridge running west to east from the Algar Valley above Bolulla to Calpe, and is best studied from Pinos to the north, or Altea la Vieja to the south. One day I hope to be able to complete a traverse of the ridge for the enjoyment of walkers or scramblers, but, at present, only one-third of it has succumbed to my advances, including, happily, the summit ridge from the tooth to the western col, and the summit at the eastern end with its ridge dropping down towards the sea. You can also gain the ridge from the Bernia Circuit and spend a happy hour exploring until you come up against serious rock climbing. There is much of interest on this mountain: fuentes on both flanks, an ancient fort (in ruins), and a forat, or hole in the ridge rocks through which you can crawl.

Access

Most walks start from the Bernia Plateau where the AV1424 from Jalon meets the AV1425 from Benissa, via Pinos, although there are other approaches from Altea la Vieja which are not described in this book.

ROUTE 4: MAIN SUMMIT VIA WEST RIDGE Sc(C) 7km 5h

Making A Start

Leave the car park at Bernia (near to the Restaurant Sierra Bernia) and walk towards the ridge (south) for about 5min on an unsurfaced road, until the road forks. Take the left-hand road (east) towards the fuente; the other track can be seen zig-zagging up to the western col, and is your return route. After passing two casitas on the right, you see another house higher up the slope, and your road enters a shallow barranco, where you leave it, as a narrow path ascends the steep slope (due south) towards the ridge. *10min*

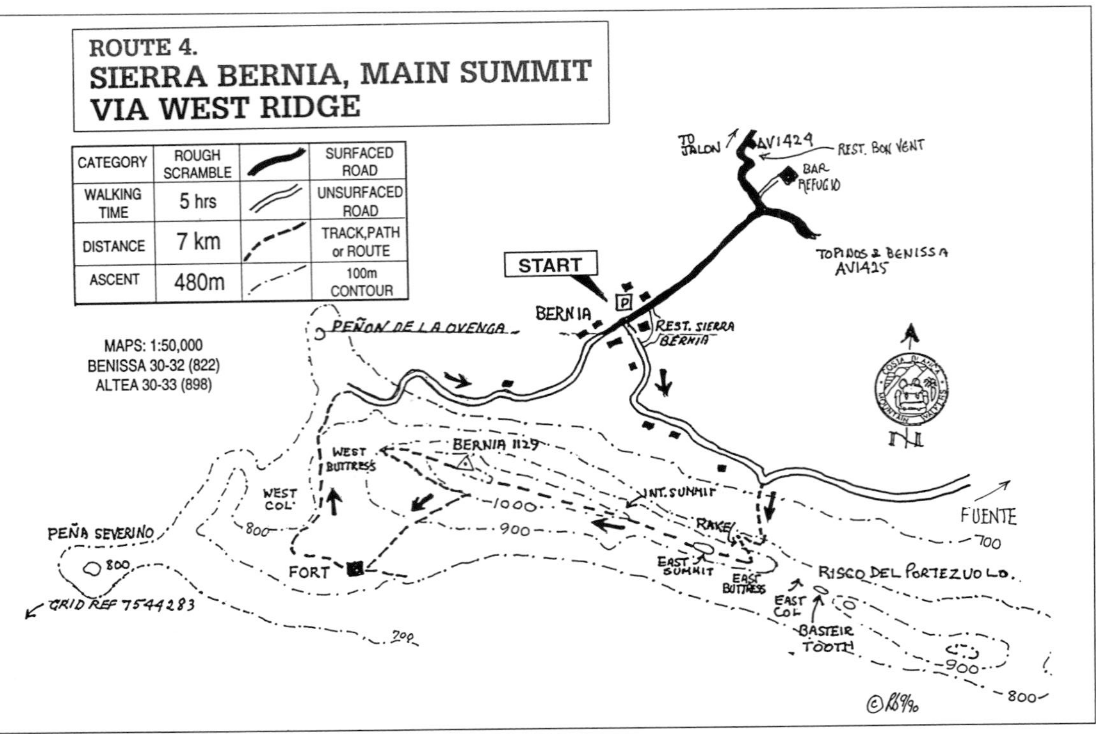

ROUTE 4.
SIERRA BERNIA, MAIN SUMMIT VIA WEST ROUTE RIDGE

CATEGORY	ROUGH SCRAMBLE		SURFACED ROAD
WALKING TIME	5 hrs		UNSURFACED ROAD
DISTANCE	7 km		TRACK,PATH or ROUTE
ASCENT	480m		100m CONTOUR

MAPS: 1:50,000
BENISSA 30-32 (822)
ALTEA 30-33 (898)

For the first 1½h, in classical style, the route heads straight for the ridge over very steep and rocky ground. It will be 4½h before you tread a good path again!

Getting To Grips With The Mountain

The path soon disappears, and there is nothing for it but to use your mountain skills to find the easiest way through the boulders, rocks and vegetation, always going as directly upwards as possible, towards a group of white boulders which will be reached in about 10min, and another 10min will bring you to the top of this shoulder, and a welcome rest at some larger rocks with a red marker. *30min*

Now you can see clearly your route on to the ridge (due south). Your markers for the first stage are three huge boulders on a steep scree slope. You head for the gap between some small crags and the right-hand boulder, where the vegetation is less troublesome. Immediately above is a band of small crags, and once these are reached, move right (west) for a short time to climb up a rake (sloping terrace), then back left to gain the top of East Buttress. You can see in all three rakes, dropping from left to right across the buttress wall. The lower one is only a narrow groove, the middle one is yours, and the upper one is a difficult rock climb.

To The Rock Wall

Cross a little terrace and another knoll, and start the steep climb through broken rock and scree (no path) heading for the boulders, which can be reached in 20min I'm sure you will now need another breather, which will enable you to enjoy the extensive views to the north. You can also contemplate the steep scree which leads upwards to the base of the band of crags (as long as it continues to flourish, there is a good guide - a crack filled with ivy), and in another 20min you will be there. *1h*

On To The North Rake

Now at last, you have a goat track to follow along the base of the crags (west) until a red marker shows the start of your rake. On the way, you can look up to see the first rake. Your rake is broad and firm, but take care, as it is exposed if you venture to the outer edge. In all too short a time, you leave it to climb a path up the slope to the main ridge. *1h 22min*

On To The Ridge

The markers going left (east) descend to the Eastern Col beneath the Tooth, and to the fuente. From the ridge you can now admire the magnificent view of the whole ridge east, right down to Mascarat, Toix and Peñon d'Ifach. To the west, the twin summits of Bernia are now visible, with the white triangulation post on the main (western) summit. You can also see a small intermediate summit between them.

The Summit Ridge

Now all the effort to reach the ridge is rewarded in full as you start your traverse to the summit. Obviously you will choose a route to suit your capabilities. Wherever possible, the ridge rocks are the normal line for the expert, but for others, there is marked a safer and easier route, avoiding some of the more difficult pinnacles.

Get on to the ridge, keeping first to the left (south) side, but in 5min, cross over to the north side and a short rock climb. *2h 5min*

Fig Tree Groove To Eastern Summit

Go up a groove with chock stones, and pass behind the fig tree, then ascend a broad gully to gain the Eastern Summit. *2h 35min*

To Main Peak Summit

Descend as best you can on the ridge rocks to Intermediate Summit, which you pass on the left (south) side, and go down a very sporting arête into a small gap from which you escape up a short rock groove on the north side to see the Main (West) Summit ahead. Pass the last remains of a watch tower on the left to gain the main Summit and the triangulation pillar (installed by helicopter in 1988). *3h*

The views, as might be expected, are extensive, and especially beautiful is the eastern aspect down the ridge to the sea.

Traverse Of West Summit Ridge

Leave the Summit, and start by descending a rough arête which has a metal stake fixed to the rock. Making sure that you are on a good stance, look down over the precipitous north side to see the only nevera (ice-pit) on the Bernia. This is a lovely traverse, as the ridge descends quite sharply, ending in a boulder-filled groove. On to another delightful rocky arête, which you leave at its end, by climbing down the left (south) side on to easier ground. Your time on the ridge is now limited, so enjoy every last moment, as, all too soon, twin cairns and red markers remind us to find a way off the ridge on the left (south) side. *3h 25min*

You now join a rough rake across the base of the crags of Holly Oak Wall (the tree is high up in a crack). There are some red markers, but you are crossing scree, and you should aim for a crag on the farthest side.

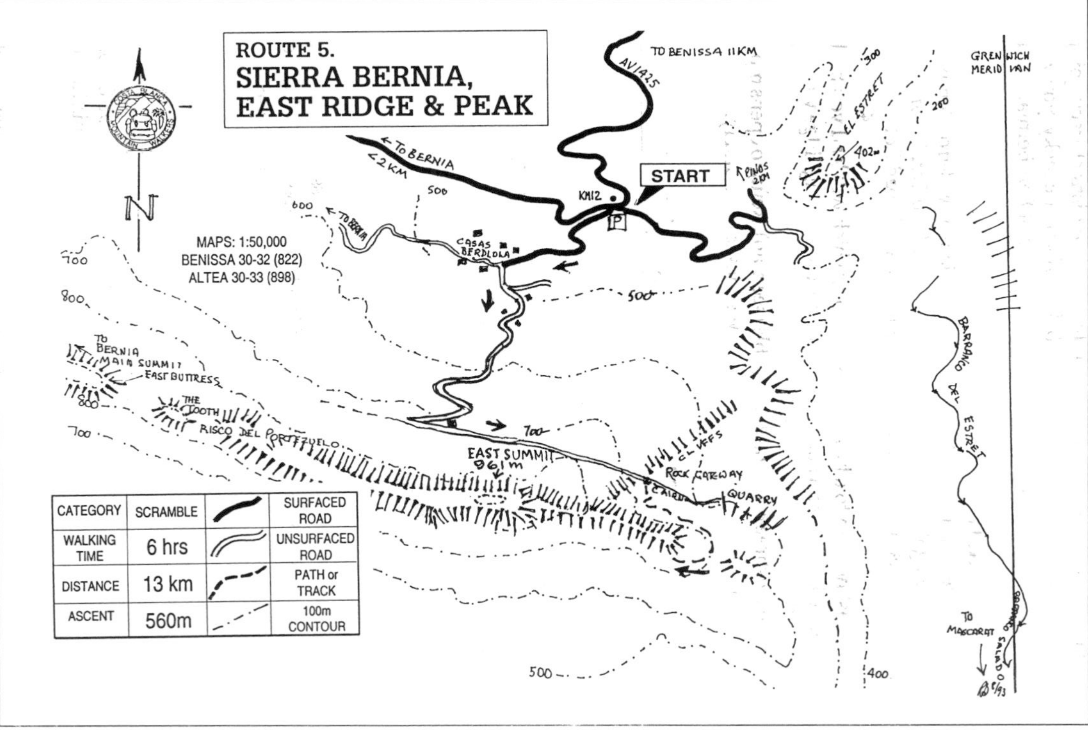

CATEGORY	SCRAMBLE
WALKING TIME	6 hrs
DISTANCE	13 km
ASCENT	560m

When you are nearly there, look out for a very indistinct track going back right, aiming for the castle ruins below. If you are lucky, you will join a good marked track, and arrive at the ruins of Fort Bernia. *4h*

A Good Path At Last!

Say goodbye to rough walking now, as you join a well-trodden path west to a rock gateway, and go round the end of the Bernia summit's western crag, as you descend the dramatic valley to Broad Col and Pena Ovenga. *4h 15min*

Go east now on to a broad forestry road, which will lead you back to Bernia village after what must be the most rewarding ridge walk in our region. *5h*

There are three restaurants available (see map). Refugio opens most days, Sierra Bernia too. Bon Vent only Wednesday to Sunday.

ROUTE 5: EAST RIDGE AND PEAK Sc(C) 6km 6h

The Bernia Ridge, at its eastern end, can be approached from a number of directions. From the east, where the rocks give out, at Collado de Fachuch, above the Mascarat Gorge, there is an easy approach by car right to the ridge itself, due to the construction of an urban road (Altea Hills). From the south, you can again take your car high on the mountain, through developed areas, (Urb, Sierra Altea), from Altea la Vieja, leaving your car near the big water tank, at the top of the development, and striking off on a reasonable path to the col. Our route approaches the mountain from the north.

Getting There

Leave the main trunk road (CN332) just south of Benissa, and turn off on to the AV1421, signposted Jalon, and in a few metres, fork left on to the AV1425, signposted Pinos. At Km.8, on the AV1425 you will pass the Pinos Restaurant, and below, on the left, the tiny church and the scattered hamlet of Pinos. At Km.12, turn off left (south), and park your car where the road splits. This is an excellent place to examine your route before setting off, to identify the main features you will pass on the walk. Below, to the west, gathered together on a small piece of high ground, are a number of farms which go under the name of Casas Berdlola. Across the valley, you can study the whole of the Bernia Ridge from Collado de Fachuch to the main Western Summit. The main forestry road, which traverses beneath the crags towards the prominent band of rocks which drop down from the ridge towards the Estret

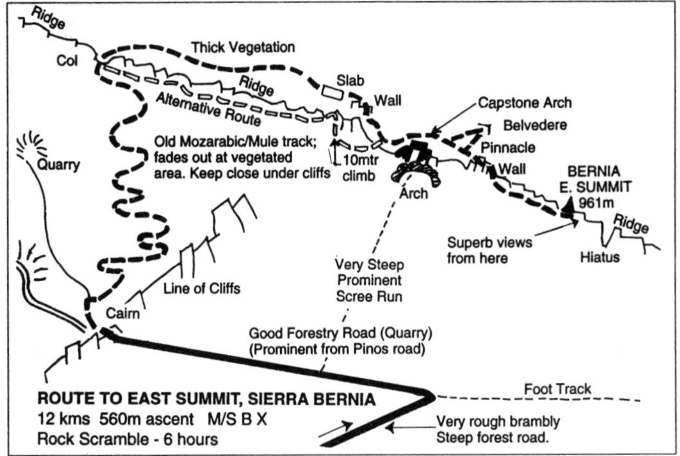

Gorge, can clearly be identified. Finding the natural bridge and stone arch up on the ridge is a more difficult task. The key is the very narrow scree run just to the left (east) of the Eastern Summit, the final objective of this walk.

Down Into The Pinos Valley

Those of you who are in a hurry can take your cars for another 2km to the bottom of the valley, but the walk down the right-hand road (south-west) is so pleasant an introduction to the walk that I strongly recommend that you walk this first 2km, anticipating as you go the delights of the ridge across the valley bottom, and on your right, the chained drive of a little villa, Casa Dolores. The road now starts to climb gently, towards Casas Berdlola (Route No.7), and, in a few minutes, your road forks off left (chained to prevent use by cars). *30min*

Towards The Rock Gateway

Follow a good unsurfaced forestry road as it climbs directly towards the ridge, and, in a few minutes, ignore a road which goes down left (Route No.7). You pass a little casita on the left (east), and then you go through other casitas as the road moves west for a short time. At an old finca, you join a good forestry road, and turn left on an eastern track towards a quarry and the rock gateway in the band of crags. You can now see ahead the deep cleft of the Estret Gorge, which leads down to the dramatic Mascarat Gorge on the coast. There are now extensive views of the whole Pinos Valley, with Casas Berdlola to the north and Pinos to the north-east. In the distance to the north-east, the great bulk of Mongto appears, and a little to the south is the gorge of La Garganta (the throat) near Gata de Gorgos, and, on the coast, the hill of Isidoro, with its radio antennae, near the village of Benitachell. You now cross the band of rocks at the rock gateway and seek out on the right-hand side a cairn which marks a vague track which climbs to the col. *1h 15min*

To The Col

The track zig-zags and disappears once or twice, but cairns have been placed to help you, as you climb basically south-east, to reach the col between two prominent buttresses. As you climb note how, to the south-east, Olta first appears, followed eventually by the Penon d'Ifach, and finally, Sierra Toix. Once you have gained the ridge you can appreciate the extensive views of the coast, including Sierra Helada, the Cortinas, Puig Campana, and even the provincial capital of Alicante with, perched high on a rocky prominence, the castle of Santa Barbara. At this point, the other two approach routes, previously described, join the ridge. *2h*

To The Belvedere

Your first objective is a small ledge beneath a yellow rock wall, and to get there, you keep to the base of the crags on the south side of the ridge, descending a little, before climbing to the wall itself, and then traversing to the ledge. *2h 30min*

The route now follows a broad groove in smooth rocks, and surmounts an easy 5m wall. Above the wall, scramble up some steep rocks to one of the great natural features of the Bernia Ridge - the Rock Bridge. The bridge is made up of a great slab of rock, which has fallen across a chasm. Beneath it is another marvel of nature, the Rock Archway, which spans the narrow scree chute which descends precipitously to the valley floor.

There are some interesting natural caves and fissures hereabouts, but you must press on to the west to reach a reasonably broad belvedere. Views are now opening up, to the south and south-west, of Aitana and the Guadalest Valley. *2h 45min*

On To The Arête

You must now take to the rocks for the final climb to the Eastern Peak, which can be seen above you. First, you must tackle the pinnacle above the belvedere by going right up a short easy rock pitch, and, once round the back of the pinnacle, addressing yourself to an easy rock staircase which will lead you on to the crest of the arête. Ahead, to the west, can be seen a sheer rock wall on the south side, with about a 5-degree overhang, above a steep drop of at least 50m on to the scree below. This feature is called "The Billboard", and it can be clearly identified from Altea la Vieja. The northern side of this wall is less precipitous, but is made up of sharp flakes of limestone, which is not the easiest terrain to negotiate. I recommend that you traverse for only about 5min, just below the crest, popping up now and then to peep over the edge to relish the sheer drop on the southern side. After crossing the arête in about 5min of easy walking, you reach your ultimate objective, the East Summit of Sierra Bernia. *3h*

The Summit

Once more, the views are truly magnificent. To the west, the ridge continues with impressive pinnacles and arêtes to the buttress which leads on to the main (western) summit of the Sierra Bernia. To the right (north) of the ridge is little Peña Ovenga, and to the left (south), the twin summits of Peña Severino, joined by a razor-sharp arête. You can see the whole of the Aitana Ridge, from Puig Campana, with its attendant Cortinas, to the great summit of Aitana itself, the highest peak in the Province. There are extensive views of the Guadalest and Algar Valleys. In the foreground, down below you, on the right-hand side of the ridge, you can identify the undercut crags, which the shepherds once used as a shelter; you pass these on the way up from the Fuente Bernia to the Forat (the hole which pierces the ridge). The Forat itself is hidden from view. I am particularly impressed with the view down the ridge to the east, as the crags fall away, ultimately dropping into the Mediterranean as Moro del Toix, and the monolith of Peñon d'Ifach, with the attractive little resort of Calpe nestling between them.

Further West?

Sadly, at present, there is no walking route beyond the Eastern Peak, as further exploration is restricted to well-equipped rock climbers.

Descent

I strongly recommend reversing the ascent route, and have always been able to resist the temptation to climb down, through the arch, and run down the steep, rough scree. There is a route from the Arch which climbs a 10m wall on the northern side of the ridge to the crest and then down the north side back to the col. The going is very rough and I prefer the southern route. *6h*

Refreshments are available at the Pinos Restaurant, but be careful if you are ordering the "Menu del Dia", as the first course is always sardines (the speciality of the house). A visiting friend, a devotee of the sardine, ordered them as his main course, and, subsequently, had to eat them as starter and main course, some twenty sardines in all. Fortunately, this did not extend to the dessert!

ROUTE 6: FORT AND CIRCUIT M(B) 14km 4$^{1}/_{2}$h

This fort (built for a Spanish King in 1565) was used as a last refuge by the Moors fleeing persecution and expulsion in the seventeenth century. The Moors were evicted and the fort demolished in 1612. Extensive ruins lie on the southern shoulder beneath the summit crags at the western end of the ridge.

The walk is about 14km, an anti-clockwise circuit of the ridge, crossing south to north by means of a forat, or natural tunnel. Walking is often on good paths, but there is some scree and a little easy rock work. The ascent to the ridge itself starts with a short easy rock climb.

Getting There

A start can be made by parking cars at the end of a short road leading from the main road, Km.15 from Benissa (AV1425) and 12km from Jalon (AV1424), and walking west towards the ridge. Ahead you can see the zig-zags of an unsurfaced road which leads to a broad col between Bernia and Penon de la Ovenga, which can be reached in 30min, (some brave souls take cars as far as this col). A short diversion to the top of Penon de La Ovenga will be rewarded with dramatic views down into the Paso de los Bandoleros (allow 40min).

The Col

The track now turns left (south-west) to climb steadily along the flank of the Bernia to reach a rocky col between the mountain and Pena Severino. This is a good track, so take time to appreciate the great gully on your right which leads to the source of the Rio Algar. Tarbena can be seen perched high on a small plateau with Bolulla below it. Behind you can see the tortured red strata of the Sierra Ferrer leading to Col de Rates. There is a small cave on the left, and then you are at the col with uninterrupted views to the south from Altea to Aitana. *50min*

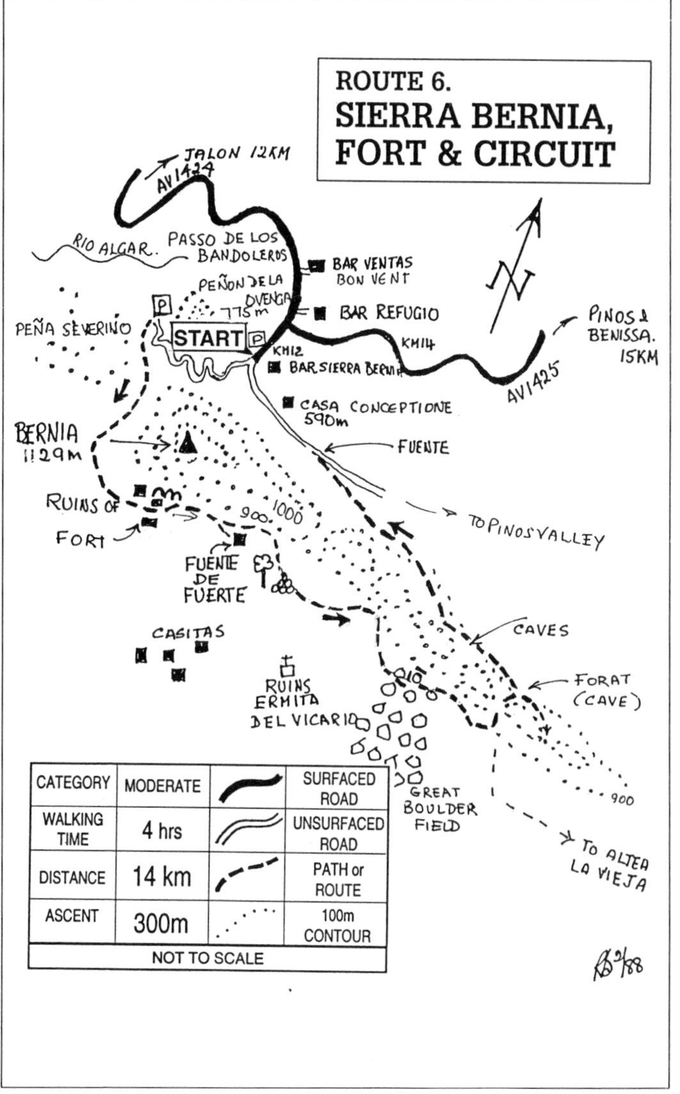
ROUTE 6.
SIERRA BERNIA, FORT & CIRCUIT
JALON 12KM
AV1424
RIO ALGAR.
PASSO DE LOS BANDOLEROS
BAR VENTAS BON VENT
PEÑON DE LA OVENGA
775m
BAR REFUGIO
PEÑA SEVERINO
START
KM12
KM14
BAR SIERRA BERNIA
PINOS & BENISSA. 15KM
AV1425
CASA CONCEPTIONE 590m
BERNIA 1129M
FUENTE
RUINS OF FORT
900
1000
TO PINOS VALLEY
FUENTE DE FUERTE
CASITAS
CAVES
RUINS ERMITA DEL VICARIO
FORAT (CAVE)
GREAT BOULDER FIELD
900
TO ALTEA LA VIEJA
CATEGORY
MODERATE
SURFACED ROAD
WALKING TIME
4 hrs
UNSURFACED ROAD
DISTANCE
14 km
PATH or ROUTE
ASCENT
300m
100m CONTOUR
NOT TO SCALE

The Fort

This is reached by turning left (south-east) on well-defined paths for 10min. Although the fort was demolished, and has since suffered from the attentions of treasure-hunters, the extent of this great fortification can still be seen. *1h*

From the fort maintain height and take a path going parallel to the ridge (south-east). You will first find a painted boulder, and then two squarish boulders on line. Near here, red markers will lead you in 1$^{1}/_{2}$h to the forat, high on the summit ridge near the eastern end. The track is good for 15min but then becomes rough with a number of scree chutes (loose rock), and a few rock scrambles.

The Route To The Forat

You have a clear view ahead to your next objective, which can be seen at the base of the bare crags with a few trees at its mouth, about four small buttresses from the eastern end of the ridge. The track will climb fairly steadily, keeping high but under the crags. There are a number of trees surviving on these high slopes, and one magnificent specimen is our first objective, marked by a rock cairn.

Follow the red markers, and descend some rocks to a broad scree run, and immediately climb left up the scree. To continue ahead would lead to the Del Fuente, and this route should only be used if you are in need of water. Below you is a small settlement of casitas and orchards. *1h 30min*

In 20min, the cairn under the large oak tree is reached, and then it is necessary to cross more scree, and descend a little by a large juniper tree. You should now be directly beneath a small col on the main ridge, with two distinctive pinnacles, and directly above the ruins of the Ermita del Vacario. *2h*

After another 15min, you enter the great Boulder Field, which takes 15min to cross, and entails a little rock work. *2h 30min*

The path now starts to climb steadily towards the forat, which should now be clearly visible above. Cross some flat slabs, and, in another 30min, you have reached the magnificent portals of the cave, and an excellent place for lunch. Note particularly the rock plants and trees which have colonised the rocks. *3h*

The Forat (Cave)

It is now necessary to pass through this low cave, in order to gain the northern side of the ridge, and continue your circuit. Some people crawl through on hands and knees, others try to maintain a more dignified posture, but, unless you are particularly small, you will have to bend very low to make this, thankfully, short traverse (5min). On reaching the northern side you have equally extensive views The drop in temperature can be most noticeable. On your right-hand side, you will see red markers on the rocks, which will lead, after a short and easy rock climb, to a path which will give access to the actual rock ridge of the mountain. Take care, however, as the gradient is steep, but the intimate views of this beautiful ridge make it well worth the effort. (Allow ³/₄h for this diversion).

Descent To The Bernia Plateau

A good path now moves left (north-west), keeping at first close to the crags and passing under some overhanging rocks (used as shelters by shepherds) In 20min there is a short rock scramble to a good path leading in easy stages to a large fuente (spring), then along a broad track back to your starting point. *4¹/₂h*

ROUTE 7: PINOS VALLEY M(A) 12km 6h

This valley runs alongside and below the jagged crags of Bernia Ridge from the dramatic Estret Gorge (which continues to become the even more dramatic Mascarat Gorge on the coast between Altea and Calpe) to the high plateau of the Bernia. There is, however, no river, on the surface at least, but it contains many small farms which benefit from its sheltered position. Many of the farms are only occupied during the weekends and at fiestas when the owners come out from the town to tend their crops. A few, however, are still occupied even though they have none of the benefits of modern living. Unlike most of our other walks which end on top of a mountain, this one is spent ascending the valley to the Bernia and returning by an alternative route back to Pinos, and throughout the rather long day you will have the chance to admire the northern crags of the Bernia and the distant views of the coast.

Mostly on very good tracks, there is one short section of an old mozarabic trail on the ascent and about 10min linking two tracks by climbing up through terraces on the way back. The route follows a figure-of-eight with the cross-over near Casas Berdlola, so the walk can be shortened if required. It is a walk which most walkers can enjoy and, if you are sure that one of the restaurants is open, you can travel very light. It is unusual on my walks to pass through farmyards, but on this one, you pass through a number of them. Please respect the owners' property and privacy.

Making A Start

Leave the AV1425 (Benissa to Pinos) road at Km.12, and park in clearing, where two metalled roads lead down into the valley. Get your bearings, and you will see Pinos's little church on a ridge to the north-east, and, to the south-east, the small hamlet of Casas Berdlolas which is the halfway point of our walk. Take the left-hand road east towards the jaws of the Estret Gorge and Olta, passing two white fincas with the same name, "La Lloma" (the hill), and in 10min a finca with a palm tree, "Finca de Francisco Ferrer", which you will again pass at the end of the day. As you walk downwards the surfaced road ends and you turn off right on a rather rougher road for a short while, to rejoin the surfaced road, which comes down from Pinos village, at the bottom of the valley. *15min*

Cross the dry stony river bed as it enters the gorge, and turn away from it (north-west), on a good road parallel with the Bernia Ridge. Go through the stone gate posts, and start to climb under two casitas as the track zig-zags upwards to a third finca with unusual stucco work on its wall. It is necessary to go behind this finca to find a mule track (if the finca is occupied, seek permission; in any case, you can climb the two terraces just before reaching it) which traverses gently at first, and then zig-zags upwards. In 10min (marker), leave the track and walk along the almond terraces to another occupied finca, where you cross the farmyard to gain a good road going north-west. *1h*

To Casas Berdlola

As you walk this section, you can admire the steep crags of the Bernia and try to identify the rock bridge on the very crest, with a beautiful natural arch below it (these are directly above a long narrow scree run). Also in the distance, just below the crags, can be seen a small white casita which you will pass in about one and a half hours' time, and at the head of the valley is the hamlet of Bernia, which is your lunch stop. Another road joins us from the left and the tiny hamlet of Casas Berdlola appears ahead. Glance backwards for a lovely view of Moraira Castle, framed in the jaws of the Estret. We now join a good road coming up from the valley bottom. Turn left, and in 15min you will pass through the hamlet of Casas Berdlola. Continue upwards. *1h 40min*

To Bernia Village

As you climb, look for a very unusual finca, built against a massive boulder on your left under the ridge, and you get a clear view of our next objective, a small white casita higher up the valley. Pass a ruined casita,

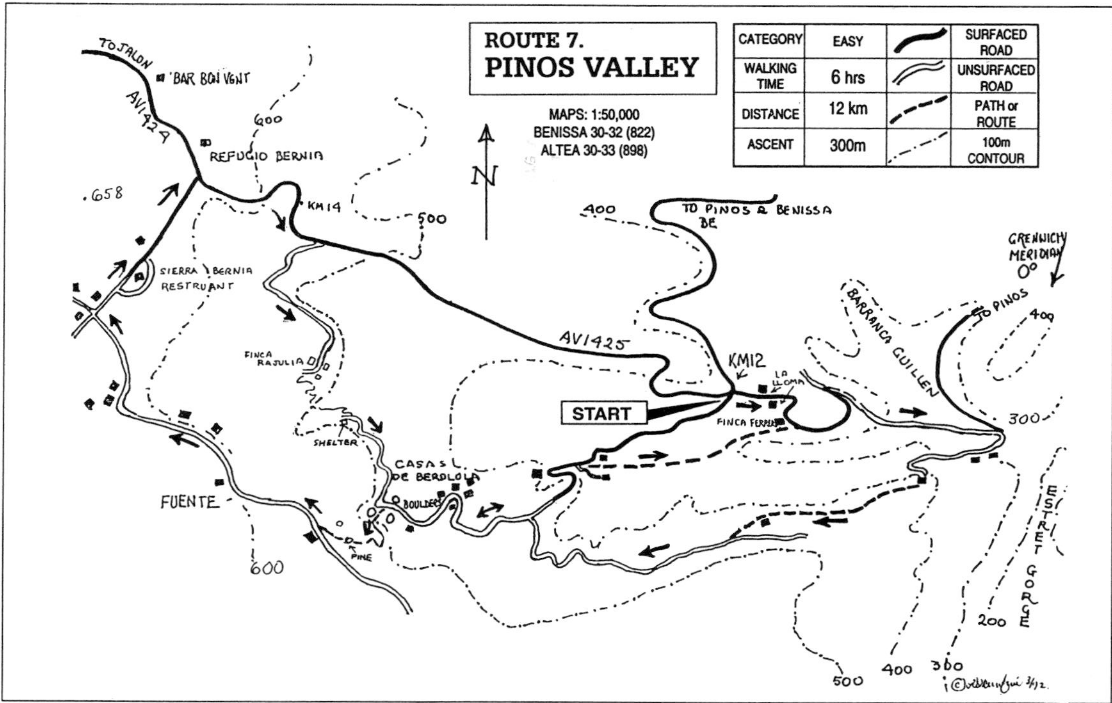

ROUTE 7.
PINOS VALLEY
MAPS: 1:50,000
BENISSA 30-32 (822)
ALTEA 30-33 (898)
CATEGORY
EASY
WALKING TIME
6 hrs
DISTANCE
12 km
ASCENT
300m
SURFACED ROAD
UNSURFACED ROAD
PATH or ROUTE
100m CONTOUR
N
TOJALON
AV1424
REFUGIO BERNIA
.658
KM14
SIERRA BERNIA RESTRUANT
FINCA RAJULIA
SHELTER
CASAS DE BERDOLA
BOULDER
PINE
FUENTE
AV1425
TO PINOS & BENISSA
KM12
LA LLOMA
START
BARRANCA GUILLEN
TO PINOS
GRENNICH MERIDIAN 0°
ESTRET GORGE
400
500
600
300
200

then some flat, exposed slabs and enter a shallow barranca with some large boulders. *2h 10min*

This is where you leave the good road (it is your return route), and move left towards the ridge on a badly eroded track. Follow my markers to find an old Mozarabic trail upwards until the little white casita comes into view. Head directly for the casita, taking care not to lose the path. Once at the casita, with its stone seat around a tree, you can take a break to admire the extensive views, with the Ferrer Ridge seen to the north and the hamlet of Bernia ahead. Now join a good road (north-west) under the ridge and pass the fuente (spring) which flows all the year round. This is the starting point for the ascent to the ridge and to the forat, the hole in the rock which gives access to the southern side of the ridge. (This is another route which will take about an hour). Carry on past the fuente and in half an hour reach the junction with the track coming down from the West Col and the fort, turn right, passing the Sierra Bernia Restaurant, onto a surfaced road and the junction of the Jalon and Benissa roads. Near the junction is the Refugio Restaurant and about a kilometre on the road to Jalon the Bon Vent Restaurant, which has never refused me refreshment. *3h 20min*

Down Into The Valley Again

Having refreshed yourself, start your return route from the junction of the Jalon and Benissa roads and follow the AV1425 south-east towards Pinos for just over a kilometre. A few metres after you have passed Km.14, turn right, onto a good, unsurfaced road which goes down to the south. The road eventually ends at an old finca, Casa Ratulia. I have obtained permission from the owner to establish this route, nevertheless, it always pays to be polite, and, if he is in residence, always greet him, and you may have to accept a glass of wine. *3h 50min*

The next short section needs care if you are not to lose your way as the path is overgrown, and you must keep a lookout for red markers. Pass through the building of the finca, keeping the house to your right, and turn right onto another track. Across a shallow barranca you can spot a small shelter amongst the terraces, which is your next objective, as it marks a good road which will lead you back to Pinos. The track leads us down to some cultivated terraces which you cross, following red markers, to cross a small barranca, climbing out the other side and up the terraces to the small shelter where you find a broad unsurfaced road which contours in and out of a number of barrancas and brings you to the large boulders which you passed earlier in the walk.

In 20min you pass, once more, through the Casas Berdlola and in another 10min the junction with your morning's route where you keep left, passing under a small villa, Casa Dolores, to reach the valley bottom, where we join a surfaced road which climbs up to our starting point in half an hour. A much more attractive route is to seek out the narrow path, which starts just above a concrete road, on the right-hand side. There are red markers to help you keep on course as you walk high above a gorge, with a lovely little finca below you, until you reach Finca Francisco Ferrer. Join the surfaced road and turn left, up the hill, back to your starting point. Refreshments are on hand 3km along the road to Benissa, at the Pinos Restaurant. *6h*

ROUTE 8: PEÑA SEVERINO (with Peña Ovenga) M(B) 9km 4h

The attention of the legions who make the, justifiably, popular walk from Bernia village to the fort is, of course, claimed by the mighty peak of the Western Summit which soars to 1100m and then runs east as a dramatic jagged ridge for 4km to the sea. Ignored by most is a beautiful peak on the right of the path up to the port. This is the object of today's walk, the Western Peak of Peña Severino.

There are in fact two peaks, each over 800m and between them a delightful arête. It has long been my ambition to achieve a complete traverse of this arête but, whilst both peaks can be safely ascended by walkers, the traverse is sadly the province of a strong, well-equipped rock-climbing party, prepared to nail themselves to rotten rock! On this walk you will visit both of the peaks and enjoy the inspiring views along the arête without having to suffer the discomfort of the traverse itself. (Within a few metres of the Western Summit the way is blocked by sheer pinnacles.)

Getting There

Leave your transport at the parking place near the Bernia Restaurant. (Start A) Km.15 on the AV1425 from Benissa, or Km.12 on the AV1424 if you are coming from Jalon.

To The Broad Col And Peña Ovenga

Head south-west along a good, unsurfaced road and in a few minutes the road to the fuente forks off left. We keep straight on towards the Western Summit of Bernia to follow a well engineered forestry road up to the col. People with sturdy cars can take them to the col in normal conditions. Near the last zig-zag there is a short-cut, marked in yellow

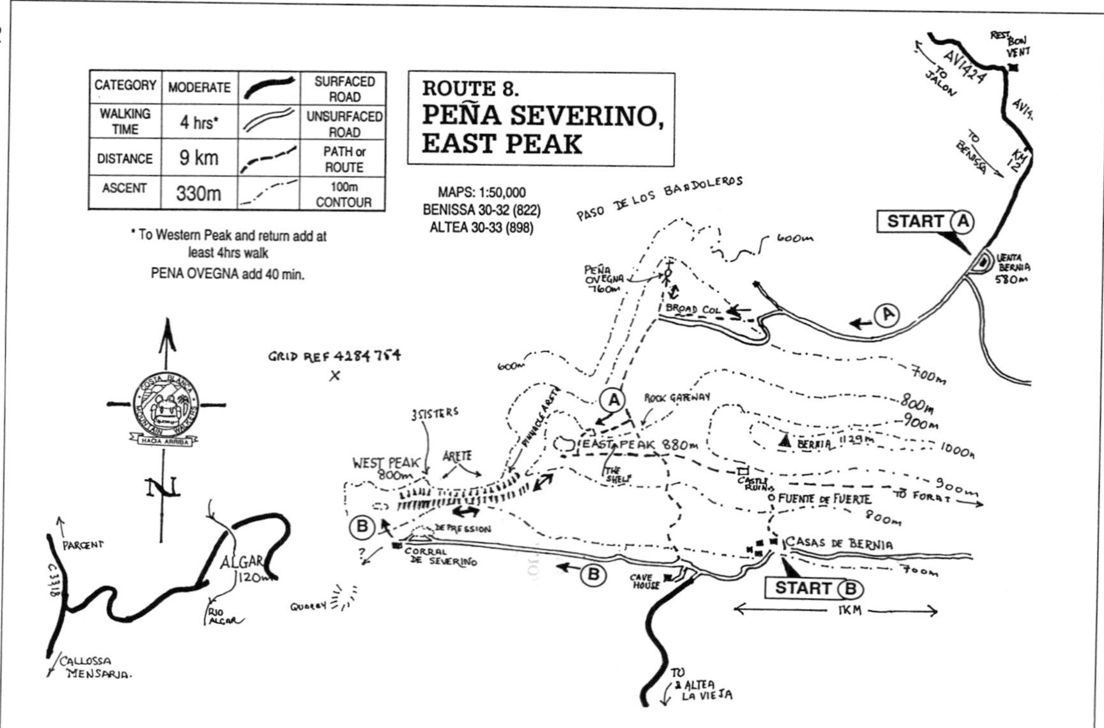
CATEGORY
MODERATE
SURFACED ROAD
WALKING TIME
4 hrs*
UNSURFACED ROAD
DISTANCE
9 km
PATH or ROUTE
ASCENT
330m
100m CONTOUR
* To Western Peak and return add at least 4hrs walk
PENA OVEGNA add 40 min.
ROUTE 8.
PEÑA SEVERINO,
EAST PEAK
MAPS: 1:50,000
BENISSA 30-32 (822)
ALTEA 30-33 (898)
PASO DE LOS BANDOLEROS
REST. BON VENT
AV1424
TO JALON
AV14
TO BENISSA
KM 12
START A
VENTA BERNIA 580m
600m
PEÑA OVEGNA 760m
BROAD COL
GRID REF 4284 754
600m
700m
ROCK GATEWAY
800m
900m
3 SISTERS
EAST PEAK 880m
BERNIA 1129m
1000m
WEST PEAK 800m
ARETE
PINNACLE ARETE
THE SHELF
CASTLE RUINS
900m
FUENTE DE FUERTE
TO FORAT
800m
DEPRESSION
CASAS DE BERNIA
PARCENT
CORRAL DE SEVERINO
ALGAR 120m
700m
CAVE HOUSE
START B
C3318
QUARRY
RIO ALGAR
1KM
CALLOSSA MENSARIA.
TO ALTEA LA VIEJA
HACIA ARRIBA
N

and white. Use it by all means if you find the broad forestry road not to your liking. On arriving at the end of the road at Broad Col consider, if you will, an ascent of a minor rocky crest to the north, Peña Ovenga. The ascent will take you only 20min, admittedly over very rough broken limestone, but the sheer drop down into the Paso de los Bandoleros is worth the effort. The summit is crowned by a wooden cross so someone must love this little peak. (Its name, I think, means forgotten peak.)
30min + 40min for Ovenga

To Peña Severina East Peak

Now you have a pleasant half hour, on a good track, with some sensational views down into a deep barranco which joins the Paso de los Bandoleros, with Tarbena perched on a shelf high above the valley and under the mountains. To your left there are intimate views of the crags of the Bernia and ahead the rock gateway leading to Bernia Fort with our mountain on its right. Just as you make the final climb to the rock gateway seek out another path going right (south-west) under some crags. *45min*

There is a mini col to aim for near a prominent flake, then keep traversing upwards to the skyline (there really is a path) but avoid tracks going downhill. Keep left, under the crags (there is a pine tree to aim for) and you will gain the Shelf with views now to the south, Altea and Benidorm. Take a breather and enjoy the view; you are only a few minutes from the Eastern summit. *1h 15min*

For some reason there is a path up to the summit of our mountain which is a bit rocky and moves out to the right a bit at the end to traverse over rocks to a cairn. *1h 40min*

The Eastern Summit

To the east the Bernia, and the western end of its ridge, presents a magnificent spectacle, but it is to the west that my eyes have always been drawn, to the Arête. Walkers, should they chose to do so, can descend for about 20min to the start of Pinnacle Ridge for sensational views of an overhanging north wall which looks pretty rotten, and a ridge which is only held together due to the fact that it never freezes. (One Pennine winter and most of it would fall off!) Below can be seen a good track which leads to an abandoned finca, Corral de Severino. The views of the tortured strata of the end of Sierra Ferrer (beloved of geology tutors) are an attraction to the north. There is more to see but I leave it to you to check your map whilst you enjoy a rest on this lovely summit.

Peña Severino, Pinnacle Arête with Sierra Aitana in the distance. Photo: Author

The Western Summit

It is possible for experienced mountaineers to drop down (not literally) from Pinnacle Ridge to the track below. Others should reverse the route to the Rock Gateway or take a direct route, east, across the Shelf to reach the track to Bernia Fort. From the gateway keep a look out for a track descending south which will join the next described route. (Allow 1h 15min from summit to lower path.)

Approach From Altea La Vieja (Start B)
Leave Altea la Vieja and head towards Callosa D'Ensarria on the A150 for 2km (since the road was upgraded there are no kilometre posts!). There is a prominent round-headed pine on your left and you pass through a gateway on to a narrow, but well surfaced road which will take you in about 5km to the unbelievable hamlet of Casas de Bernia, perched on a level bit of ground right under the fort at an elevation of 700m. At 4km from the main road, note a house built into a cliff on the left-hand side and a chained track also on your left. This is the start of your walk with parking for a few cars only.

To Corral De Severino
Turn off the surfaced road onto an unsurfaced one, which is chained, and zig-zag upwards, passing the Cave House, someone's weekend home. Now settle down to an easy walk along a contour, slightly north of west and, at a wider point, note a waymarked Mozarabic trail heading upwards (north) to near the Bernia Fort. On this lovely traverse you get extensive views and can inspect the Arête, which looks benign from this side. Ahead is the Western Peak. In half an hour you will pass a depression on the right-hand side which has in the past been cultivated just before you arrive at the ruined finca, Corrall de Severino. *45min*

Ascent Of Western Peak
Unlike its sister, this peak has no path to help you and the only advice is to head for the skyline from the finca. If you head for the crags which join the peak to the Three Sisters (the pinnacles which join the peak to the Arête) you will have to do some easy rock scrambling. The safest route is to keep over to the left (west) where the ground is still steep but less complicated. In about 45min you should be on the summit with its cairn. *1h 30min*

In all directions the views are sensational and I find it difficult to mention any particular one. The view along the arête, of course, is favourite. Below is Algar and the Aixorta, with Callosa and the whole of the Guadalest Valley. Cocoll, with its new air-strip, and Col de Rates with Tarbena and Bollula, and even the Segaria Ridge near Orba, can be identified.

At present there is no alternative return route surveyed but there is the possibility of descending to Algar from the finca, to the quarry, or even leaving the summit and following a faint path which heads down into the Paso de los Bandoleros. (We still have to look at these routes. If, meanwhile, you should manage to find them, please let us know.)

ROUTE 9: PASO DEL BANDOLEROS M(C) 7km 4h

El Paso del Bandoleros (the Pass of the Brigands) is a deep gully between two high Sierras, the Bernia and the Ferrer, and at some time long ago, a substantial river flowed down this gully to join the Rio Algar. The river has long since gone underground, but the barranco remains, and is the object of this walk. Like most other ravines in this part of the world, it is not possible to traverse the whole way down to the Algar Valley, due to the river having formed high waterfalls when it encountered strata of harder rock. The resulting drop of about 50m might be attractive to mountaineers using ropes, but not to walkers. Whilst this is a modest walk you seldom have the benefit of good paths and there is quite a lot of very rough walking.

Getting There

The walk starts and ends at the Bon Vent Restaurant on the Bernia plateau, near to Km.12 on the AV1424 from Jalon. From Benissa, you can take the AV1425 via Pinos, to reach the Bernia plateau. The Bon Vent is normally open from Wednesday to Sunday, when the proprietor Juan Manuel is in residence.

Making A Start

Leave the restaurant, and walk along the road towards Jalon for about 2km, which gives you plenty of time to admire the majestic views of the Bernia and the Ferrer. Between these two is the Paso, and beyond, in the distance, Bolulla, Callosa d'En sarria, and the whole mountain range from Puig Campana to Aitana. Overlooking the gorge, on the southern side, is the shapely peak of Pena Ovenga behind which is the very end of the Bernia Ridge, Pena Severino. At the bottom of the first major hairpin bend, near Km.9, an unsurfaced road leads off left (west) to an old finca. In 10min, at the old finca, turn off left (south-west) towards Pena Severino, and walk through almond groves until a good path appears (red markers). *1h 40min*

Into The Barranco

A reasonable track now follows the right-hand (west) side of a deep barranco, which will lead us directly down into the Paso. The track ends

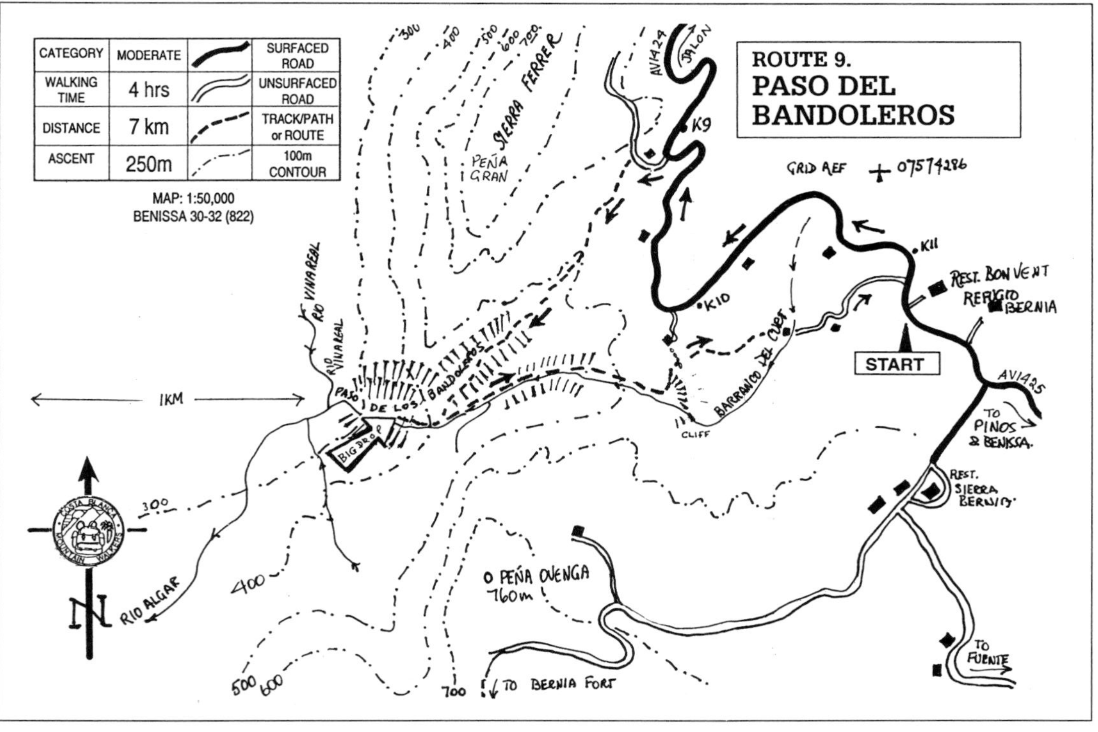
ROUTE 9.
PASO DEL BANDOLEROS
CATEGORY MODERATE
WALKING TIME 4 hrs
DISTANCE 7 km
ASCENT 250m
SURFACED ROAD
UNSURFACED ROAD
TRACK/PATH or ROUTE
100m CONTOUR
MAP: 1:50,000
BENISSA 30-32 (822)
GRID AEF 07574286
START
1KM
K9
K10
K11
AV1424
JALON
AV1425
REST. BON VENT
REFUGIO BERNIA
TO PINOS & BENISSA
REST. SIERRA BERNIA
TO FUENTE
SIERRA FERRER
PEÑA GRAN
BARRANCO DEL CUET
CLIFF
PASO DE LOS BANDOLEROS
BIG DROP
RIO VINAREAL
RIO ALGAR
O PEÑA OVENGA 760m
TO BERNIA FORT

in about 30min, and we take to flat slabs which lead down into the boulders of the old river-bed, where the Barranco del Curt joins it from the north. *2h*

Above you, on the right-hand side of the gorge, is a cave which energetic folk have explored and emerged from the roof. Most of us, however, will enjoy a brief rest before exploring further down the gorge.

To The Old Waterfall

For some 10min it is possible to follow the route of the old river, clambering between the large boulders, which make progress rather slow, before you are confronted with the impressive drop over what once was a waterfall. You now have good views down into the Algar Valley, and upwards towards the crags through which the water once thundered. To continue down into the Algar Valley it is necessary to climb the scree leading to the crag on the left-hand side of the gorge. Circumvent it, and descend over very rough ground into the Algar Valley. To return to the Bernia plateau, however, retrace your steps upstream to the junction of the two barrancos. *2h 30min*

Climbing The Barranco Del Curt

Walkers may wish to retrace their steps, others, prepared for a bit of rough walking, may prefer to make this a circular route and tackle another barranco. We now head north-east on a good path on the northern side of the barranco, until there is a small rock scramble, and ahead can be seen a red-coloured crag, which overhangs some caves. This is another old waterfall. By all means explore the caves, but the best route upwards is to avoid the crag, keeping left (north) on easier ground. You climb up close to an outcrop of rock (thankfully on red markings), and head for the gap between two other outcrops on the skyline. *3h*

It is debatable whether there is really a path over this rough ground, but the markers should help you to reach the top, marked by a large cairn and a boundary wall (marked on the M.O.P.U. map). *3h 45min*

Back To The Bon Vent

Follow the line of the wall until an old ruined finca is reached and you have views to the north-east of the Bon Vent Restaurant.

Those who have tired of the rough walking can, quite justifiably, follow the unsurfaced road north for 5min, join the road, and turn right for just over 1km back to the restaurant. Other hardier souls (or masochists) can plot a course towards the Bon Vent, crossing some shallow terraces to a casita, from which a broad unsurfaced road leads directly to the restaurant. *4h 30min*

I have watched Juan Manuel and his wife Antonia struggle to improve the facilities at this idyllically placed little restaurant. Their home is in Denia, and whilst their daughter Yolanda is at school, Juan carries out all the duties necessary to provide you with refreshment. The facilities still need to be further improved, but there is no need for any improvement in the quality of his food, or his cheerful service.

Prickly pear

Sierra Serrella

ROUTE 10: SUMMITS AND PLA DE LA CASA   S(B)13km $7^{3}/_{4}$h

The Cordillera de la Serrella is the 12km ridge which runs parallel with, and to the north of, the Aitana Ridge in a west-to-east direction from near Benisau in the west to Peñon de Castillo in the east, above the Guadalest Reservoir. Its main peaks are the twin Serrellas which are both credited with 1359m (although many do not agree that they are of equal height), Pla de la Casa (1379m), Mala del Llop (1361m), Peñon de Castillo (1120m) and, finally, the outlying ridge of Borrell (1250m), which is immediately above the road, just below Puerto Confrides.

On this walk you tackle the first three summits in a circular walk, starting from the Puerto Confrides at the head of the Guadalest Valley.

Making A Start

Park your transport as near to the Puerto (pass) as possible, at about Km.26 on the C3313 beyond Confrides. It might be convenient to make arrangements with the proprietor of the Rincon del Olvido Restaurant, just below the pass, to have a meal at the end of the walk, in which case, your vehicle will be welcome in his car park. Start by taking the road which leads north from the highway near a culvert and a fire precaution sign, and continue to climb upwards under the cliffs, with good views of the road twisting and turning downwards from the pass towards Alcoy. You now have good views of the northern cliffs and the summit of Aitana, along with the high plateau beneath them. To the west, Monte Cabrer and the heights of Plans are visible. Go through a small gateway, and the path can be seen zig-zagging upwards under the Serrella peaks. *30min*

You will only be going part-way along this road, and leave it on a bend going left on another good track going west through young pines. Your objective is the western ridge of the Serrella, and when the pines give out, you climb up through the terraces, then the broken ground, and finally, on to the rocks which lead to the ridge. The village of Alcolecha now appears below you. To the east The Bernia is seen end on, looking like the Matterhorn, with Peña Severino below it, and to the south-west Benicadell, Cocentaina and Alcoy appear. *1h*

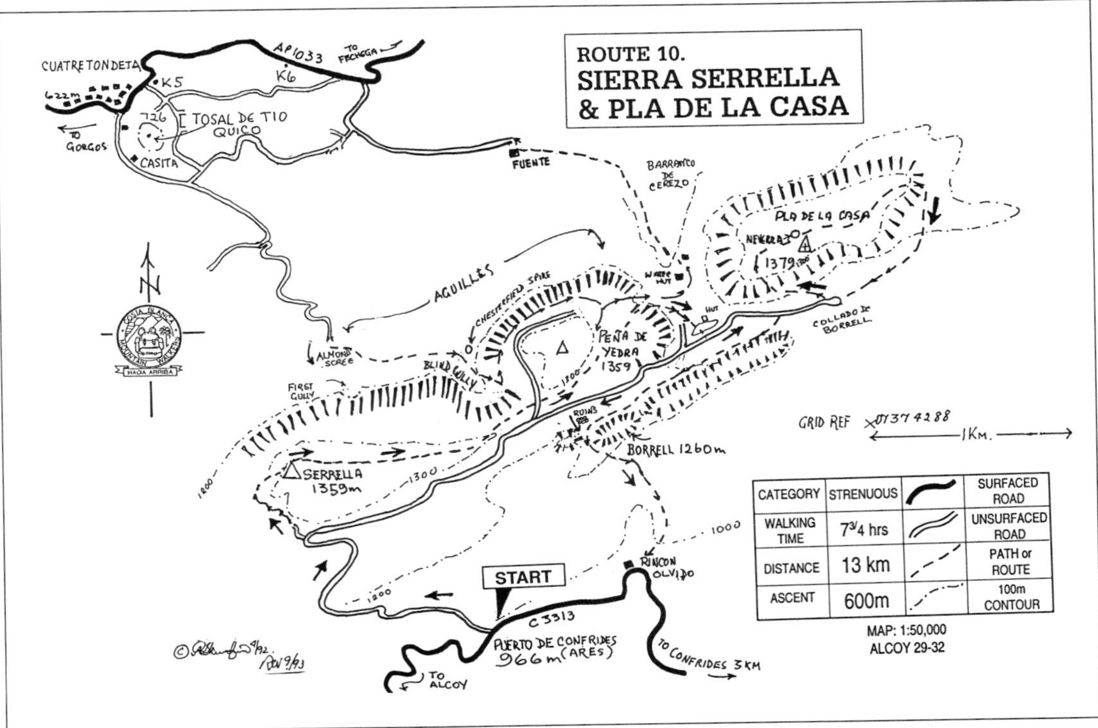
ROUTE 10.
SIERRA SERRELLA
& PLA DE LA CASA
CUATRETONDETA
622m
TO GORGOS
K5
K6
AP1033
TO FACHECA
726
TOSAL DE TIO QUICO
CASITA
FUENTE
BARRANCO DE CEREZO
PLA DE LA CASA
NEVERA
1379
WATER HUT
HUT
AGUILLES
CHESTERFIELD SPIRE
PEÑA DE YEDRA
1359
COLLADO DE BORRELL
ALMOND SCREE
BLIND GULLY
FIRST GULLY
RUINS
BORRELL 1260m
SERRELLA
1359m
GRID REF 0137 4288
1Km.
1000
1200
1300
RINCON OLVIDO
START
C 3313
PUERTO DE CONFRIDES
966m (ARES)
TO ALCOY
TO CONFRIDES 3KM
CATEGORY
STRENUOUS
WALKING TIME
7¾ hrs
DISTANCE
13 km
ASCENT
600m
SURFACED ROAD
UNSURFACED ROAD
PATH or ROUTE
100m CONTOUR
MAP: 1:50,000
ALCOY 29-32
COSTA BLANCA MOUNTAIN WALKERS
HACIA ARRIBA

To The West Summit

Finally, as we struggle up the steep slope, Guadalest and its castle come into view as we gain the ridge, and move east towards the Summit, with the forestry road visible in a trough below us to the south. Take to the north side of the ridge for a while, and find a broad forestry road, which traverses under the main Summit to a col, from which the West Summit can be reached in 10min. *1h 45min*

To The East Summit

Return to the forestry road, and carry on to a crossroads, and straight on in an easterly direction on a faint track, and reach the East Summit in about 15min. Now the shapely pinnacles of Pla de la Casa are ahead and to the left, across another trough, are the rocks from the top of the Pinnacle Route. *2h 15min*

Cross yet another forestry road in order to continue your traverse of the ridge, and note that you can see to the right (south) below you, The Rincon del Olvido Restaurant (forgotten corner). To the north is the remote village of Cuatretondeta in the Ceta valley. Guadalest Reservoir is now in full view, as well as the rest of the Serrella ridge, Mala del Llop and Serrella Castle. Finally is the Barranco de Borrell, the deep gorge separating us from our next objective, the Pla de la Casa. To the south are the distant peaks of Jijona, Peña Roja and Mignol. *2h 55min*

Leaving The Ridge

You now have to descend to the col before tackling your next peak. There is no path, the scree and rocks are unstable and need care. Below you can be seen a large flat area with a small shepherd's hut, which is your next objective. *3h 20min*

Cross this flat area, and

Looking west from Pla de la Casa to the Serrellas. Confrides below

drop down to a forestry road, and head east towards Pla de la Casa and the Collado de Borell, which is a good place to stop to study your line of ascent of the next peak. Where the forestry road ends, a small cairned track leads off north through the scree at the western end of Pla de la Casa. The track zig-zags upwards through the rocks and gains the ridge. *4h*

Ascent of Pla de la Casa

Follow the route already described in the last paragraph. If in doubt, keep moving left a little to find red markers, which will lead you to the top of the western buttress of the mountain. Once the ridge has been achieved, move east towards the Summit, and you will see how the mountain got its name. Pla means a level area, and whilst the top of the mountain is no bowling green, it is more gently undulating than most. Keep going east, and when you meet a small hill, turn it on the right, and you will find the rocky arête and the pinnacles of the summit to your right. Beneath the summit is another large flat area, which in spring is covered with prickly blue hedgehog broom (*Erinacea anthyllis*), and in the centre of which is the largest and deepest nevera (ice-pit) that I have ever seen. *4h 30min*

It will take only 10min of an easy rock scramble to gain the highest point, an elegant pinnacle with a cross and a letter-box installed by the Callosa de Segura Mountaineering Club. As might be expected, both foreground and distant views are sensational. Note to the north in the far distance the mountain of Almisira and the Forada Ridge near Pego.

The Return To Collado De Borrell

The descent is far from pleasant, as the path which goes right off the eastern end of the buttress soon disappears into scree and rocks which are extremely unstable. Keep going down until you can see below you a large crag set in the middle of the scree slope, and make this your first objective. From the crag, move further south, avoiding any temptation to use tracks which go in any other direction, as they will surely lead you into the depths of Barranco del Moro, on the wrong side of the ridge. Eventually, when Aitana comes into view, set a course for the array of aerials and domes on its summit. Take your last look at the coast, with Altea and Sierra Helada, and find a narrow track leading south-west towards Collado de Borrell. *5h 30min*

You will have to negotiate the head of a small barranca, descend a little to pass under some slabs, and finally, pass through a boulder field to reach a small rise, from which, at a cairn, another track leads left down towards the Guadalest Valley. Ignore this track, and rejoin your morning route under the screes of Pla de la Casa. *6h 15min*

To The Puerto Del Contadores

A sensible route, after such a demanding day, is to follow the forestry road west, as it descends a little into a hollow, climbs up a little (bearing left at a junction), to traverse under the summits of the Serrella back to the shepherd's hut on the flat area which we visited earlier. *6h 45min*

Keep on the forestry road, until another flat area with extensive ruins of fincas is reached. Go south down through the ruins, and climb to a small gap in the rocks, between the summit of Borrell and the rest of the ridge. This is the Puerto del Contadores, which leads down to the Rincon del Olvido Restaurant, which can now be seen below you. Contadores means the counting place for sheep and goats. *7h*

Ascent Of Borrell (Diversion)

Those with inexhaustible energy, and a spirit of adventure, will ignore the sensible route, and head for the base of the Borrell Ridge to the south. There is a well-defined goat track which leads directly to the Puerto del Contadores, but there is one small problem: as goats do not tend to reach a height of more than a metre, climbers over this height will impale themselves regularly on the spiky vegetation. In 25min, after passing some sheep folds, built against the crags, you will note a tempting rake which leads upwards to the right, and leads to the summit ridge. It is quite an exposed rock scramble, and once on the ridge, you will have to share it with the wild mountain goats, who are the sitting tenants, and much given to posing artistically in impossible situations on the pinnacles. When you tire of this diversion, return to the track, and join the walkers' route at the Puerto.

Down To The Rincon Del Olvido

There is no continuous track down the steep slopes to the road and the restaurant, which can be seen below you. Try to keep moving east as you descend, in order to avoid the crags and the depths of a barranco. A useful marker is a small crag with two large boulders on top, which you should pass on the upper side. Eventually, below you appears a large flattish area, from which a reasonable track descends to the road. The restaurant is a most welcome sight at the end of such a full and satisfying day, and it has a well-earned reputation for Valencian cuisine.

7h 45min

Bernia main summit with Casas Berdlola (Route 7). Photo: Maurice Gibbs

Lomo Largo with summit of Silla de Cao and Bernia in distance (Route 14) *author*
Severino Ridge looking south with Puig Campana and Aitana in distance (Route 8) *Eunice Gibbs*

ROUTE 11: AGULLES DE LA SERRELLA Sc/S 7½km 6h

The Serrella Massif, which stretches from Puerto de Confrides in the west to the Paso del Castillo in the east, has many attractive features. There are six summits over 1000m, the largest, highest and deepest nevera, and the highest and most magnificently placed castle in the area. On its northern flank, between the villages of Fachega and Cuatretondeta, overlooking the Ceta Valley, stand the Aigulles. These rocky pinnacles stand in serried ranks, high up on the scree slopes, beneath the northern cliffs, of which they were once part. It is sometimes difficult to pick them out, as they tend to merge with the cliffs behind them, but, in clear conditions, and with oblique lighting, they present a unique sight in these mountains.

The main expedition is for experienced mountaineers only, used to rock climbing and crossing difficult terrain. For such people, it will be a long but exhilarating day. For those who feel unable to tackle the rocks, the good tracks through the cultivated terraces beneath the pinnacles will prove to be a memorable walk in magnificent surroundings. Hardy walkers should have no difficulty in reaching the Chesterfield Spire at the bottom of the scramble, and following tracks which descend to the nearest road.

Getting There

From the coast, leave the Jalon Valley, and continue past Castell de Castells on the A120, until you reach Fachega. On the outskirts of the village take the left-hand fork on the AP1033, signposted Cuatretondeta, and soon the pinnacles will come into view, high on the northern slopes of the Serrella. The countryside is made up of shaly soil and there are very few identifiable features on this road, but as you come to the top of a small rise, at about Km.6.5, note two unsurfaced roads on the left-hand side, and park your car here. The first road, just below the top of the rise, is your return route and the next road, which heads approximately south-west, is where you start your walk.

The Scramblers' Route - Country Walk

For the first half-hour the route is along good country roads across cultivated land, which in season is a mass of almond and cherry blossom. Avoid any road going down into the Ceta Valley, keeping roughly parallel with the mountain. Your route is generally to the west although at times the road swings away from the mountain for a few minutes. When confronted with a small hill, take the track which passes

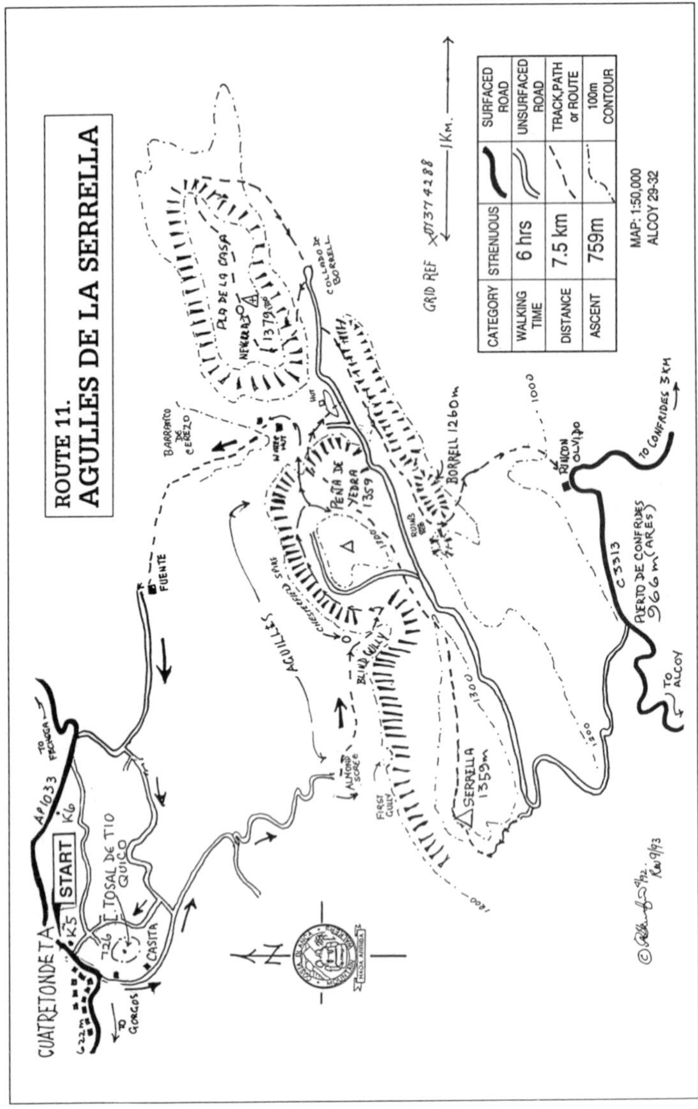
ROUTE 11.
AGULLES DE LA SERRELLA
CATEGORY
STRENUOUS
WALKING TIME
6 hrs
DISTANCE
7.5 km
ASCENT
759m
SURFACED ROAD
UNSURFACED ROAD
TRACK,PATH or ROUTE
100m CONTOUR
MAP: 1:50,000
ALCOY 29-32
GRID REF X0737 4288
1KM.
CUATRETONDETA
START
K5
K6
AP1033
TO FACHECA
TO GORGOS
TOSAL DE TIO QUICO
CASITA
FUENTE
BARRANCO DE CEREZO
WATER HUT
HUT
PLA DE LA CASA
NEVERA
1379
COLLADO DE BORRELL
PENTA DE YEDRA
1359
RUINS
BORRELL 1260m
RINCON OLVIDO
TO CONFRIDES 3KM
C3313
PUERTO DE CONFRIDES
966m (ARES)
TO ALCOY
AGUILLES
SPIRE
CHESTERFIELD
BLIND GULLY
ALMOND SCREE
FIRST GULLY
SERRELLA
1359m
1300
1200
1000

it on the south side (left), and in 20min you are joined by a good unsurfaced road coming up from Cuatretondeta. Turn left now, directly towards the mountain and climb gently, in zig-zags, until the road ends in a grove of olives, flourishing in a field of shale. You are now directly beneath First Gully, with its large fan of scree. *30 min*

To The Chesterfield Spire

This is the end of good tracks for the next 5h, as you leave the stony grove to find a rough track going upwards, then traversing east across the scree shoot. How these scree paths survive, I cannot guess, as there are now very few goats in the hills. It may be the hunters who tread out the paths each year after the winter rains. After crossing the first scree, the path continues between scrub and rocks towards Blind Gully, keeping fairly level. When you reach the second scree shoot, it is easier to ascend the right-hand side, where the vegetation and rocks give you something to hold on to. When you reach the base of the cliffs another rough track appears, going east, and leads into the pinnacles, which are now visible ahead. You will pass a narrow fissure on the right-hand side (Willie's Folly), which separates a tooth of rock from the rock wall on the west side of Blind Gully. This fissure always seems to attract walkers, but after struggling through it, you will only emerge higher up on the great stone shoot of the gully. It is better to keep straight on until you reach an elegant but leaning spire of rock; Chesterfield Spire.*1h 30min*

This is as far as the prudent walker should go. The views down the valley towards Cocentaina and Muro de Alcoy are impressive when seen against the foreground of the pinnacles. It is also possible to explore the pinnacles to the east, although there are no reliable paths, and it is also possible, with luck, to join the scramblers' return route near the fuente.

Hancliff's Route (for scramblers only)

This route is the only civilised way to the top of the Serrella Ridge. The alternative is by way of the wide gully filled with unstable rocks and scree, which, after half an hour, is blocked by a rock wall. The gully continues to the east, becoming even steeper and more unstable. By comparison, this scramblers' route is on rock, sometimes vegetated, but sound, and giving intimate views of the pinnacles, which become even more dramatic when seen from above. Red markers have been placed, and the route takes about one and a half hours to complete.

Start your climb above the tooth of rock next to the Chesterfield Spire, climb a modest rock wall between two pinnacles, and cross some scree towards a prominent crag, which is passed on the right-hand side. Now ascend by slabs and a groove to a rocky staircase. The sound rock gradually deteriorates into scree and scrub, as the summit of the Serrella appears to the west. Below you can be seen the wall blocking Blind Gully. Keep going up until you find yourself on a nice little arête, which leads to a small shelter at the top of the climb. You now have time to take in the extensive views of the Ceta Valley as far as Gorga, and you should be able to see your car parked along the valley road. *3h*

Across The Serrella Ridge

Ahead of you to the east, the ridge continues towards the beautiful peak of Pla de la Casa, and to the south, the aerials on Aitana are visible. You are also made aware of the complex structure of the Serrella, which is, in fact, made up of three separate ridges, with forestry roads in the valleys between them. To the west can be seen the main summit of Serrella, with its triangulation pillar. Continue going east and you will come to a grassy col at the end of one of these forestry roads. From here I recommend that you climb south to gain the top of some crags on Peña de Yedra, which gives excellent views down into the Guadalest Valley. *3h 30min*

Down Into The Barranco Del Cerezo

Return to the col, and head east in the direction of Pla de la Casa, to descend the end of the ridge. There is no path, but head for a lower col where some tracks cross at the Puerto del Cerezo between the two mountains. This is somewhat difficult to find in poor visibility. *4h*

Now turn left (north) down the ravine, which will eventually lead to the Ceta Valley below, and in a few minutes, arrive at a small hut, used to collect drinking water for the villages below. It is tempting to follow the partially buried water pipe as a guide to the valley, but beware, the pipe does some pretty desperate things when it encounters crags. Climb instead up behind the little hut, to find a higher path, which passes through a small rock gateway and then across some scree to another rock gateway, where a well-engineered path zig-zags down and finally ends in an almond grove and a fuente. *5h*

Second Country Walk

A good unsurfaced road now leads west from the almond grove, descending all the time, until you join another road and can turn east towards your starting point. The views of the pinnacles from below are equally delightful, as you pass a shaly depression before reaching the

road, at the end of an exhilarating day. Sadly, no refreshments await you, but the bars and restaurants of Cuatretondeta and Fachega are close at hand.

6h

ROUTE 12: SERRELLA CASTLE M(A) 13km 3½h

The history of the Moorish occupation of this part of Spain for over seven centuries is well documented elsewhere, but the remains of watch towers and castles are still to be found throughout the region on many strategically situated crags, and certainly add interest to a day in the mountains.

Our first castle, the highest in the region, is right on top of a sheer crag overlooking the northern side of the Guadalest Valley forming part of the Sierra de Serrella. This range runs in a shallow arc from east to west and excellent views of the range can be had from Guadalest and the C3313. The zig-zags of the forestry road can be seen crossing the front of the castle crag and disappear over a col to the right of the crag. At the bottom left of the zig-zags a small red building marks the pumping station. The castle is not marked on the military maps, but its water supply is Pozo de Castellet.

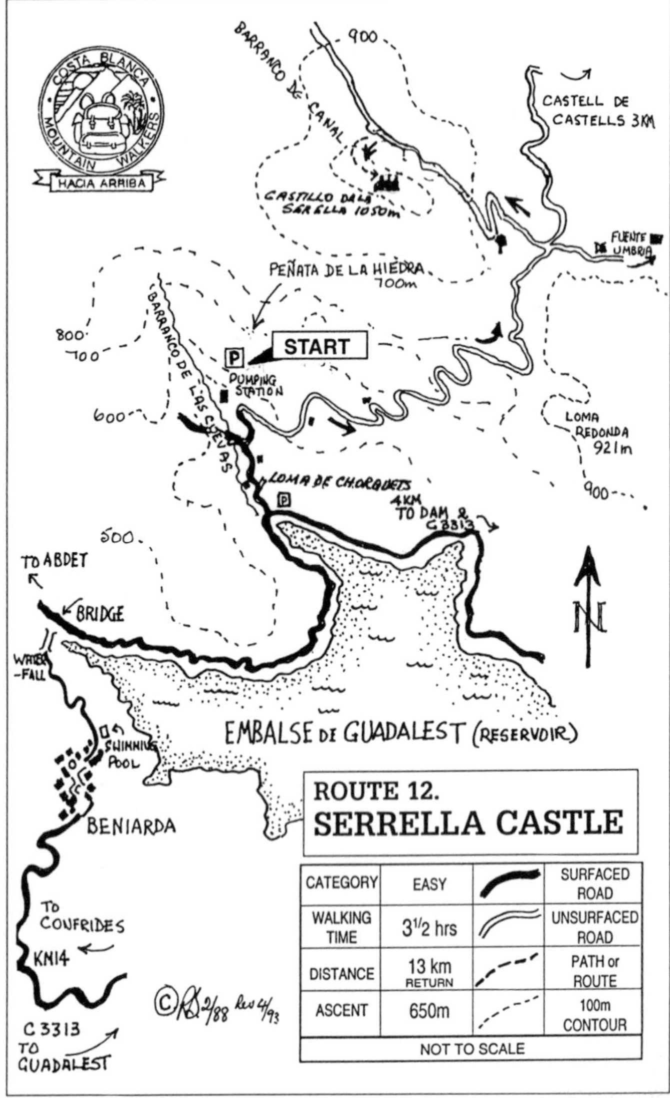
COSTA BLANCA
MOUNTAIN WALKERS
HACIA ARRIBA
BARRANCO DE CANAL
900
CASTELL DE
CASTELLS 3KM
CASTILLO DALA SERELLA 1050m
FUENTE DE UMBRIA
PEÑATA DE LA HIEDRA
700m
800
700
BARRANCO DE LAS CUEVAS
START
PUMPING STATION
600
LOMA
REDONDA
921m
LOMA DE CHORQUETS
4KM
TO DAM &
C3313
900
500
TO ABDET
BRIDGE
WATER-FALL
SWIMMING POOL
EMBALSE DE GUADALEST (RESERVOIR)
BENIARDA
To
CONFRIDES
KM14
C 3313
TO
GUADALEST
N
ROUTE 12.
SERRELLA CASTLE
CATEGORY
EASY
SURFACED ROAD
WALKING TIME
3½ hrs
UNSURFACED ROAD
DISTANCE
13 km RETURN
PATH or ROUTE
ASCENT
650m
100m CONTOUR
NOT TO SCALE

'Glacier' de Serrella and Mala del Llop from Route 12. Photo: Author

The Route

Our route follows forestry roads except for the final climb to the castle ruins which necessitates some easy, if exposed, scrambling. Cars can be taken as far as the pumping station, but beyond this, the road is subject to erosion. Forestry vehicles and Jeep Safaris also use this road, so be prepared to share it with them! Make a start from the road along the northern side of the Guadalest Reservoir where a very tight bend negotiates an arm of the reservoir, formed by the rocky bed of the Rio Cuervos (2km from the western end, and 4km from the dam). There are some red marks on the wall and the surfaced road leads north-west, following the dry bed of the Rio Cuervos for the first half-hour. After 5min, ignore a track on the right, and shortly afterwards, when the road forks, keep to the right, following the water-pipes until the pumping station is reached (30min). Our road now bends right to move north-east across the base of the castle crag on a well engineered road (unsurfaced), which zig-zags upwards in order to gain the col. Some of the gradients are very steep, so take your time, stopping to admire the views. Above you are the ruins of the castle. After 20min, you pass a prominent crag to the right. Here is a good place to stop for excellent views of the Guadalest Valley (first views of Confrides at the western end) and behind you the Barranco de Canal, which in most of the guidebooks is called the "Glacier" of the Serrella. Whilst it has none of the characteristics of a true glacier, the twin jagged ridges somehow suggest it, and I too, on seeing it for the first time, thought of it as such. Thankfully, the gradient now eases a little, and shortly afterwards, you reach a broad col with a crossroads, Puerto del Castillo.

The Broad Col

You now have extensive views to the northern side of the Serrella Range - not a village to be seen, only the mountains in all their glory dominate everything, from Mala del Llop (1361m) to the west, to the Sierra Aixorta to the east. To the north-west is Corral de Alt and Paso Tancat with its rocky gorge. From the col, the road straight ahead goes down to Castell de Castells, the road to the right (east) leads in 10min to the Fuente de Umbria (on the left, blue sign on tree). Our way goes left (west) to zig-zag upwards towards the base of the crag. After 10min, at a lone pine tree, look back to get your first view of Castell de Castells below in its lonely valley. Some rocky pinnacles are passed, and then a second col is reached. *1h 35min*

The road (constructed 1987) continues to the edge of the glacier ridge, then dips down to the Castell de Castells-Alcoy road west of the village. Up to the left, can be seen the castle ruins which can be reached in 10min by following a well-worn path, first, to the right of a deposito (still containing water) then to the right until the rocky ridge is reached, then traverse back left to enter the castle ruins.

The Castle

Despite the neglect of nearly five centuries the ruins are impressive and the views of the surrounding mountains even more so. The Guadalest Valley, with all its many villages, is probably here seen from its most attractive viewpoint. The old "glacier" dominates the western aspect with Mala del Llop beyond. Altea and the coast are in the distance to the south-east, and Aitana is to the south with another Moorish castle, El Castellet, on its flank, a few degrees right of Benifato village and the transmitting station on the summit. To the north, range upon range of mountains lead to the distant horizon.

The Descent

Those with kind friends or chauffeurs, can now look forward to a comfortable walk down to Castell de Castells by either of the forestry roads. Most, however, will have to retrace their steps down to the Guadalest Valley, reflecting on a day spent in some of the most magnificent mountain scenery of our province. There is a bar and an excellent restaurant, the Mustique, in the village of Beniarda. *3½h*

Val De Jalon

ROUTE 13: CORDILLERAS DE ALMADICH M/S 17km $5\frac{1}{2}$h

This is a most scenic walk and, for once, we do not climb to the summit of the mountain but first start by walking up this attractive valley, then climbing a ravine to a high plateau and, finally, enjoying a 5km traverse along a broad ledge 300m above the valley floor. The walk is all on good tracks and the high level traverse is broad enough for the local farmer to graze his cows on in summer!

Getting There

Leave the lush lower Jalon Valley at Parcent and follow the A1202, signposted Castell de Castells, towards Benichembla. Just past Villa Menlu on the right and near Km.3.5, turn left (south) on a narrow, surfaced road for about half a kilometre until another road joins from the left. This is in fact the return route. Leave the car here.

Up The Valley

This delightful, unfrequented valley makes a lovely walk in itself. First walk south on the road climbing gently with plenty of time to admire the views. Behind you rises the Caballo Verde Ridge with Pena Roch at its western end. High above you on your left rise the cliffs of what the Mapas Militar call, rather unimaginatively, Cordilleras, which simply means a mountain range, and the many bands of cliffs contain a number of summits with its highest point, Morro Enserra, 1000m. Across the valley, guarding the entrance, is El Mirabo, 695m, and to the left of this peak (north-west) is the bulk of Cocoll, 1141m. To the left of Cocoll, right at the head of the valley, is the shapely cone of Tossalet del Vaguer. The Traverse is on the northern slopes of the Cordilleras.

To The Ancient Settlement

The road continues to rise and ahead can be seen the great buttress of Pena Finestres, which you will pass close to later. In half a kilometre ignore a concrete road on the left-hand side, our road continues to zig-zag upwards. Look over your shoulder to see Orba Castle and Montgo on the coast. The road now loses its surface and you pass a casita in course of restoration and later a ruined one. *1h*

You now pass very close to the base of the crags, as the path narrows, and you pass a tiny casita with a fireplace and descend a little to negotiate the head of a small barranca. You should now start to find red markers to help you. Climb to a small col with a crag and a rock cairn. *1h 15min*

Below can be seen the road which follows the valley bottom to the Fuente Pena Blanca at its head, and nearer, the ruins of an ancient settlement lie ahead, which you will pass through in 10mins time.

To Fuente Pena Blanca

Now negotiate another narrow ravine and climb to another shoulder with an oak on it. Look back to see the village of Murla nestling under Pena Roch as you walk down to the troughs of the fuente (restored 1985), much used to water grazing animals including cattle which, thankfully, are always in the charge of a vaquero (herdsman). *2h*

The Ravine

The unsurfaced valley road ends here and at the head of the valley is a rocky stream bed in a narrow ravine (normally dry). To negotiate this obstacle follow a very indistinct path which climbs to the cliffs on the right-hand side, then under them to cross over the stream bed. Now follow a good path which heads generally east, gaining height. Over your shoulder lies the distinctive peak of Tossalet del Vaquer (Hill of the herdsman), and the higher one of Cocoll with its new forestry road to the summit. First there is a shallow ravine to negotiate, then descend into a terraced barranca under Llometa d'Albordo, a good place for a break before starting the traverse. *2h 30min*

The High Level Traverse

Start by climbing out of the barranca on a good path moving basically east. The traverse is 5km and will take about 2h, depending on how often you stop to relish your position some 300m above the valley floor, following approximately the 800m contour. There are, however, six major ravines to cross to prevent the route becoming boring. There is no need for waymarkings as the cattle keep the way clear (and well fertilized).The only reason for grazing this dangerous route is that, facing north, it probably retains grass during the summer when grazing in the valley is scarce. There are no walkers' routes off the traverse. There are a number of enticing gullies which, however, all seem to end in vertical drops, only suitable for those with plenty of abseil rope and a strong nerve. You will be walking under some very impressive cliffs, but only at the ravines is there any possibility of leaving the traverse to

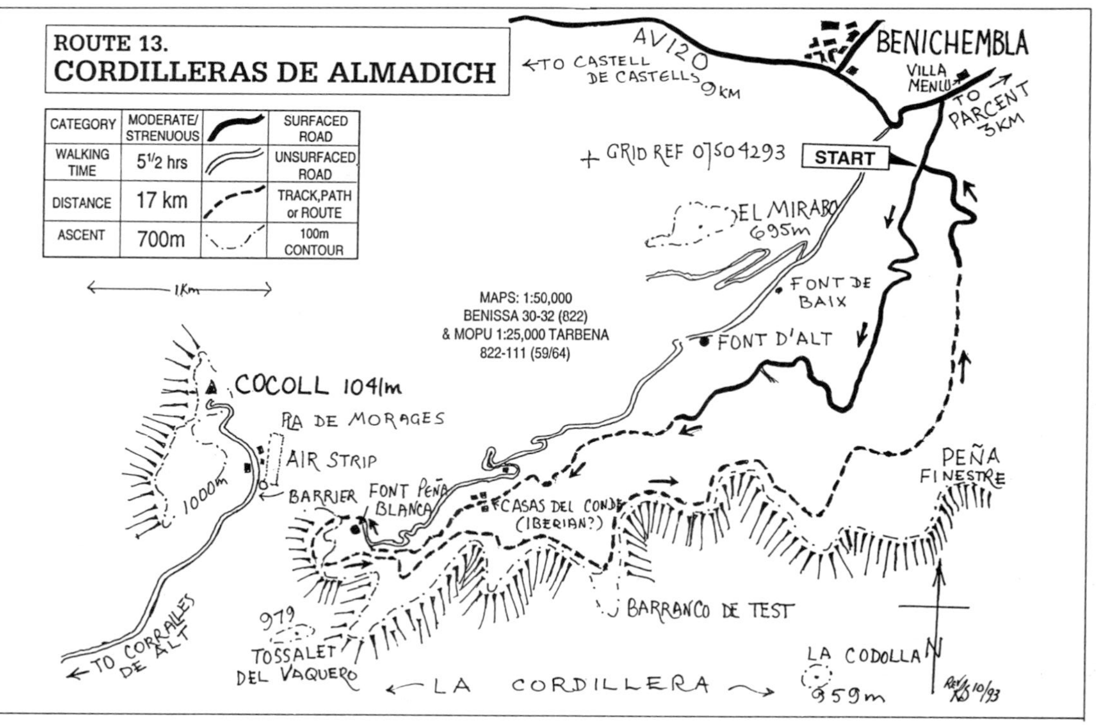
ROUTE 13.
CORDILLERAS DE ALMADICH
CATEGORY
MODERATE/ STRENUOUS
SURFACED ROAD
WALKING TIME
5½ hrs
UNSURFACED ROAD
DISTANCE
17 km
TRACK,PATH or ROUTE
ASCENT
700m
100m CONTOUR
1Km
BENICHEMBLA
AV120
TO CASTELL DE CASTELLS 9KM
VILLA MENU
TO PARCENT 3KM
GRID REF 07504293
START
EL MIRADOR 695m
FONT DE BAIX
FONT D'ALT
MAPS: 1:50,000
BENISSA 30-32 (822)
& MOPU 1:25,000 TARBENA
822-111 (59/64)
COCOLL 1041m
PLA DE MORAGES
AIR STRIP
BARRIER
FONT PEÑA BLANCA
CASAS DEL CONDE (IBERIAN?)
1000m
PEÑA FINESTRE
BARRANCO DE TEST
979
TOSSALET DEL VAQUERO
TO CORRALLES DE ALT
LA CORDILLERA
LA CODOLLA
959m
N

climb to the summit. The views are sensational and you can pick out your morning's route up the valley, including the dam constructed to hold back flood water, which you may have missed on the way up.

In some 2h, under Peña Finestres (Peak of the Windows), leave the traverse by crossing the last ravine and striking upwards towards a shaly area which marks the end of a development road. Below you can be seen your cars and the surfaced road leading down to them. Descend through new villas until the road gains a surface and you reach your cars after a dramatic and beautiful walk. There is plenty of hospitality in the bar at Benichembla and more sophisticated fare in Parcent.

5h 30min

ROUTE 14: LLOMA LARGA M(B) 9km 4½h

When I first looked upon these mountains of the Costa Blanca I was excited by the rugged ridges of the Bernia and the exquisite shape of Puig Campana, but realistic enough to accept that such bare rock might well be outside the capabilities of a retired mountaineer. But one mountain, which stirred memories of our British hills, gave hope of rather less exacting exercise and, in fact, has proved to be a great joy to me. That mountain is Cao which is the next best thing to a British fell walk in Spain (without, of course, the bogs and the driving rain).

The Mountain

The ridge runs north-east to south-west from the Jalon Valley to Pinos, and is 3km west of Benissa. You can see the two main peaks at the end of Benissa's main street and from most parts of Calpe, but the best view of all is from the CN332 as you climb out of Calpe towards Benissa, from which the whole ridge can be clearly seen. Cao has no great crags, but it does have impressive bands of rock and deep gullies. Some of these small cliffs have been identified as old sea-cliffs. The mountain has a distinct advantage over other peaks. It has excellent Spanish restaurants at each end! Some experience is required in finding the best route to follow on the ridge, and boots are essential as much of the walking is on bare rock. The ideal way to do this walk is north-west to south-east, and obviously needs two cars.

The Start

Originally the route started near Venta Roja Restaurant, just inside the Jalon Valley at the northern end of the Paso de Molinos but the area has now been developed for housing. It is now preferable to tackle the ridge

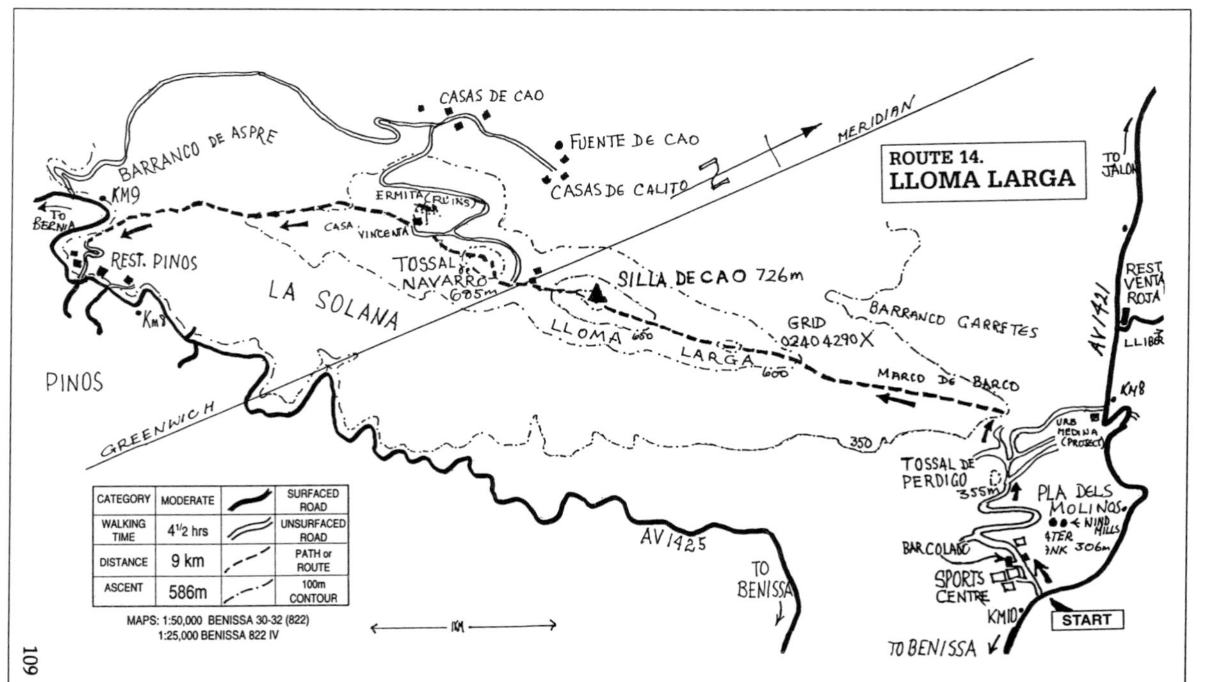
ROUTE 14.
LLOMA LARGA
CASAS DE CAO
FUENTE DE CAO
CASAS DE CALITO
MERIDIAN
TO JALON
BARRANCO DE ASPRE
KM9
TO BERNIA
ERMITA (RUINS)
CASA VINCENTA
REST. PINOS
TOSSAL de NAVARRO 605m
LA SOLANA
SILLA DE CAO 726m
REST VENTA ROJA
AV 1421
LLIBER
BARRANCO GARRETES
GRID 0240 4290 X
LLOMA 600
LARGA 600
MARCO DE BARCO
KM8
URB MEDINA (PROJECT)
PINOS
GREENWICH
350
TOSSAL DE PERDIGO 355m
PLA DELS MOLINOS
WIND MILLS
WATER TANK 306m
BARCOLAR
SPORTS CENTRE
KM10
START
TO BENISSA
AV 1425
TO BENISSA
CATEGORY | MODERATE
WALKING TIME | 4½ hrs
DISTANCE | 9 km
ASCENT | 586m
SURFACED ROAD
UNSURFACED ROAD
PATH or ROUTE
100m CONTOUR
MAPS: 1:50,000 BENISSA 30-32 (822)
1:25,000 BENISSA 822 IV
1KM

from the southern side at the col (Collado), near Km.11 on the AV1421 from Benissa to Jalon. (Signpost to the Sports Centre for Benissa (Polydeportivos)).

Follow the surfaced road, passing the Bar Collado, where refreshments are available, as it climbs and swings left at the water tanks. Pass two fincas and bear right at a junction and you are on one of the developer's access roads which contours, twists and climbs, eventually right up to the ridge at Tosal de Perigor. *45min*

The Ridge
At times there are good paths, and at times there are only bare rocks, and in some places, there are even red markers, but treat these with caution, because *some* are only boundary markers. Best to keep as near to the crest as possible, and do not be deceived by false summits: there are between 7 and 9 intermediate summits on this ridge. Remember that Cao is 1h 20min away, so settle down to enjoy the magnificent views in all directions. Note the Jalon Valley to your right, and the distinctive limestone flora. *2h*

Silla De Cao (726m)
There is no mistaking this summit, with its lofty triangulation station of the Institutio Geografico. It is a true mountain summit, all rock, with extensive views in all directions. Note especially the vines of Maserof in the valley to the west. The views of the Pou Roig Valley and its railway bridge and the distant Peñon d'Ifach and to the north-east a far-away vista towards Pego can all be enjoyed from this point. Due south-west, but out of sight below, lies the col with its casitas, behind which is the Tosal de Navarro, and it is not a bad idea to plan your route up to this from the summit of Cao. To descend to the col keep as near to the right of the ridge as is prudent, as the nearer the edge the easier the going. Continue until you can see the col and its casitas. *2h 30min*

At The Col
This is a lovely place for a meal break, right on the Greenwich Meridian of Longitude. The peak Silla de Cao, to the north-east, is in the Eastern Hemisphere, whilst Tosal de Navarro, on the other side of the col, is in the Western one. There is a modern structure, right in the col, but to the north of this is an old finca with an era, and in season there is watercress in a small stream. A road which has come up from Pinos, via Casas de Cao, can be followed to Casa Vincent by the faint-hearted who do not wish to ascend the Tosal.

Tosal De Navarro (683m)
Do not attempt a direct ascent from the casita, as the lower slopes are full of dead trees and debris. Better to traverse left until clear ground is encountered, and then traverse right to find the weakest point in the rock bands, to reach a rock summit with a cairn (3h). From here keep as near to the crest as possible and eventually you will descend to another col with a casita, and join the road previously mentioned.

Turn left, south, along the road until you come to a finca, still occupied, Casa Vincent. Keep going south-west, dropping down to a ruin on the right and a path which crosses the ridge at right angle to our route. Ignore this and keep on the same bearing to the north of a small hill, with the Barranco de l'Aspre and Casas de Cao below on the right (north-west). The ridge has been ripped up for planting pine trees, but you will still be able to find a path heading down to the surfaced road to Bernia (AV1425) which soon comes into view, at the bridge over Barranco de l'Aspre, near Km.9. If in doubt bear left, a little away from the bridge, and find a good track, which becomes a road, passing a finca and reaching the surfaced road, a few metres to the east of the Pinos Restaurant, where refreshments are available. *4h 20min*

ROUTE 15: ORBA CASTLE M(B) 6km 3h

As you drive on the C3318 from Parcent towards Orba and Pego, you will be treated to a good view of the ruins of this ancient castle on the left as you approach the pass. Returning by the same route, the eastern aspect is even more impressive. This is a lovely walk with rewarding views, first of the Jalon Valley with its vines and almonds to the south, then the contrasting vista of the Girona Huerto to the north, lush with citrus groves. This is a circular route with few good paths, but is well within the capabilities of most walkers. If you only wish to ascend to the castle then start from Murla (an unsurfaced road leads north-east from a stone cross at the eastern end of the village) as this is a much easier route.

Making A Start
The Pavo Real Restaurant is just to the south of the watershed between the Girona and Jalon valleys. It is the start and finish of this walk, at Km.14 on the C3318 at Murla. First walk along the car park on the south side of the restaurant for a few metres to an almond tree set in a wall. Here, turn right through the orchard and a path will appear marked in

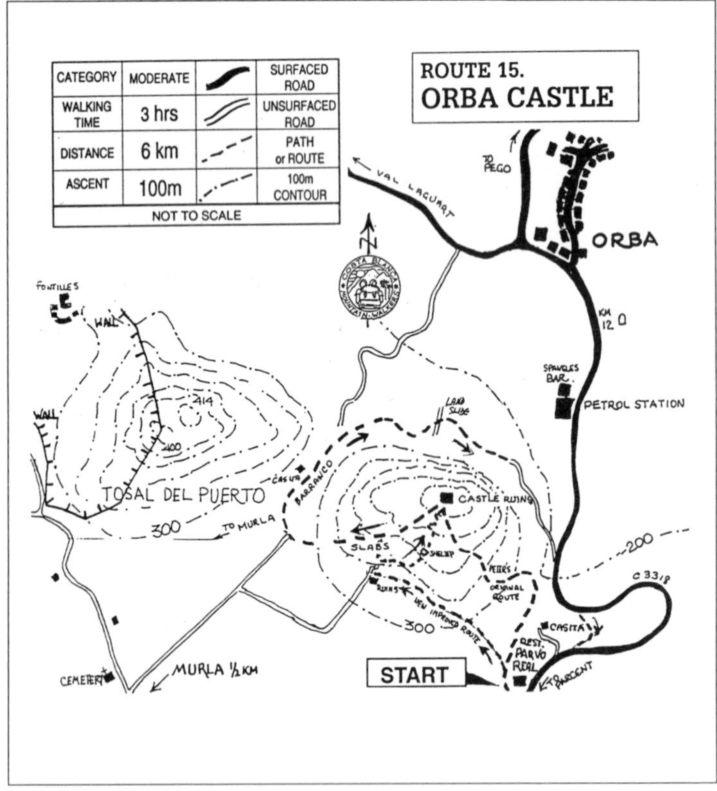

red. It will lead in 25min to a broad road coming up from Murla. Go along this road until it turns into a track near an old ruin.

To The Castle

From here, it is 15min to the castle, which is directly above. Whichever route you choose you will not have a continuous path. Avoid the vegetation by keeping to the rocky slabs as much as possible. If you keep to the left (west) you will find more bare rock, and eventually pick up the marked track to the Col. If at the ruins you traverse right (east) for some time, you will come to a cairn under a carob tree, which marks a good path to the shelter, and then on to the summit. There is little to choose between these routes in getting to the top. The western view is of the continuing ridge of Tosal del Puerto and the impressive boundary wall of Fontilles Sanatorium. To the left of the ridge can be seen the Caballo Verde Ridge and Peñon Roch with the Ermita of San Sebastiano perched high above the tiny village of Murla. Note Benimaurell high in the Val de Laguart with the village of Campbell below it.

Walking through the ruins to the eastern side you look down into Orba and the lush Huerto of the Girona, backed by the Sierra Segaria, with the sea in the distance. *1h*

Descent And Circuit

At the south-western end of the summit a track leads on to bare sloping slabs and some more red markers. Care is needed at one or two points to negotiate the rocks. Move slightly right (following the direction of the ridge) for a short time, passing a water deposit, to arrive at a small Casita with a corral. Here an unsurfaced road joins from Murla, and you can break off the circuit to visit the village which is half an hour away. Turn right along a reasonable track and enter the small Col on the ridge along almond terraces. Watch out for a red marker which indicates the need to drop down one bancale to join the rough track which descends the stony barranca between cliffs. Below can be seen a large water reservoir. The tracks swings north-east through a grove of pines, and drops down to a badly eroded area. A broad track to Orba should be ignored. Look for a red marker on the right. *2h*

After a rough start a passable track appears through the pines, moving east with the crags of the castle above on the right. After 20min there is much evidence of erosion, and the going is again rough, but take heart, the best track of the walk now appears, and leads gently down to the main road just above the petrol station *2h 40min*

Turn right towards the pass, and at the first bend, look for a red marker on the wall indicating a path which zig-zags upwards avoiding the hair-pin bends of the road and the traffic. Rejoin the road again near the pass, always being careful to walk on the left-hand side of the road, facing the oncoming traffic. Happily, it is then only a few metres back to the restaurant and welcome refreshments. *3h*

ROUTE 16: FIG TREE WALK TO EL FORAT NEGRE E(A) 15km 5h

To those who love the pastoral scenery of the lower Jalon Valley (Val de Pop), with its lush growth of vines and picturesque Riu-Raus, the upper valley beyond Benichembla provides a contrast, as the now dry river bed meanders between the crags of high mountain ridges. The ridge to the right (looking up the valley) is Cabello Verde with its dramatic peak of Peñon Roch hanging over the tiny village of Murla. The Ermita San Sebastian, high on the mountain behind the village, seems to protect it from the threatening Peñon. To our left is another ridge, which is the objective for the day.

Making A Start

Leave Parcent by taking the AV1201 towards Castell de Castells and past Benichembla. Stop at Km.4.5, (new road bridge). This upper valley, has, over the years, suffered devastation in the winter storms, and, as recently as 1988, the road to Castell de Castells was swept away in three places as flood-water destroyed quite substantial culverts. Reconstruction work is nearly complete, and it is at one of these newly-constructed bridges, where the Barranco Galistero joins the Jalon River that you start your walk. Here, a few years ago, stood a grove of old and fruitful fig trees. Sadly, the construction work has taken its toll, and only one wounded specimen survives. I still keep my original name for the walk, as a tribute to the sympathetic engineer who converted the old mule-track, which we shall use on our walk, into a forestry access road, and stabilised the edges with young fig trees. This is a gentle walk, and suitable even for perambulators [if fitted with 4-wheel drive, good springs (and a shock resistant infant!)] The objective of this walk is not an isolated mountain, or a castle perched on a rock, but a lovely walk in majestic scenery, first, above the upper Jalon Valley, then looking down into the Val de Alt. The newly made forestry road makes the going comfortable, and there is little need for route-finding. With your back

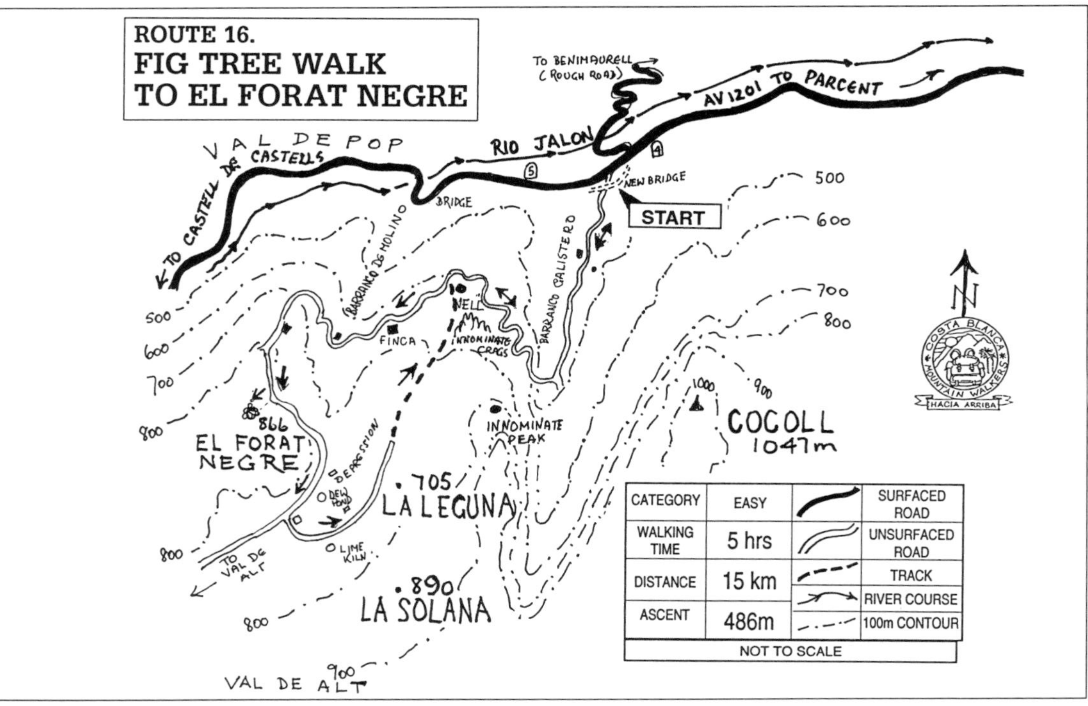
ROUTE 16.
FIG TREE WALK
TO EL FORAT NEGRE
TO BENIMAURELL
(ROUGH ROAD)
AV 1201 TO PARCENT
VAL DE POP
VAL DE CASTELLS
TO CASTELL DE CASTELLS
RIO JALON
5
4
NEW BRIDGE
START
BRIDGE
BARRANCO DE MOLINO
BARRANCO GALISTERO
WELL
FINCA
INNOMINATE CRAGS
INNOMINATE PEAK
866
EL FORAT NEGRE
DEPRESSION
DEW POND
LIME KILN
TO VAL DE ALT
705
LA LEGUNA
890
LA SOLANA
VAL DE ALT
COCOLL
1047m
1000
900
800
700
600
500
N
COSTA BLANCA
MOUNTAIN WALKERS
HACIA ARRIBA
CATEGORY
EASY
WALKING TIME
5 hrs
DISTANCE
15 km
ASCENT
486m
SURFACED ROAD
UNSURFACED ROAD
TRACK
RIVER COURSE
100m CONTOUR
NOT TO SCALE

to the road, look up a broad valley (east of south). To the left is the bulk of Cocoll (1047m). Immediately ahead is a broad track and an unnamed peak (part of La Laguna); on the right the summit ridge ends in a rock gully, and between these points can be seen the new forestry track zig-zagging up over the ridge.

To The Barranco De Molinero

Follow the track up the Barranco de Galistero alongside the dry river bed, passing a casita on the right, and a fuente on the left, and in 15min reach a junction. Take the right-hand fork, which leaves the valley and starts to climb in well-engineered zig-zags to the right-hand flank of Innominate Peak. As you gain height, look back to see the Cabello Verde ridge appear to the north, and finally arrive at Innominate Crags, where you will find an old finca. Carry on round the edge of the ridge to a gully (which is the return route), where there is a fuente. *45min*

After a short climb, around another bend, is an old, quite extensive finca with a well, oven and era (threshing floor), a wonderful spot to rest for a while with commanding views. *50min*

To the north-east is Peñon Roch, the end of the Cabello Verde ridge, and Montgo is visible now. Leave the old finca, probably reluctantly, now moving south-west, and press on down into the Barranco de Molinero. Below, you can see the new substantial road bridge over the Jalon River. Seeing the river in its normally dry state, it seems hard to justify such a bridge, but, when winter comes with the storms, it will certainly prove to be of great benefit to the people of Castell de Castells and beyond. It seems a long way down to the head of this barranco, and a long climb (now north-west) up to regain the height lost, but soon, turn south-west again to reach another ruined finca, and a deep roadside well on the left. *1h 30min*

To El Forat Negre

This last stretch is very pleasant and more gentle. Go in a southerly direction up to an old casita on the left, then turn left (south-east). The track now levels out, with a small ruined house on the left. Follow the track for about 20m, then strike upwards (no path) amongst the rocks to reach the highest point, where there is a rock cairn and a small shelter. You are now at El Forat Negre (869m) with extensive all-round views, which include the Bernia, Aixorta, Serrella Castle, Mala del Llop, and the highest of them all, Aitana. Only one village, Famorca, can be seen to the north-west. *2h 15min*

Return Routes

Those who have become deeply attached to the forestry road can reverse the route; those seeking a little variation, and not afraid of a bit of rough walking, can rejoin the forestry road at the fuente, by following the original direction (generally south-east and south-west), passing a ruined casita on the left; follow this route for 20min before turning left at a junction near a dew-pond. After 5min (generally north-east) pass an old limekiln on the right and the road then ends. *40min*

Now the rough walking starts, as we turn off left into a barranco (north-east) to enter a gorge. Keep to the right-hand side (east), and descend carefully until a goat-track appears and leads down to the fuente on the forestry road, which we saw on the ascent. *1h*

There is no handy bar for refreshments but Benichembla is only 4km away.

Rush leaved daffodil

Val De Laguart

ROUTE 17: CABALLO VERDE RIDGE S(C) 14km 5h

In 1609 a great battle occurred on this ridge, as the troops of the Spanish king subdued the last remnants of the Moorish occupation, destroyed their castle of Peñon Roch, and deported every man, woman and child to Africa via the port of Denia. The last refuge of these Moriscos had been this long high rocky ridge, which divides the Jalon and Laguart valleys, running due west to east, with the rocky mountain El Peñon Roch overlooking the little village of Murla at the eastern end. The Moors had defied the expulsion orders of the Spaniards, and continued to lead a peaceful co-existence with their Spanish neighbours, but, by 1609, they had been joined by other refugees, and totalled over 20,000, which eventually caused alarm amongst the Spaniards. The name El Caballo Verde is based on a mystical Moorish knight who was said to ride from the mountain on a green charger to drive out the Christians.

This walk offers a complete traverse of the ridge from the western end to the col under Peñon Roch. The rest of the ridge to Murla needs some rock-climbing, and cannot be considered a walk. The approach and the first and last sections of the walk are on surfaced roads. The ridge itself is rough walking, mainly on rock with hardly any paths. The ridge rocks are very dangerous in wet conditions and in poor visibility route-finding is difficult, especially at the broad western end. So far, no safe way has been found off the ridge on its flanks.

Making A Start

Leave the C3318 at Orba with signs Fontilles and Val de Laguart, and follow the AV1433 until it ends at Benimaurell. Park near the Bar Oasis. A narrow surfaced road to the Jalon Valley continues past the Bar Oasis and climbs the northern flank of the ridge to a col where there are a few casitas. *40min*

Onto The Ridge

Leave the road to join an old track with some stone steps on the east side. This is all that remains of an old mule track between the Jalon and Laguart valleys and will take you down to Benimaurell, so you leave it after a few minutes, to follow the orange-coloured markers onto another narrow track which continues on the north side of the ridge towards Pt

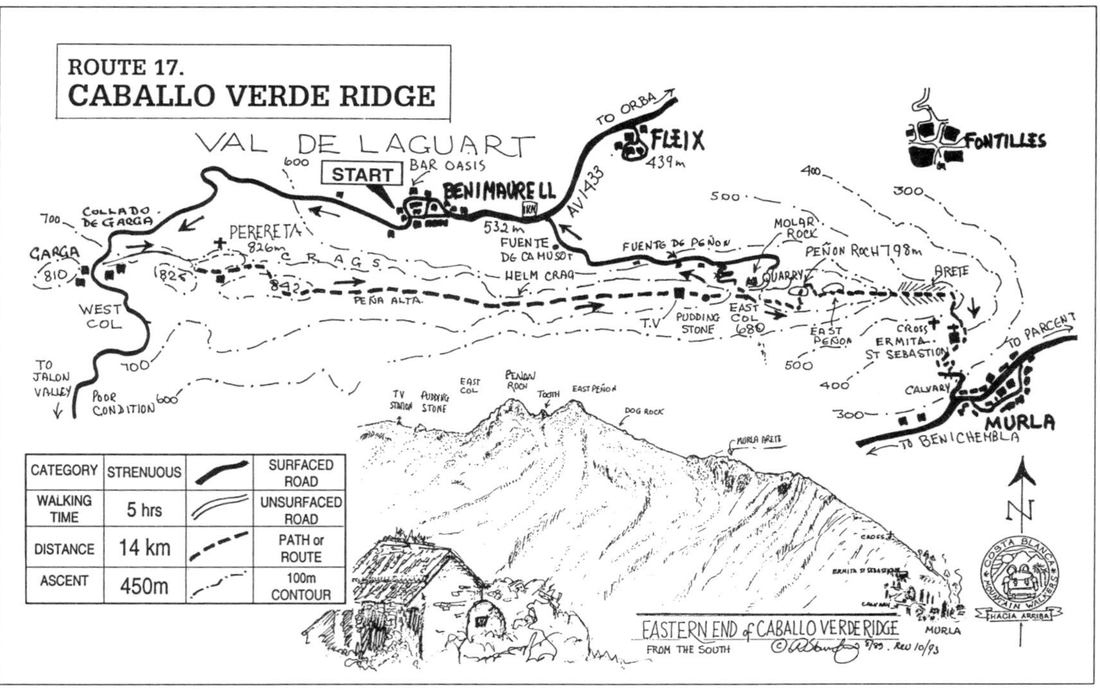

CATEGORY	STRENUOUS		SURFACED ROAD
WALKING TIME	5 hrs		UNSURFACED ROAD
DISTANCE	14 km		PATH or ROUTE
ASCENT	450m		100m CONTOUR

824. You now reach a small col with bancales (terraces) and here you cross over to the south side of the ridge, and towards Pt 847. At times, there is no path, and at other times, its seems that there are two or three. Try not to lose height, and reach a small ruined casita with Pt 847 ahead (the highest point on the ridge). Overhead on a crag (Perereta 826m) on the north side of the ridge is a stone cross from which views of the valley are obtained. At this point the ridge is very broad. *1h 20min*

Keep going towards the col, then move right to aim for the summit rocks, in which you will find a rock gateway leading to the south side of the ridge and views of the Jalon Valley and the eastern part of our ridge, terminating in Peñon Roch.

1h 40min

From here to the Peñon there is seldom a continuous path, and it is often better to keep to the ridge rocks. First, pass a small cairn, then reach a small col with bancales coming up from the northern side. For another half-hour, keep on the ridge, until you reach a small depression with crags on the far side. *2h*

Keep left going down and avoid the crags, bypassing them on the south side. Use a narrow terrace, and pass a circular shelter with views of the narrowest part of the ridge and some prominent pinnacles of rock (Helm Crag). *2h 50min*

On the north side of the largest pinnacle is a large cave, well worth exploring. This is a wonderful place to stop for lunch.

Descend from the pinnacles on flat slabs to a craggy ridge, which is a very sporting scramble for those with good balance and nerve. Ahead on the right is the Cao Ridge near Pinos. Slowly the ridge broadens again, and we can see first the Peñon and its quarry on the northern flank, and the walls of the sanatorium at Fontilles also appear, and then, at a small shelter, the blue TV cabin and Pudding Stone. *3h 20min*

Pass the TV transmitter (overturned when last I was on this ridge).

3h 50min

Then pass the Pudding Stone which you pass on the left (north) to reach the col under Peñon Roch. *4h*

Ascent Of The Peñon (Diversion)

To reach the summit of the Peñon is a rock scramble, and to cross the two summits, follow a rocky arête and ridge down to the Ermita San Sebastian, and then via a Calvary to the village of Murla. It is a very rough expedition, with no paths, but is very rewarding. Allow $2^{1}/_{2}$ hours to Murla. There are orange markers on the ascent and descent of the summits ONLY. For those experienced in rock-climbing ONLY.

Start on the south side of the summit crags by crossing a maze of large boulders, well vegetated with spiky plants. If this does not put you off, perhaps the 4m wall will. This obstacle, however, has its weakness, and is the last obstacle before traversing carefully upwards towards a small belvedere. From here, strike straight up to the summit on broken ground. The small holes made by treasure seekers, and a few broken pots and tiles indicate that you are nearing the summit. To descend, go down a short rock pitch (easy) on the north side, which is a little exposed, and traverse up to the eastern summit. From here, keep to the ridge as far as possible, passing Dog Rock on the left whilst descending slabs, to gain the short but delightful Murla Arête, then make for the metal cross above the village, descending through old terraces to the Ermita, then down to Murla on a good track.

Linger awhile, because this is where you will leave the ridge to return to Benimaurell. The next section is very overgrown, and is notorious for its briars (shorts *not* recommended). Go down on the north (left) side, and keep wherever possible to the bare rock. Keep left of a large boulder with a garden on top, and aim for a rock shaped like a tooth (Molar Rock). At this rock, you strike a good track which goes right to the quarry and the surfaced road. A better and shorter route is to go left until a new casita is reached. *4h 10min*

There, look for a path on the right (orange markers) and go down in zig-zags on an old mule track to the surfaced road near a casita. Turn left and walk back to the main road, then left towards the village and the Bar Oasis. On the way, it is fun to pick out the pinnacles and other points on the ridge, and bask in the satisfaction of a hard walk well done. *5h*

There are three bars and three restaurants in the village of Benimaurell.

ROUTE 18: DAY OF 5000 STEPS S(B) 18km 6½h

I do not pretend to be able to date or explain the ancient stepped mule tracks which can be found all over these mountains, and are commonly known as Mozarabic trails. The word Mozarabic is usually reserved for those Moslems who accepted the Christian religion after the reconquest. They are well-constructed tracks, showing considerable engineering skills, as they take in their stride precipitous ascents and descents across the gorges and valleys of the rugged mountains. Begin this walk by crossing the Ebo Gorge (Val de Infierno), from Fleix towards the village of Val d'Ebo (a descent of some 300m). It is a circular route of some

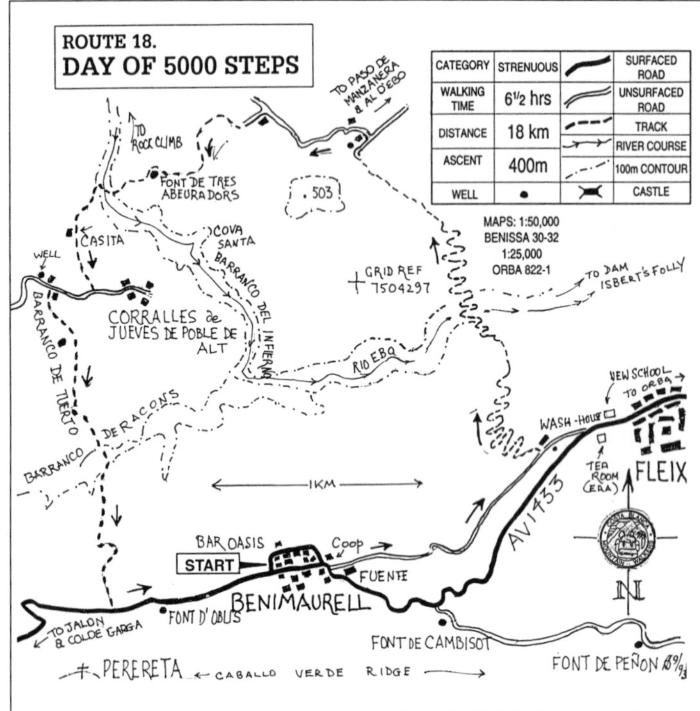

CATEGORY	STRENUOUS		SURFACED ROAD
WALKING TIME	6½ hrs		UNSURFACED ROAD
DISTANCE	18 km		TRACK
			RIVER COURSE
ASCENT	400m		100m CONTOUR
WELL	•		CASTLE

18km. In one or two places, even the solid Mozarabic construction has succumbed to the forces of nature, and the track becomes difficult to follow, but generally, the whole long day is spent on good trails with magnificent views. You will not pass a single inhabited dwelling during the whole walk, but there are good water supplies at three wells on the route.

Making A Start

Benimaurell is the last and highest village in the beautiful Val de Laguart. Seen from Montgo, you can really appreciate its elevation of 532m at the head of the valley. To reach the village, leave the C3318 at Orba, follow the AV1433 (signposted Val Laguart), and start the walk at the Bar Oasis at the western end of the village.

Go down through the village in an easterly direction until you reach the Cooperativa Agricola San Roch, and turn left down to the village well and wash-house. From here, a lovely lane descends gently through orchards of cherry, almond and apple, until in 20min you see the wash-house of the neighbouring village Fleix ahead. Just before reaching the wash-house and its fuente, turn left to join your first Mozarabic trail, which will lead us to the very bottom of the gorge. *20min*

Down To The Rio Ebo

Across the valley as you descend you can see a complementary trail zig-zagging upwards on the other side of the gorge. This is on our route. In another 15min cross a small stream, and go down through a cave in the cliff. Descend now by zig-zags, and get your first view of the beautiful waterfall, which drops some 70m from near the cave to the base of the cliff. Sadly, the stream dries up in the summer, but in winter, or after rain, it is worth doing this part of the walk to appreciate the beautiful cascade. After another 30min, recross the stream to reach the east side of the valley. *50min*

Keep to the trail as it passes under some cliffs, and zig-zags down to the rocky bed of the Rio Ebo. For most of the year there is no water in the river, but after stormy weather, not only does the river flow, but the dam downstream (Isbert's Folly), holds water for a few weeks, and a lake is formed. Diversions upstream to the Val de Infierno, and downstream to the dam, are possible.

Camino De Juvias

Cross the dry river-bed to find the Mozarabic trail, which keeps to the left-hand side of a deep ravine for about 30min. After passing a squarish boulder, the track climbs left away from the ravine. On this section, you get good views up into the Val de Infierno, and back to the Fontilles Sanatorium, with its great boundary wall, the Caballo Verde Ridge, and in the distance, Montgo on the coast. Eventually, a stream invades the trail, which becomes very eroded and overgrown. Thankfully, this section is very short, so push through to reach a level area with almond groves and a well. This is Pou de Juvias. *2h 25min*

Leave the well, and go uphill on a broad unsurfaced road in a west-north-westerly direction, passing some small casitas, until in about 5min the track levels out, and comes to an extensive ruined finca. To continue on this road would lead over the Paso de Manzanas to Pla de la Molino above the village of Val d'Ebo. Turn left, once more down into the gorge in a generally south-west direction. The track at times is badly eroded, but there are dramatic views down into the gorge as you pass under some cliffs to arrive at a flat area with a spring, Font de Tres Abeuradors. *3h 15min*

Down Again To The Rio Ebo

There was once a good trail leading to the river-bed, just above Cova Santa, but sadly it has nearly all disappeared. As there are cliffs immediately below the Font, it is necessary to move left (south) downstream for a while to avoid them and reach the stony bed of the river. Turn right upstream, and in a few minutes you should find a crag with two cairns on top, on the left-hand side, which indicates the start of the ascent. Avoid the gully immediately above by keeping to the left (south side of it), and head for a small casita, seen high up amongst the terraces. *4h*

To Corrales De Juvees Del Poble De Alt

From the old casita, a reasonable Mozarabic trail leads upwards towards a well seen on the skyline, which is reached in 20min. Once there, you will find the Corrales, a collection of restored casitas. Turn west on a good road (which would eventually lead in 5km to Collado de Garga) until you reach a level area with a well and some ruined fincas.
4h 20min

Down Into The Barranco Del Tuerto

On the opposite side of the road from the well, close to one of the farm buildings, find yet another Mozarabic trail which, in 2h, will take you down into the Barranco de Racons (a tributary of the Ebo), and up again to join the road near Collado de Garga. First follow the trail down the east side of the Barranco del Tuerto, passing an extensive finca on the other side. In 30min the track levels a little, is invaded by a stream, and crosses the larger Barranco de Racons. *4h 40min*

Ascent To Benimaurell

Your final objective can be seen above, a large buttress to which the trail leads via many twists and turns. It offers beautiful views down into the Val de Laguart. *5h 20min*

Pass to the right of the buttress, and in a few metres you reach the top of the slope, and the track becomes a wide lane, which leads you in a few minutes to the road. *6h*

Turn downhill to return in 30min to the fleshpots of Benimaurell, after a very full and happy day following in the steps of the Moorish muleteers. *6h 30min*

Barranco del Infierno and Rio Ebo from Camino de Juvias. Photo: Author

Val De Gallinera

ROUTE 19: FORADA RIDGE M/S 9km $6^{1}/_{2}$h

This ridge walk is mostly trackless, so you need to be well shod and capable of picking a good route. It is difficult to imagine a route with so much interest. It starts at an ancient wash-house and the remains of a water mill, then visits an ancient monastery, the ruins of an Iberian settlement, and an interesting cave-dwelling. The eastern summit has a large forat, a natural hole in the rock, and even more Iberian ruins. The final peak has an unusual iron cross, and the walk ends at a Moorish king's castle with a modern mountain refuge installed.

Leave Pego on the C3311 to Cocentaina, along the beautiful Gallinera Valley, and start the day at the village square of Benisiva where the Bar Placeta will provide refreshments and food. There are also good bars at Beniali. It is worth first making a small detour along the road to the west, where you will find, on the right-hand side of the road, the village fountain, wash-house, and the remains of an ancient water-mill.

To The Monastery

Across the road from the square is the village bakery (Panadero Alphonso) and a set of concrete steps by the side of a steep road leads up through the pretty sister village of Benitaya. Walk through the village houses until in 10min an impressive new gateway is passed on the right. The remains of the old monastery are within the walled area to the right of the gate, which is planted with pines. El Convento de la Gallinera was founded in 1611 by Franciscans under the patronage of the Duke of Gandia. It is said that the spot chosen for the monastery is where the sun shines through the forat on the Forada on the saint's day. The area is now private property but if you walk through the gates and along the new road for a few metres, you will find the old spring opposite a new reservoir. The Font de L'Hort de Mengual bears the date 1741. The old ladies in the village can still remember the monastery bell being rung to announce the distribution of food to the needy. Keep going upwards, and pass further ruins on your left, before reaching a surfaced road, which you follow south (right) for a short time before turning west (right) onto an unsurfaced road (partly concreted). Now step off left on to a mule track. *30min*

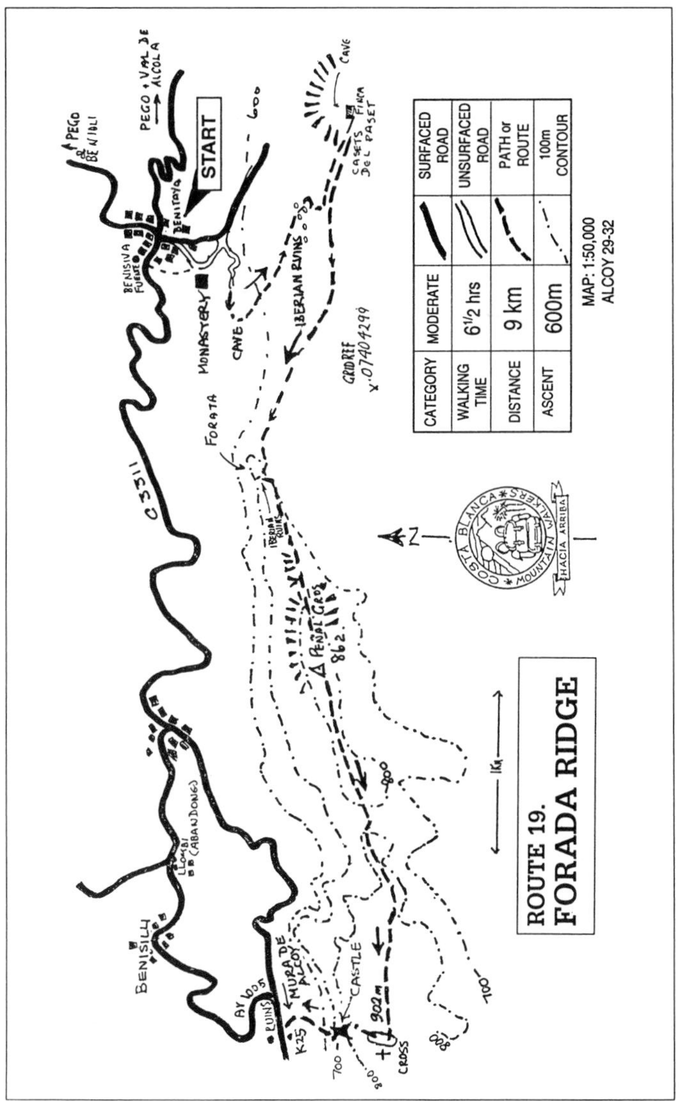
ROUTE 19.
FORADA RIDGE
START
PEGO + VAL DE ALCOLA
BENISIVA
FUENTE
MONASTERY
CAVE
IBERIAN RUINS
CASETS DEL PASET
FINCA
CAVE
GRIDREF
Y.07404299
FORATA
C3311
PENAL GROS
862
BENISILI
MURA DE ALCOY
CASTLE
902m
CROSS
RUINS
K25
1Km
600
700
800
N
COSTA BLANCA * MOUNTAIN WALKERS *
HACIA ARRIBA
CATEGORY | MODERATE
WALKING TIME | 6½ hrs
DISTANCE | 9 km
ASCENT | 600m
SURFACED ROAD
UNSURFACED ROAD
PATH or ROUTE
100m CONTOUR
MAP: 1:50,000
ALCOY 29-32

To The Ruins And Cave House

This old Mozarabic trail is much decayed, and you have good views ahead of you of the Forat, on the eastern summit. After passing a water-worn cave on the left side, the track changes direction towards the east. The cave was once a spring and legend has it that such was the flow of water that a bale of hay which fell from a passing donkey was found 5km away in the valley bottom. Ahead, just below the skyline, can be seen the remaining stones of the old Iberian settlement which you pass through. *1h*

Up above can be seen the large caves in the cliff face, which have been walled in to form dwellings, and in a further 10min you reach the broad ridge, and turn left (east) towards a large ruined finca. On entering the finca, you find a large cave with a domed roof, and sockets in the walls, no doubt to provide for a second floor, to accommodate the shepherd above his flock.

To The Forat

You now start your traverse of the Forada Ridge, and will be travelling west for the rest of the day. There are no reliable tracks, so some route-finding is necessary as you head for the eastern summit, with its graceful rock arch. You will have to scramble through the rocks to reach the arch, from which you get excellent views of Benisili Castle, and in the far north-west, the distinctive peak of Benicadell near Muro del Alcoy. *1h 45min*

To Peñal Groso

The main peak of the ridge at 862m can be seen ahead with its white triangulation pillar. First descend to a col, and then strike upwards, passing some distinctive crags, one of which bears a strong resemblance to Kilnsey Crag in the Yorkshire Dales. After passing an intermediate summit, you arrive at the main summit. *2h 40min*

To Peña Alta

The way ahead can now be seen clearly, with your objective, Peña Alta, identifiable by its metal cross, and below it, to the north, the beautifully situated ruins of the final objective, Benisili Castle (Castillo de Alcala). Across the valley can be seen Lorcha Castle in the Serpis Valley, and there are magnificent views east down the whole length of the Val de Gallinera. To the south are extensive views of the wild wastes of the Val d'Alcala. Between you and your objective, however, are a number of undulations which it is necessary to avoid. At the first depression, with

Above:
The Peña Divino.
Route 29 traverses the back of the ridge.
Brian Evans

Right:
The Forat on the Forada Ridge.
(Route 19)
Peter Reason

Looking towards Barranco del Infierno from Camino de Juvias (Route 18) *Maurice Gibbs*

Climbing towards Bollulla Castle from Pasa Tancat (Route 23) *Maurice Gibbs*

Benisili Castle - Peña Alta with Benicadell from Forada

a small almond grove, avoid rocks by traversing a little left. *3h 30min*

Avoid a broad barranca at a cairn with a hunting sign by traversing left (south), to avoid losing height, and make for a large boulder, on which the owner of the hunting rights has staked his claim in paint. *4h 15min*

At the top of a shallow valley, move right a little to follow a short rocky arête, which gives access to the final ascent to the cross. The unusual metal cross on the summit has recently been vandalised by some mindless persons, however they cannot destroy the beautiful views across the Val d'Alcala and the southern mountains. *4h 50min*

To Benisili Castle

It is now necessary to leave the main ridge, and descend the spur to the north, which leads to the castle seen below. There are two tracks, one on each side of the rocky arête, before you reach the grassy plateau on which the beautiful ruins stand. There is a fuente at the end of a small path to the west of the arête. The castle is strategically placed to command the whole valley, as far as Beniarrama Castle, clearly seen

Forada Summit with 'Kilnsey Crag' looking west. Photo: Author

10km to the east. Benisili Castle is of Moorish origin, having been built by Al Azarach, the Moorish king. It passed to Jaime I in 1258, and he in turn gave it to his heir Pedro. The castle therefore has right royal connections, but these failed to save it in the disastrous earthquake of 1644. If you climb the parapet, you will find a small bunk-house built into a turret on the northern side, equipped as a refuge by local mountaineers. The first-aid kit is very basic, but included a full bottle of brandy when last I visited this hut! *5h 40min*

Back To The Road

There is an old mule track which zig-zags down to the north, to reach the road near Km.25. The track was always difficult to follow until, in 1990, an extensive forest fire removed all the vegetation, and it was rediscovered. The nearest reliable refreshment place is Benisiva.

6h 15min

ROUTE 20: ALMISIRA VIA ALTO DE CHAP Sc(B/C) 14km 5h

Almisira (757m) is easily recognised by its array of antennae, which occupy the summit. On approaching Pego from Vergel there is a particularly attractive view of this mountain and as you drive towards Adsubia to enter the beautiful gorge which leads to the Val de Gallinera, you can admire its bold northern crags. To the north of the summit on a small lower spur, is the ancient Castillo de Gallinera. Beyond the gorge lies the unspoilt and fruitful Val de Gallinera, famous for its cherry orchards, which are a mass of blossom in spring.

The route described here is only for those hardy souls who can climb steep rocks, undeterred by spiky undergrowth. During the ascent of Alto de Chap it is necessary to endure these conditions for about an hour. Thereafter, once the high plateau is reached, there are good tracks all the way.

Those who seek a more gentle route should reverse the descent route via the castle. There is little need for route-finding to reach Pla de Almisira in about 2h. Start from the school in Beniarrama, and go down the lane by the Restaurant de Val. Head towards the castle for a short while, but at the first junction, bear right to contour round a large barranca.

Making A Start

From the isolated unspoilt village of Beniarrama (school, shop, bar and restaurant all closed 1993), look upwards to the south where the skyline is dominated by a line of crags, Alto de Chap (626m). It is, in fact, part of the Forada Ridge, which forms the southern side of the Val de Gallinera. From the village the cliffs seem impregnable, but there is one noticeable weakness. By making for a prominent buttress, which is passed on the west side, it is possible to climb through the crags to reach the top of the escarpment.

Start from the Calle Almassera in the west end of the village, and take the small concrete road leading to the cemetery and then an unsurfaced track past the Stations of the Cross with their ceramic

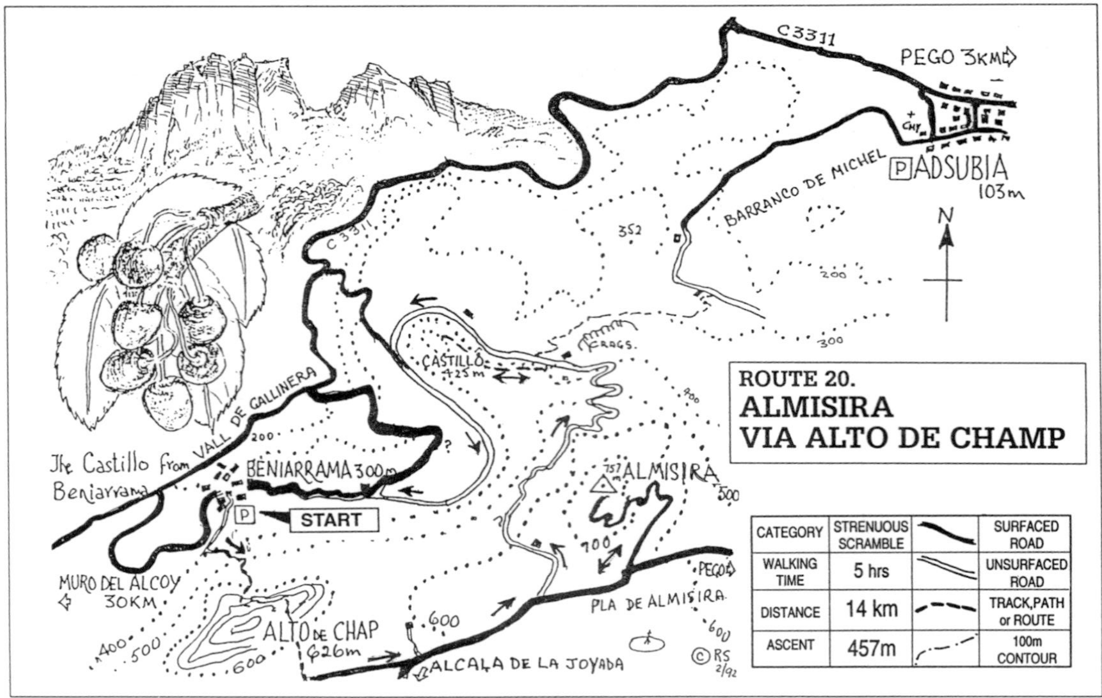
ROUTE 20.
ALMISIRA
VIA ALTO DE CHAMP
CATEGORY
STRENUOUS SCRAMBLE
SURFACED ROAD
WALKING TIME
5 hrs
UNSURFACED ROAD
DISTANCE
14 km
TRACK,PATH or ROUTE
ASCENT
457m
100m CONTOUR
C3311
PEGO 3KM
ADSUBIA
103m
BARRANCO DE MICHEL
N
352
200
300
CRAGS.
CASTILLO 425m
400
757m ALMISIRA
500
700
PEGO
PLA DE ALMISIRA
600
ALCALA DE LA JOYADA
© RS 2/92
The Castillo from Beniarrama
VALL DE GALLINERA
BENIARRAMA 300m
START
MURO DEL ALCOY 30KM
ALTO DE CHAP 626m

pictures. Ignore a track leading to the left, even though our track seems to be heading away from the buttress. After a few zig-zags, in about 15min, turn off left (red marker), heading straight for the castle. Level at first, then climbing a little on a good track. Finally on a bend, the track ends in an almond grove. *30min*

Scree Grove To Lower Combe

The almonds are growing in scree, and the campesino has made a rough mule track which goes upwards through the trees. It can, however, be detected only by those with a well-developed imagination and supreme optimism: mule droppings confirm the route. The next section is rather difficult.

When the almond trees end there is still a vague track up to the base of the buttress beyond which it is extremely overgrown and difficult to find. In 10min reach the wall of the buttress. Turn right (west) in order to get round it. For the next 10min you will have some misgivings, but the track *is* there, under all the shrubbery. Persist in trying to find it as the terrain on either side is even more difficult. (Secateurs, pangas, gloves and thorn-proof clothing are a distinct advantage here.) Eventually, a track emerges from the undergrowth, over scree and then rock, to reach the lower combe with its pine trees. *50min*

To Peter's Rake

Move upwards on to a narrow path which goes left (north-east), aiming for a narrow cleft between the buttress and the main cliffs above. At the cleft, you find yourself in the upper combe. Climb upwards through the pines towards the crags, bearing just a little to the right, to find a narrow rock staircase, which leads to the rake (red markers). You have a short rock scramble upwards towards the top of the cliffs, ending in a short groove, which leads to a cairn on the summit of Alto de Chap. *1h 30min*

To Almisira

There are extensive views to the south, across the broad expanse of Val de Alcala. To the west is the Forada Ridge, and to the east your ulimate goal, the summit of Almisira. Below lies the road from Pego. Go straight down to the road (south-east), taking great care, as the terrain is broken limestone pavement, to reach the surfaced road, and turn left (east). *1h 45min*

Pass a small casita on the left, and a junction where the road comes up from Val de Alcala, to reach Pla de Almisira. On the way, note the red markers, which indicate the unsurfaced road on the left, leading back to the village via the Castillo de Gallinera. This road is your return route. At the Pla, a surfaced road leads upwards to the summit. *2h 40min*

The Summit

From this vantage point, you can spend some time identifying the peaks which can be seen in every direction. To the south are Peñon Roch and the Cavallo Verde Ridge, with Serrella Castle beyond, and Peña Mulero in the distance. To the north, beyond Villalonga, can be seen the serried ridges of three Sierras - Zafor, Gallinera and Almirante.

The Castle

Much is known of the history of the extensive castle, which once crowned this strategic mountain, but only a few stones remain. Moorish in origin, its governor was Abdalla Marhop. In 1243, it fell to Nicolas Scals. It was the scene of the signing of the important Treaty of Almisira, between the Moors and the Christians. The castle probably suffered in the earthquake of 1644, but it is more likely that what little remained was scattered when the road to the Transmitting Station was constructed. A forestry lookout cabin has been newly installed on the summit, and is manned during high fire-risk periods. Just below the cabin, on the north side, is a small section of wall with a cement coping. Some say that the wall is one of the remains of the Moorish castle, others claim that it is even more ancient being of the Iberian period.

GALLINERA CASTLE

Descent to Castillo de Gallinera

Retrace your steps to the road, and turn right, and in a few minutes, turn off again to the right (north) at the red markers. Pass a small casita, and in 15min, at the top of a small rise, you get a magnificent view of the picturesque castle below. The road starts to deteriorate, and it is hard to believe that only a few years ago it was passable with care by motor traffic. Pass under the impressive northern cliffs of Almisira until you reach a small casita beyond which a red marker shows the rough track to the castle itself. In 1990, the owner of the castle installed a gate to prevent access. (When I made enquiries at the local town hall, I was told by the mayor that everyone just walked round the gate, but to be very careful as the ruins are dangerous, especially the deep, open, cistern.) *3h 40min*

Carry on down the unsurfaced road, passing Casa de la Pradera, around the castle, to head for Beniarrama, eventually joining a surfaced road. Turn left to arrive at the village. At present, you will have to go to Adsubia for refreshments. *5h*

ROUTE 21: FORNA TO VILLALONGA M(B) 10km 5h

This is a lovely walk, between two ancient castles, crossing a modest Sierra with views of the remote valley of the Rio Serpis. This delightful walk is mainly on good tracks.

Getting There

To get to the beautiful little village of Forna, leave Pego on the C3313 towards Cocentaina, and near Km.41 turn north on the AV1004 for 4km. As you reach the top of a small hill, just before entering the village, park your car and walk up a good track to the right (east) to visit Forna Castle. The castle is in a good state of preservation, Moorish in origin, having belonged to Al Azadrach, a Moorish king. In 1262 it belonged to Don Bernardo de Guillen, whose six sons were known as Los Caballeros del Panacho Negro (Knights of the Black Plume). Notable features of the castle are its well-preserved entrance, and the four towers facing north. Unlike other castles in the Gallinera Valley, it survived the great earthquake of 1644. You will need a torch to fully explore the castle.

Making A Start

Start near the Calle Fuente, and go north up a steep concrete road between new villas. In 10min the road ends and you take to a very

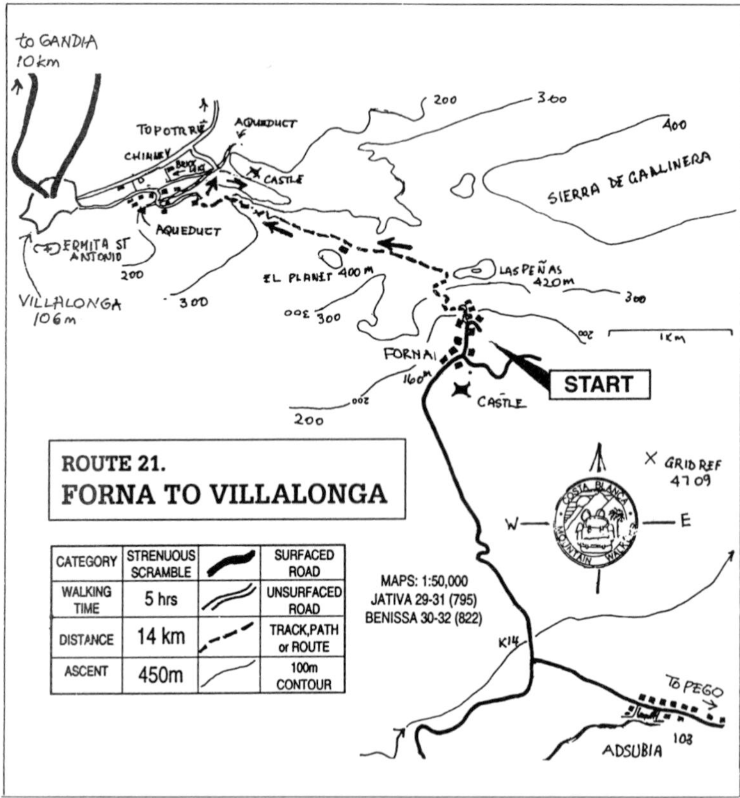

CATEGORY	STRENUOUS SCRAMBLE		SURFACED ROAD
WALKING TIME	5 hrs		UNSURFACED ROAD
DISTANCE	14 km		TRACK,PATH or ROUTE
ASCENT	450m		100m CONTOUR

eroded mule track, which zig-zags upwards on the west side of a barranca. As you climb, look back for lovely views of the village and castle, with Sierra Negre behind them. The track now contours round a broad gully, and crosses easier ground. Look back, and you catch a glimpse of Almisira, with its transmitters on the summit. At the highest point you pass an occupied casita on your left. *45min*

Down The Barranco del Castillo

Just past the little casita views start to open up to the north, first down into the barranco, then the towns of Patria and Gandia, and finally, the ruins of Villalonga Castle at the northern end of the ridge on the other side of the barranco. In the distance can be seen Sierra Ador. Now the track starts to descend quite steeply through pines, until the large town of Villalonga appears, with the Serpis Valley behind it. *1h 20min*

During the descent there are lovely views of the Sierra Ador mountain range behind the town. On a little hill just outside the town, is the picturesque hermita of San Antonio, with a calvary leading to it.

To Villalonga Castle

At a newly constructed villa join an unsurfaced road, which leads down through other villas, and will eventually lead to the town. Move north-east, and there are two routes available. The first is to watch out for a small water aqueduct, and follow it along the rear of some houses until it joins a road coming up from the road to Patria. The second route is to descend the road until you reach the villa with the name Belater Lolita (just above the brick-works) on the right, and follow a road moving north-east until you reach the aqueduct, and join the first route. Now go south up a rocky stream bed under high walls on the right, which support orange groves, and enter the Barranco del Castillo. A reasonable path traverses the slope upwards towards the castle ruins, which are clearly visible. The last few metres into the ruins is much eroded and needs care. *2h 30min*

From the castle the Serpis Valley can be seen behind the town leading to Alcoy through the Val de Infierno gorge. Only a railway occupied this valley, but it closed 30 years ago. Happily, the abandoned track is preserved as an unsurfaced road, which gives access to walkers who can enjoy the majestic scenery, the waterfalls and rapids of the beautiful Rio Serpis, and the varied wildlife, which includes kingfishers, herons and exceedingly large trout, (see Route No.24). Behind Gandia, near the coast, can be seen the Sierras of Bota and Faconera.

Villalonga (the long village) is of Roman origin, established by Colonia, retired soldiers of the Roman army who took their pensions in Spain, and were given land to farm. They built their villas in a line, probably along a reliable water supply. The castle is of Moorish origin but by 1240 was in the possession of King Jaime I of Aragon.

Sadly, there is as yet no alternative route to offer back to Forna, but it is always interesting to reverse a route, simply because the views are totally different from the outward journey.

There is a good restaurant, The Nautilus and a bar at Forna.

Val De Algar

ROUTE 22: BOLULLA CASTLE E(A) 9km 4h

Bolulla is an old world, unspoilt village 7km north of Callosa d'Ensarria on the C3318 to Pego, 3km past the Algar Falls, a great tourist attraction with many restaurants. There is at present no restaurant in the village, only a bar which can be rather late in opening in the morning. Opposite the bar lives an old gentleman who once took tourists on his donkey to the castle and still likes to offer his burro for photo calls. In May, like all villages in the valley of the Algar, it is the Nisperus harvest, and if you look through the large barn doors of these old village houses you will see the ladies preparing the fruit for the Cooperativea at Callosa. The Cooperativas canning plant sends the fruit as far as Japan, and at the height of the harvest hundreds of pickers from Andalucia throng the town, causing an accommodation problem.

As you approach the village you will notice the groves of nisperus and oranges, and these orchards continue throughout the walk following the valley of the Rio Negro towards the village's main attraction, its Moorish castle. All on good tracks, except for the actual ascent of the castle ruins, which is a rock scramble.

Leave your transport at Bolulla and walk up Calle St Joseph, north, until you reach the village's water cistern where an unsurfaced road leads off left. In a short while enter a very small rocky gorge where the concrete surface reminds us of the winter floods which rush through this narrow place. Note, on the right, some steps which lead to an old Mozarabic trail, the original way to the castle and on to Castell de Castells. This trail will keep to the barranco of the Rio Negro and as a result has suffered from erosion.

As you gain height you get your first view of the great blade of rock upon which the Moors built their castle (seen to the left of the main summit). Below, as you pass through almond orchards, can be seen the well-irrigated citrus groves, and now and then you can hear running water. Occasional glimpses can be had of the old Mozarabic trail.

30min

Ignore a road which climbs to the left and the road levels off. Stop, as always, to appreciate the views of Sierra Bernia and Peña Severino behind you.

As you approach the (normally) dry bed of the Rio Negro note a

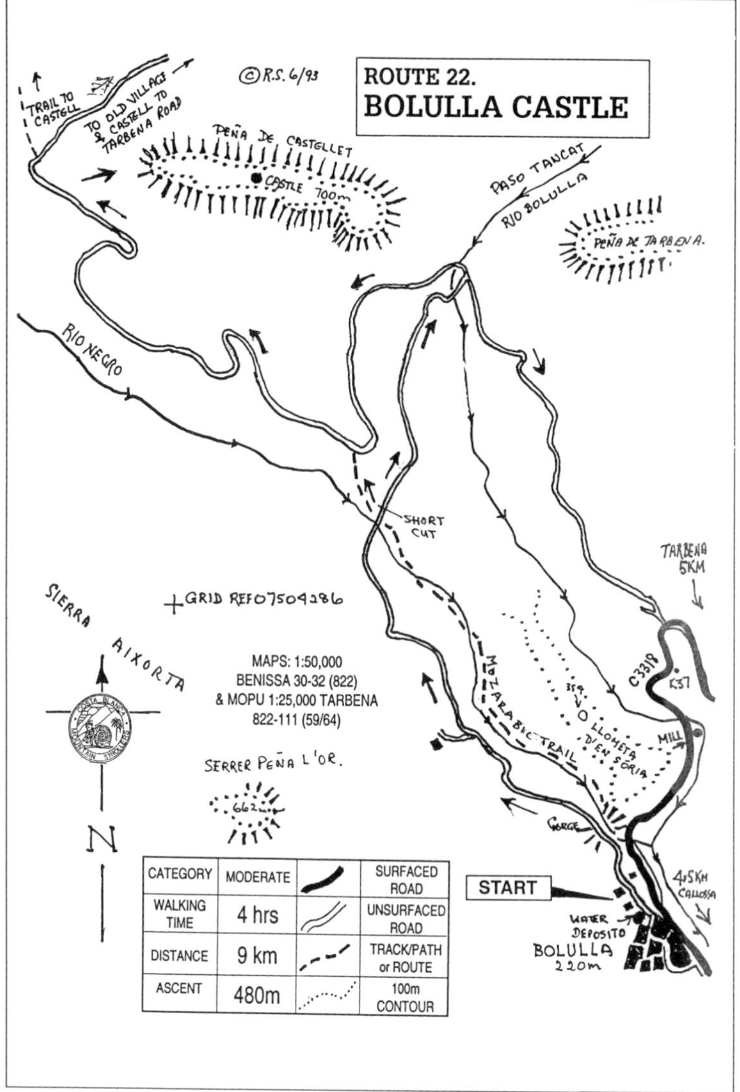

CATEGORY	MODERATE		SURFACED ROAD
WALKING TIME	4 hrs		UNSURFACED ROAD
DISTANCE	9 km		TRACK/PATH or ROUTE
ASCENT	480m		100m CONTOUR

Mozarabic trail leading off left to join the road to the castle higher up. This will save you about 15min if you take advantage of the short cut. Cross the barranco, and note also the Mozarabic trail joining from the right from the valley bottom. *50min*

You are now approaching the great Castle Crag, with the dark defile of Paso Tancat (closed pass) on its right. It really is closed as you would have to be a very dedicated rock-climber to get more than half an hour into its dark depths. Now approach and cross another dry barranco, Rio Bolulla, which issues from the Paso Tancat. *1h 15min*

Climb now to a good forestry road which, in about an hour, takes you to a col from which the ascent of the castle can be made.

You now change direction (south-west) to cross under the crag, and zig-zag upwards towards the col. After 30min, another track from the village (following the Rio Negro) joins on the left, and then the remains of an extensive finca just below the col is reached. This is known by the locals as "the old village" and, within living memory, was inhabited by some local families during the summer months when supplies were brought up by pack mule. The finca buildings are still used, and you will note that there is much dressed stone used in them, which could indicate Moorish origins, or that the castle ruins were used for building materials. The old era (threshing floor) is near to the road, with a number of rollers still in situ - please do not disturb! The col is reached in 5min. *2h 15min*

The Col

An attraction of this walk is that, from here, there are a number of pleasant short excursions you can make before having lunch:

1. The Ascent To The Castle Ruins - Rock Scramble

Allow 1h return. Start either from the finca or the col by keeping just below the rock ridge on the southern side. Unless you are a rock-climber, *do not* keep to the crest, as in 10min it will lead to a gap with some exposed moves. After 10min, descend a little to a fir tree, cross a scree run, and head straight for a gap in the outer defensive wall. Aim upwards towards the right-hand edge of the ruins, then enter the inner wall, and head left to enter the tower. As you might expect, the views are extensive and impressive. If you can bear to look over the edge, it is now clear why the Moorish builders went no higher along the ridge. Take great care here - the walls lack maintenance! Only to the north is the view restricted by higher ground.

2. Walk Along The Southern Rim Of The Paso Tancat

Allow 1h return. Continue over the col on the same track for 100m, and, at some red way-markers, go up left along the old mule track towards Castell de Castells, following the red markers, until you get good views of the dramatic crags of the Paso Tancat Gorge.

3. Walk To The Valley Of Paso Tancat
Allow half an hour return. Continue along the road as in Walk 2. You can now explore the old settlements in this remote valley.

Descent (Allow 1½h)
Return by the same route until you reach the road junction near to the Barranco Bolulla, where instead of turning right to follow the morning's route, you keep straight on above the valley of the Rio Bolulla, descending gently to join the main road near Km.37.

Turn right down towards Bolulla remembering , of course, to face the traffic which can be heavy in summer. The Rio Bolulla is on the right at first and then cross a bridge over it. Note the ruins of a really substantial water-mill on the left which must in years gone by have had a very reliable source of water. Note also an unusual sight in the dry sierras, the many large willow trees by the stream. If you follow this route in winter the whole of the left-hand side of the valley is alive with the sound of small streams plunging down to join the river.

By now the bar in the village will surely be open and you can take refreshments and make the little burro's day. You may also meet a sophisticated old man who lived in America for many years who will undoubtably try to sell you a village house. Judging by the number of foreign residents, he has been fairly successful.

ROUTE 23: TARBENA CIRCUIT M(B) 18km 5h

Perhaps this walk could be called "A walk around El Somo" because, in the course of it, you do just that, moving anti-clockwise around that undistinguished hill. You will enjoy 5h amongst majestic mountain scenery, visit a beautiful natural rock arch, a castle, and a dramatic gorge. Mostly on excellent tracks, only one small section is badly worn and overgrown. Remember that the last section is a climb of some 400m, so save some energy for it!

Getting There
Since the new road from Tarbena to Castell de Castells, the AV1203, was opened, you can approach the start of this walk, at the Collado de Bichauca (Km.6) from either direction. The road may not be shown on

your map, so leave the C3318 at Km.30.5, just above the village of Tarbena. From Castells, leave the main road at the river bridge (Km.12).

Making A Start

Start by walking west down the road towards Castells, with views of Sierra Serrella and Mala del Llop in the distance. Below is the well-watered area Corralles de Alt, now farmed from Castells, with its well down to the right, looking for all the world like an inverted pudding basin. Beyond the well are views of the dramatic escarpment of Cocoll, and the little pointed peak, Tosal del Vaquero. Now turn off, left, at Km.7 onto a broad forestry road and head south-west.

To The Chorquet Well

Change direction over what is normally very wet ground on a broad road which turns a little before climbing the south-west flank of El Somo to Corral del Somo, passing an old finca below on the right. At the top of a rise are the ruins of Corral del Somo at a junction where you descend left in a south-east direction. *1h 25min*

Pause for a moment to enjoy views of the western mountains, with Mala del Llop (north-west) and Serrella Castle to the left of it. If you look carefully in the distance, ahead and slightly to the right of the track, and high up on the flank of the Aixorta, you will see a gully. On the left-hand side of this gully try to pick out the lovely natural rock arch, Arc de Atancos. The arch is 12m across and 10m high, and is well worth a visit.

The track continues to descend, passing two casitas until it reaches a stony barranco and, on the right of the track, a well built into a wall. This is Jibe del Chorquet, and has excellent water, despite the fact that you must use a rusty can to have a drink. Please close the door when you have finished.

Visit To The Arc de Atancos

A few metres further along the track from the well where the track bends to the left, find a track on the right, which in 10min will lead you to the base of the Arc. There is no track from here, and the ground is rocky and overgrown, but the effort involved in climbing to the Arc is well worth it. Allow an hour for this diversion.

On To Bolulla Castle

Your route now continues, and for a short time dips gently, following the Barranco del Chorquet, but this is not your destination. Keep a sharp eye out for a small cairn and a red marker as your route turns right to

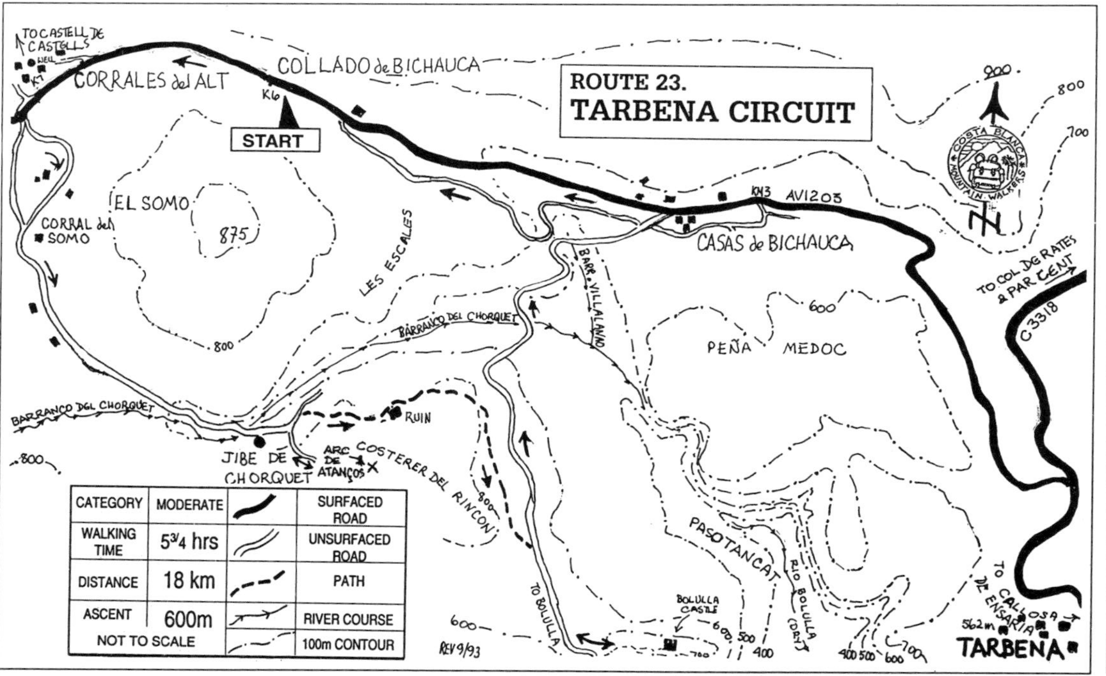

CATEGORY	MODERATE		SURFACED ROAD
WALKING TIME	5¾ hrs		UNSURFACED ROAD
DISTANCE	18 km		PATH
ASCENT	600m		RIVER COURSE
NOT TO SCALE			100m CONTOUR

traverse south-east towards Bolulla Castle. At first, the narrow track is indistinct and overgrown, but seek out the red markers which will guide you over this difficult section. After about half an hour, note a large cave on the opposite wall of the barranco (north-east). *2h*

Now, still following the red markers, cross a shallow valley with terraces, and maintain height up to a holly oak. Shortly after this you reach a ruined finca, which you pass on the left. Cross a terrace with some dead trees to climb up the last section before you get your first views of the Paso Tancat (closed valley) with its abandoned settlement below on the left.

Step by step the views ahead become more extensive and dramatic as, slowly, the path climbs and the impressive cliffs of the Paso Tancat are revealed. Eventually the Sierra Bernia comes into view, then Bolulla Castle perched on its rocky outcrop, and finally, the coast at Albir and the Sierra Helada. This last section of track down to the Col at Bolulla Castle is badly worn and overgrown (hell in shorts!) but eventually you gain a broad road which has come up from Bolulla. *4h 10min*

If you have the energy, turn right for about 100m to the col, either to admire the coastal views or to climb to the castle ruins. There is no real track to the castle, but keep away from the ridge rocks, and on the southern side make your way by means of an easy rock scramble to the ruins in about 20min.

Down Into The Paso Tancat

Go left on a broad track (north), climbing a little at first, but eventually winding down to the Barranco del Chorquet, where it joins the Barranco de Villalanao to enter the gorge, and go into the jaws of the Paso Tancat. Cross the dry bed of the river, and start the long slow climb (400m) back up to the Collada de Bichauca. *4h 40min*

In 5min pass a casita on your left and a short section of concrete road follows, before you reach a fuente with bowls for the animals. Now, above you to the east, can be seen a small casita, Casa de Bichauca, which is on the road. Watch out for another road, on your left, which switches back in a westerly direction, following the northern side of Barranco de Villalanao (changed to Cova Roja on 1:25,000 maps). Follow this good track to the head of the barranco, cross over to the other side and head for the col, with the road for company on the right-hand side. A short way from the col, join the road near an old casita on the right-hand side, and walk up it to your starting point, Collado de Bichauca.

You will have to drive either to Tarbena or Castell de Castells to find a bar or restaurant.

Other Sierras

ROUTE 24: LORCHA TO VILLALONGA and RIO SERPIS VALLEY M(A) 20km 8h

This walk is a little longer than usual, but the gradients are easy and it is all on good, unsurfaced roads. It is also on the edge of our normal area for walkers staying in the south of the Costa, but easily accessible to those staying in the north, around Gandia, who can, of course, start their walk from Villalonga if they choose.

You first of all cross a spur of Azafor (1011m) and descend to La Reprimala, 2km from Villalonga. The return to Lorcha is along the old railway track, which follows the fast flowing Rio Serpis, through a most picturesque gorge, El Barranco Del Infierno, rich in wildlife, to the ruins of the ancient Moorish castle at Lorcha. It is important to carry torches for negotiating the tunnels, especially the first one, and to make yourself visible to any traffic using the road.

Getting There

Lorcha is reached by leaving the CN332 at Vergel and following the C3311 through Pego and the Val Gallinera to Planes, where you turn off right to Beniarres via the dam, and then turn right onto the AV1001 to Lorcha. There is now a narrow, surfaced road from Al Patro direct to Lorcha, which shortens the journey considerably, but, sadly, is not signposted.

Take the first road to the right, just after the village street, in Al Patro, and go down past the wash-house to the abandoned village of Llombay where you turn off right towards Villalonga. At the top of a rise, in about 2km, take the first left north-west onto the new road, over Sierra de la Albureca, to Lorcha. This road is not, however, for the faint-hearted.

Villalonga is reached by leaving the CN332 1km south of Gandia, taking the VP1012, near the village of Bellrequart, and in 8km enter the town and turn right at the Guardia Civil Barracks towards the river, following signs for the Reprimala and Dos Hermanos restaurants, which you reach in a further 2km.

To Fuente de Olbist

Leave Lorcha, where there are five bars to delay your start, and leave the main road (AV1001) just above the beautiful fuente, Font Grota, with its

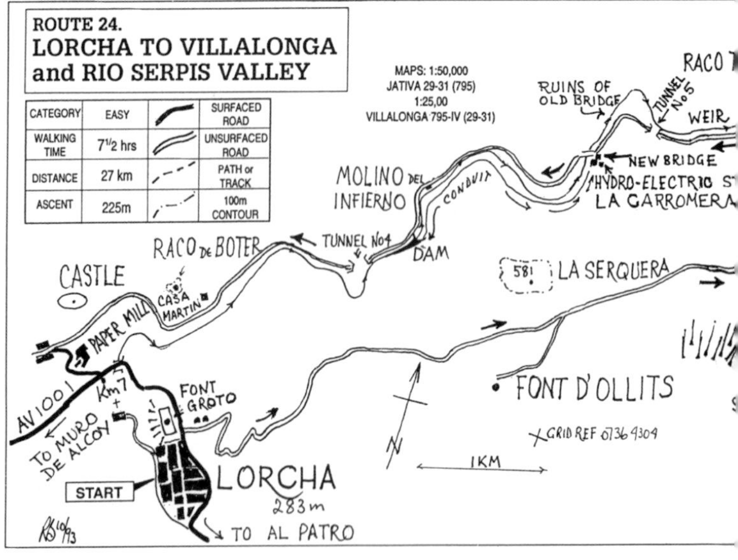

CATEGORY	EASY		SURFACED ROAD
WALKING TIME	7½ hrs		UNSURFACED ROAD
DISTANCE	27 km		PATH or TRACK
ASCENT	225m		100m CONTOUR

tables made of old millstones, cross the dry river-bed and take a broad, unsurfaced road which will lead to the first objective, Fuente de Olbist. The road is well graded and heads north-east. It ends at Villalonga, some 14km away. Note some old cave houses built against the cliffs on the left. The road now starts to zig-zag to gain height, with the Barranca de Basiets on the right-hand side. Soon there are extensive views to the south, with Lorcha and its little calvary in the foreground, the impressive eastern buttress of Benicadell, and a wide view of the Serpis Valley. An unusually large and unnecessary notice announces that the mountain is for "Public Use". Another barranco, Vertiente de la Carrasco, joins from the right and you get a view to the south of the end of the Forada Ridge. The gradient eases a little and you reach a viewpoint on the left where you can look down some 400m, into the Serpis Valley, with the old abandoned railway track that will be the return route. *1h*

Continue along the road, climbing gently as the bulk of Azafor's southern slopes come into view ahead. After a while note another deep barranco on the right and, across on the other side, a track and the fuente. This is the route and you have to go around the head of the barranco, where there is some red shale. Reach a junction. Leave the road to Villalonga and take the right-hand road, changing direction to south-west. *1h 20min*

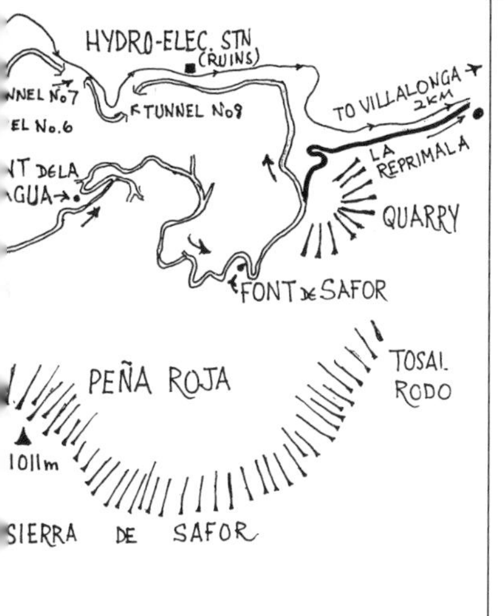

The road now passes under some smooth, exposed slabs which look like granite and seem to be glacial, and another track forks off to the left. This is the route for the ascent of Azafor (1011m). You are now high enough to see the town of Muro de Alcoy to the south and in another few minutes arrive at the beautifully laid out Fuente del Olbist. In addition to the spring there are tables and benches and a delightful barbecue. Enjoy the extensive views down the valley of the Rio Serpis, with the western buttress of Benicadell in the distance, looking like the Matterhorn. *1h 30min*

Down To La Reprimala

Retrace your steps to the main forestry road and continue east along a fairly level section with magnificent views on the right of the great semi-circle of crags which form the northern escarpment of Azafor. Across the valley, to the north, are extensive views of Sierra Ador, but little can be seen of the Rio Serpis in its deep gorge below you. Eventually, the road starts to descend and views to the east open up to show the huerto of Gandia and eventually Villalonga and the coast. After passing Font de la Pagua there is some development and you must avoid being diverted from your descent (see map) until you reach the quarry, and the road becomes surfaced. In the quarry note a road going off to the left. This is your route and leads, in half a kilometre, to the river and the old railway track. There is sometimes a signpost here! Pass through some villas and reach the old track with the old hydro-electric station on the opposite side of the river. The station, which is in ruins, was converted from a flour mill and the old conduits can be seen above the buildings. This makes a lovely spot for lunch. Those who demand more than a picnic can continue down the metalled road, for slightly more than another kilometre, to Font de la Reprimala, with its gushing fountains and its two excellent restaurants with terraces overlooking the fast-flowing Serpis. *3h 30min*

Along The Side Of The Rio Serpis To Lorcha

Leave La Reprimala and retrace your steps to the quarry, where you turn off right to drop down, on an unsurfaced road, to join the old railway running beside the river and the old hydro-electric station described above. *4h 30min*

The railway was completed, by an English company in 1893 to carry coal and other materials for the developing industries of Alcoy, from the port of Gandia. No doubt influenced by the decline of coal as a fuel and the improved road systems, the line was closed and dismantled in 1969. It was quite a feat of engineering as the track clings to the side of a deep gorge, Barranco del Infierno, through eight tunnels and numerous bridges and cuttings until, at Beniarres, it becomes the main road to Alcoy. Because of the seclusion and the abundant water, wildlife and wild flowers abound. There is a wide variety of fish in the river with trout which look more like young sharks. The track has been designated as a public road and surveyed by the highways authority. The section west of Lorcha station has been widened and graded, but the rest of the line will present some considerable difficulties, especially the bridges and tunnels which are one train wide only. Pressure is mounting for the area to be designated as a Natural Park, meanwhile be prepared to meet some traffic, especially at weekends and fiestas - another good reason for carrying torches.

A short distance along the old track come to the first and longest tunnel (No.8) and in half a kilometre another, shorter one (No.7). The river below runs in rapids and small cascades over rocks. Cross some bridges, without the benefit of parapets. After a short cutting enter another tunnel (No.6) and on leaving it, enjoy the views ahead of a wide weir stemming the river to provide water for one of the mills which once worked in this valley.

Most of the little stations and workmen's huts have disappeared, but you now pass one on the right and shortly after this watch out ahead for your first view of the stone supports, all that remains of the bridge which carried the track to the other side of the river for the remaining 5km to Lorcha. When the railway closed, the metal spans were dismantled, and a culvert constructed to cross the river lower down near the hydro-electric station. This structure was destroyed when the river was in spate in the winter of 1986. The Spanish Army Engineers constructed the more substantial bridge, which so far has resisted the flood waters. The road now leaves the line of the railway beyond the bridge supports and drops down to the old mill which is still used as a reserve generating station. This mill was called La Garromera and is

Rio Serpis - entrance to Barranco del Infierno. Photo: Author

worth exploring. You will find the sluice gates well greased and in working order. *5h 30min*

Cross the river and in a few minutes you are back on the track. Watch out on the opposite bank for the conduit, which carried the water to power the mill from a dam 1km ahead. Pass another old station and then reach the dam across the river, still in good order due to its substantial construction.

You are now high above the river as you enter the last, short tunnel (No.4). Pass through cuttings and curve around a barranco with an old ruined finca on the right, Casa Martin. *6h 30min*

Just round the bend after Casa Martin you get your first, dramatic view of Lorcha Castle, high on a spur of rock. Below on the left can be seen Lorcha and the paper mill by the river. When you reach the old buildings of Lorcha station, you turn off left (south), pass the paper mill, and reach the main road near the bridge across the Serpis. The comforts of the restaurants and bars of Lorcha are now only a few minutes away as you turn right, just past the delightful fuente, and walk up into the village. *27km - 7h 30min*

ROUTE 25: SIERRA DE OLTA M(C) 10km 4¾h

Antonio Calero in his book *The Mountains of Alicante* dismisses Olta as insignificant. On the other hand, Roger Massingham describes it as 'A tough nut to crack'. Well, on this walk, we will crack it and discover that Olta, although perhaps insignificant in comparison with the giants further inland, is still a true mountain worthy of exploration. It has all the best characteristics of a mountain, rocky summits, all its flanks protected by sheer crags and an isolated position ensuring all-round views. Don't be deceived by its height (591 metres), as small coastal mountains rising directly from the sea can be almost as demanding as the Alps.

The Mountain

Olta is the mountain whose southern summit greets the motorist as he emerges from the tunnels of the Barranca de Mascarat on the NC 332, and its eastern cliffs keep him company as he skirts Calpe towards Benissa. The northern summit seen from the road to Benissa, near the rather exotic Moorish-style building on the left of the road (Disco), is also very impressive with many rugged pinnacles. Only the western cliffs are difficult to study at close quarters - the best views are from the Autopista but this is not a place to loiter and we have to be content with distant views from Pinos or Bernia. On all sides Olta is surrounded by steep cliffs, no trouble I am sure to rock climbers, but preventing the ordinary walker from reaching the top except by one straightforward route which climbs up Broad Gully on the eastern side.

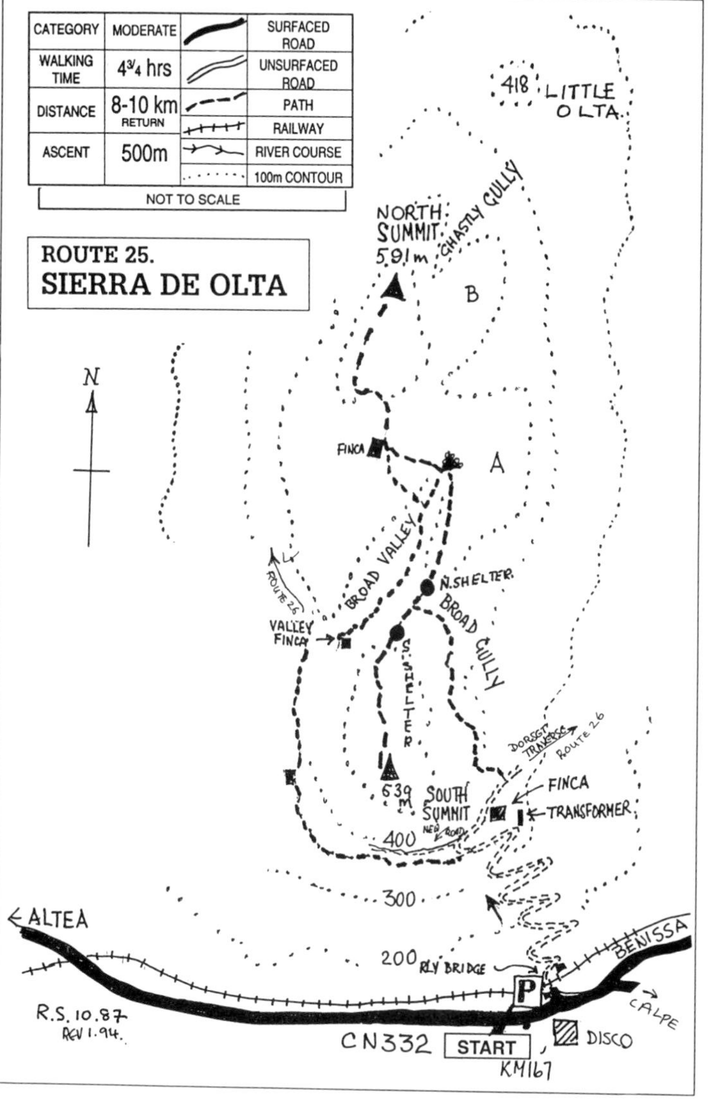
CATEGORY
MODERATE
SURFACED ROAD
WALKING TIME
4¾ hrs
UNSURFACED ROAD
DISTANCE
8-10 km RETURN
PATH
RAILWAY
ASCENT
500m
RIVER COURSE
100m CONTOUR
NOT TO SCALE
ROUTE 25.
SIERRA DE OLTA
N
418
LITTLE OLTA
NORTH SUMMIT 591m
GHASTLY GULLY
B
FINCA
A
BROAD VALLEY
N. SHELTER
BROAD GULLY
ROUTE 26
VALLEY FINCA
S. SHELTER
DORSGT TRAVERSE
ROUTE 26
FINCA
TRANSFORMER
539 m
SOUTH SUMMIT
NEW ROAD
400
300
ALTEA
200
RLY BRIDGE
BENISSA
P
CALPE
R.S. 10.87
REV 1.94.
CN332
START
DISCO
KM167

During the summers of 1991 & 1992 there were extensive forest fires on Olta which burnt off all the vegetation and this has made walking and route finding much easier. The estate roads have been improved and extended, and fire breaks constructed so look out for roads not shown on the map. It is evident from the log book on the north summit that Olta is now a popular excursion for both Spaniards and visitors which means that in places there is a semblance of a path. This state of affairs cannot last for ever and the spiky vegetation is growing well and in future years will return to harass walkers.

The Approach

Leave your car on the estate road, (west side of the NC 332) about 75 metres east of the KM 167.3 Disco. Before you set off get your bearings. The great rock buttress to the west guards the southern summit of the mountain, the rocks to the right of the summit form the eastern buttresses and, somewhere in between is the only reasonable pedestrian route to the summit, Broad Gully, which is our first objective. You should be able to follow the zig-zags of an estate road hewn out of the mountain many years ago, but happily never developed. Follow this rough but well-engineered route for the first 40 minutes of the walk. It is steep. Once beyond the electricity sub-station pick up yellow markers (dots for ascent, circles for the Dorset Circuit, which girdles the mountain).

In about 30 minutes there is a transformer station on the right of the track and then, at the next bend an old casita on the right. From now on do not take any left turns and follow the road which skirts the crags, generally in a northern direction. *45 min*

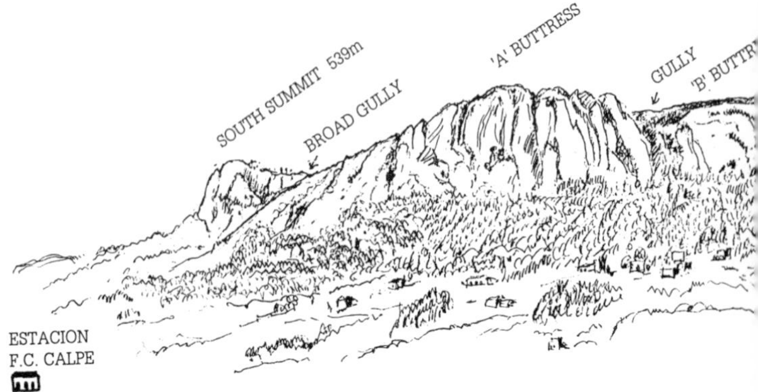

SIERRA DE OLTA EASTERN ASPECT

The Gully

Soon you have a good view of the summit crags on your left but ahead you can see Broad Gully and the narrow scree-filled path by which we can gain the top. Turn off at a cairn which indicates a short rocky scramble up the deepest part of the gully and, in 20 minutes you reach the summit plateau of Olta. The Broad Gully route comes out between two small shelters (see sketch), and from now on you have a choice of routes based on fitness or endurance, because most of the summit is limestone pavement, much eroded by water and overgrown with every spiky plant known to man! *1hr*

Summit Routes

a. South Summit Route

b. North Summit Route

The summit of the plateau of Olta is geologically complicated. The waterworn limestone precludes the development of any reliable paths and the western side is sunken into a shallow valley which, at one time, was terraced and must have supported two small fincas, one at the head of Ghastly Gully (north) and one at the southern end. Care is needed walking in this area, but you can, in 20 minutes, reach the South Summit and in 1 hour 15 minutes reach the North Summit with dramatic views to the Bernias and into the many deep crevasses which scar this, the highest point of the mountain.

Southern Summit (539 metres)

On reaching the top look for a small bothy, (shelter) made of rocks, in a generally southern direction and once past this there is a defined path and in minutes you have a commanding view of the coast from Moraira to Albir, an intimate view of the Barranca de Mascarat, with its three tunnels carrying road, rail and autopista. *1hr 15 min*

Northern Summit (591 metres, some say 586 metres)

This walk is a little more demanding, (remember that you have to come back the same way you went), but really, this is the most exciting expedition on Olta.

Turn right (north) on reaching the plateau, look for the northern bothy and aim for the old finca just 10 degrees left of the North Summit (yellow arrows). Your first objective is a small cairn reached in 30 minutes when you can clearly see the old finca and its well to the northwest. Aim for these objectives by traversing the terraces and pass to the east of the finca to find a small track leading generally north across the eastern flank of the crags. In a short time cross a small col to a false summit and change sides of the summit ridge (west). In 10 minutes you are on to another limestone pavement with a clear view of the Northern Summit (90 minutes). Take care here, especially in windy conditions, but do try to take advantage of the close views of these dramatic gullies and the view to the north (Montgo - Benissa - The Balearics). To the west is Bernia in all its glory and Puig Campana, Benidorm and even Alicante to the south. At the time of writing a Postbox and Visitors Book exists on this summit provided by the Grupo Muntanya, Calpe. *2hr 45min*

Descent

A descent by Broad Gully is recommended, but there is also an agreeable but more energetic alternative - Circuit Route by Broad Valley - **CARE NEEDED.**

Broad Valley is the shallow valley running south north on the summit, which at one time, was obviously well-cultivated. At its southern end - between imposing crags is Valley Finca (ruins).

It is best to start the descent by following the good track,along the western side of Broad Valley which goes through some pines until it eventually descends to the bottom, where there are some terraces. Here cross over to the other side to pick up another track to the finca ruins. *3hrs 45min*

Below the finca ruins the path is subject to erosion each winter as rains funnel through Broad Valley and there will never be a really reliable path. This is the crux of the descent - get it right and you have 40 minutes of delightful walking to regain the old finca on the Estate Road - get it wrong and you add about 2 hours and much effort into your descent. There is a yellow marker on the southwest corner of the finca and you should aim in this general direction for about 50 metres in the direction of a ridge with pine trees. Look for a path descending - but only for about 50/100 metres and you should find a good mule track heading first south then east which keeps to about the 350 metre contour, and continues round the summit crags - you will descend to another finca, then, in about 40 minutes you will regain the Estate Road just above the finca previously mentioned in the ascent. *4hr 45min*

ROUTE 26: DORSET CIRCUIT OF SIERRA DE OLTA M(B) 15km 4½h

Olta is the mountain behind Calpe, whose southern summit cliffs greet the motorists emerging from the Barranca de Mascarat on their way to Benissa. The eastern cliffs fill the sky on the left of the road and, from Benissa, the northern summit with its pinnacles can be seen to their best advantage.

The Approaches

Being a circuit walk, the route can be joined at any number of access points. Here are two:

Hard Man's Route

Park your transport near the disco on the CN332, close to Km.167.3, and go up a short surfaced road opposite the disco for a few metres, towards the mountain. After going under a railway bridge, bear right on a wide but rough road, pass a villa, and then zig-zag for 40min until the first route marker is found, just past an old electricity sub-station. The original route has, however, been obliterated during the construction of a forestry road a few metres higher up, which is to give access to fire-fighting vehicles. Use it to gain access to the route near the ruined finca. Allow 40min.

Lazy Man's Route

Leave the CN332 road at Km.169.1 and bear inland on the AV1394, signposted Estacion Ferrocarril (railway station). Pass Calpe railway station, cross the railway line, and drive 2½km along the main access road, climbing gently in a general northerly direction. Watch out for a large sign, Casa Such, because, just beyond it, you take a left-hand fork at a junction with many villa signs, but look for a large black one, Casa Lilly. Drive on for 1½km looking for another minor road on the left, with metal posts, a "Privado" notice, and your first yellow marker, opposite the sign "Casa D'Agostino". You (and your car) are now on the circuit route (3½km from the CN332). There is room to park a few cars here taking care not to inconvenience the residents. Alternatively, cars can be taken up another kilometre past Casa Lilly, and along an unsurfaced but passable road to the lower shelf (probably an era - threshing floor) where there is good parking.

The Circuit

This description starts from the Lazy Man's Approach, and runs clockwise. The route throughout keeps between the 300m and 400m contours. For convenience it is split into four sections. Waymarking can

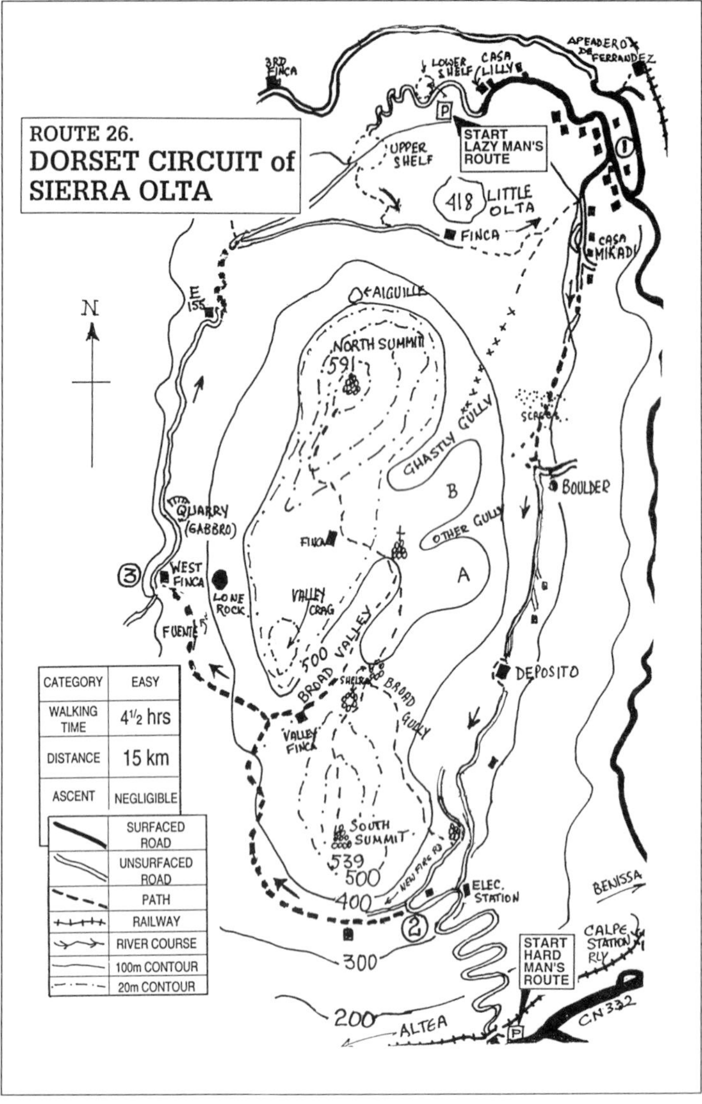
ROUTE 26.
DORSET CIRCUIT of SIERRA OLTA
N
CATEGORY
EASY
WALKING TIME
4½ hrs
DISTANCE
15 km
ASCENT
NEGLIGIBLE
SURFACED ROAD
UNSURFACED ROAD
PATH
RAILWAY
RIVER COURSE
100m CONTOUR
20m CONTOUR
START LAZY MAN'S ROUTE
START HARD MAN'S ROUTE
3RD FINCA
LOWER SHELF
CASA LILLY
APEADERO DE FERRANDEZ
UPPER SHELF
418
LITTLE OLTA
FINCA
CASA MIKADI
AIGUILLE
NORTH SUMMIT
591
GHASTLY GULLY
BOULDER
B
OTHER GULLY
A
QUARRY (GABBRO)
WEST FINCA
LONE ROCK
FUENTE
VALLEY CRAG
500
BROAD VALLEY
BROAD GULLY
DEPOSITO
VALLEY FINCA
SOUTH SUMMIT
539
400
300
200
NEW FIRE RD
ELEC. STATION
BENISSA
CALPE STATION RLY
CN332
ALTEA
P

only be described as lavish! Yellow dots indicate routes to the summit of Olta - yellow rings, the circuit. On Little Olta all the waymarks are red.

1. The Eastern Flank

Leave the surfaced road, go through the metal gate-posts, and bear left towards the mountain, with the gash of Ghastly Gully to the right. A yellow (G) on a rock indicates the routes to the finca in the col behind Little Olta (very rocky for 300m), and the route to the summit plateau via Ghastly Gully. (This is not a route to recommend.)

The unsurfaced road climbs steadily, passing three villas and a diversion on the right which can be ignored. The views now are of the Pou Roig Valley, Montgo, Benissa and Teulada, and to the right, the buttresses of Olta.

The road now drops down to the left. Carry on, passing the last villa, to a track through the pines. *15min*

The views are now extended to Moraira Castle and the few remaining stones of Calpe Castle. About here, a red arrow points invitingly right up to a second gully, which is probably just as disgusting as the previous one. Cross a small stone scree shoot, climbing gently upwards, then descend to a large boulder and an inviting track going down to the valley. Ignore this track, and turn right along a level track. *25min*

The Salinas and the Peñon d'Ifach now come into view, and a large water deposit is reached. Go right round it, and continue in a southerly direction. *30min*

You now have a clear view of the southern summit and a broad gully, which provides the easiest route to the top on the right-hand side. Descend through the rocks, then join a broad but overgrown level road, pass an old ruined finca on the left. Below, you can see the electricity sub-station and, ahead, the casita which will mark the end of this section. In a few minutes you join the main route up the mountain from the CN332. *50min*

2. Round The South Summit and The Western Flank

Carry on upwards for a few metres, with a casita above you on the right, until after a bend you find a new forestry road leading off to the left (west) (marker). Follow this road until you arrive at an old ruined finca. On this section there are good views of Calpe's two harbours and the one remaining wall of its ancient castle perched on a rock overlooking the Mascarat Gorge, with its three tunnels carrying road, railway and motorway. Albir Headland and Sierra Helada (Benidorm's mountain) come into view. The new road now starts to drop down, and after a few metres climb up right onto a terrace to resume the marked route. You are now travelling west for a short time. The end of the Bernia Ridge is now visible, and, in the far distance, the peaks of Puig Campana and Ponoch. Watch the path - it is liable to disappear about here. Soon the little settlement of Pinos comes into view, seen through the magnificent cleft of the Barranca de Estret. In another few minutes you get your first views of Valley Crag, a large cliff which guards another route to the summit. *1h 35min*

From this point you can see your next objective, an old ruined finca below an isolated crag to the left of the mountain. The path here has been washed away by the deluges from Broad Valley, and dead trees have also made a level path impossible. This is the only difficult section of the walk. The route scrambles up through the ruined terraces, then traverses an overgrown terrace, and eventually reaches a junction where the ascent route goes up to Valley Finca. We go down a little to a better path heading away from Olta in a north-westerly direction for a while.

After about 10min, look out for lots of rushes, a sure sign of water, and find the carved bowl of a fuenta right alongside the path, which now leads gently towards the old abandoned finca. *2h*

3. West And The North Summit

From here, the Tosal de Navarro (Cao Ridge) is seen to the north. Drop down below the old finca, and you will find a good track heading north towards the north summit crags. In about 10min, note the change in the colour of the bancal walls to dark grey as you approach the gabbro quarry on your right. You get your first view of the detached pinnacles of the north summit and, on a ridge, the ruins of a finca (E155), your next objective. Back to your left the Bernia Ridge presents its rugged profile with the settlement buildings of Bernia itself now visible. You reach E155 (the house has now lost its number) in another 5min. *3h*

The original route from the finca was a narrow path which contoured round the mountain to join the broad unsurfaced road. The route was much overgrown, but as a direct result of forest fires, the track above the finca has been improved and now goes directly to Little Olta. Ignore two fire breaks on the right as you climb upwards, directly under the aiguille, our own "Napes Needle", and the road levels off to pass to the left of "Indian Rock" before dropping down to join another road where you turn right and see the rocks of Little Olta and the ruined finca beneath them ahead. *3h 20 min*

By all means climb the summit rocks if you wish for excellent views down into the Valley of Pou Roig. Afterwards there is an alternative sporting descent down through the trees to join the route near Lazy Man's Start.

A more civilised end to the walk is to note a large, squarish boulder with red markers and follow a clear, narrow track down to the upper shelf, and the marked route. *3h 30min*

4. The Last Leg
Your route crosses the plateau and descends via zig-zags to the lower shelf, and then by a good unsurfaced road to Casa Lilly, the metalled road, and your starting point. During this section Moraira, Montgo, Gata and finally the Peñon d'Ifach come back into view. *4h*

ROUTE 27: MONTGO FROM JESUS POBRE S(B) 12km 7½h

Montgo is probably the most identifiable of mountains, a great elephant of a thing (yes, it does look like one when seen from the south). It is isolated from the other Sierras by the flat huerta, and in close proximity to the coast. Both Denia and Javea shelter under its protection. With the exception of Peñon d'Ifach, it is probably the most popular mountain on the Costa Blanca. The large cross on the main southern summit was once the object of an annual pilgrimage, with the penitents ascending the mountain from Plana de Just at night, carrying torches. There are four normal routes of ascent. This new one breaks fresh ground.

Getting There
Jesus Pobre (Poor Jesus) is an unspoilt village 3km north of Gata de Gorgos, and sustains a thriving brush-making industry. There are bars, shops and a restaurant. Leave the village, and go north to join the La Jara to Javea road (AP1320). Turn right in the direction of Javea, and within a few metres, turn left (north) through a small collection of villas, until the surfaced road ends at an electrical sub-station. The road, which continues upwards and to the north-west, leads to the Cova de la Punta, which is, in fact, the tail of the elephant, and continues south the entire length of the mountain to the summit. You, however, turn right on a track which at first goes south for a few metres, but settles down to a generally north-easterly direction, heading for the Great Gully, which splits the south-western flank of the mountain.

Making A Start
This walk is mainly on reasonable tracks, but there are some short scrambles, and the middle section, over a featureless area of limestone pavement, is difficult to navigate in poor visibility. Follow the track north-east, and note, high above you to the right, a handsome crag, Crested Crag, which you will pass on the way down. You cross a clearing, and then pass a cairn, which marks the junction with your

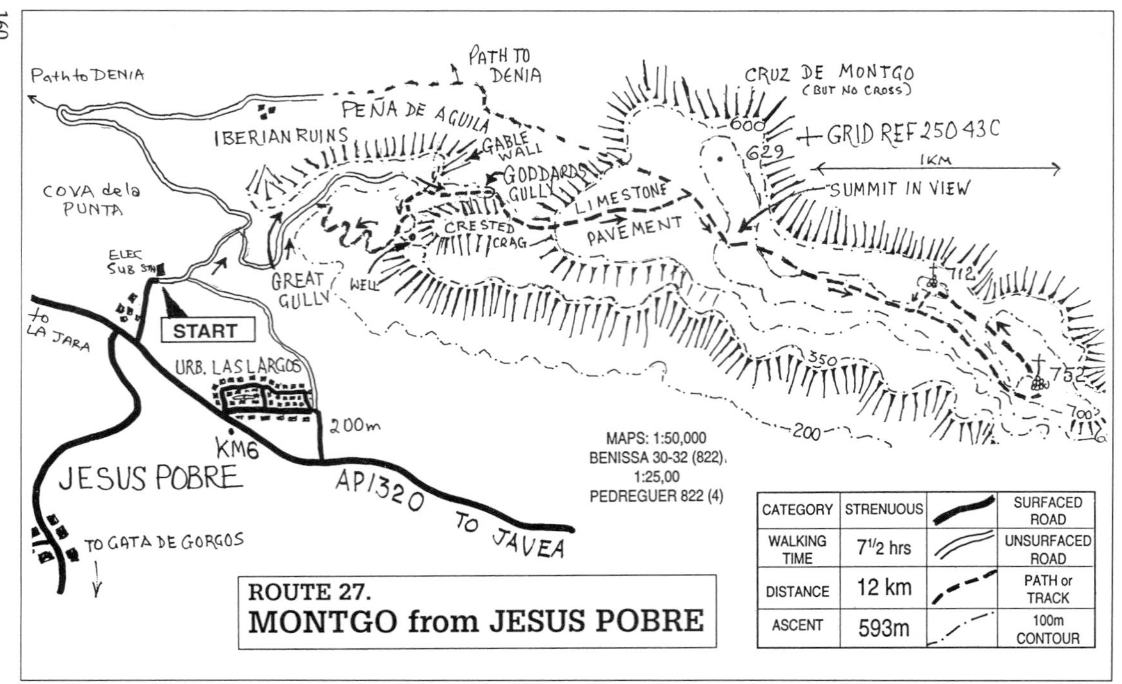
Path to DENIA
COVA de la PUNTA
ELEC SUB STN
to LA JARA
JESUS POBRE
TO GATA DE GORGOS
START
URB. LAS LARGOS
KM6
IBERIAN RUINS
GREAT GULLY
WELL
PEÑA DE AGUILA
PATH TO DENIA
GABLE WALL
GODDARDS GULLY
CRESTED CRAG
LIMESTONE PAVEMENT
200m
AP/320
TO JAVEA
CRUZ DE MONTGO
(BUT NO CROSS)
600
629
GRID REF 250 43C
1KM
SUMMIT IN VIEW
350
200
712
752
700
MAPS: 1:50,000
BENISSA 30-32 (822).
1:25,00
PEDREGUER 822 (4)
CATEGORY STRENUOUS
WALKING TIME 7½ hrs
DISTANCE 12 km
ASCENT 593m
SURFACED ROAD
UNSURFACED ROAD
PATH or TRACK
100m CONTOUR
ROUTE 27.
MONTGO from JESUS POBRE

return route. *30min*

Ahead can be seen the rust-coloured Gable Wall, which divides Great Gully from your route (Goddard's Gully). In another few minutes the track narrows, and eventually deteriorates into a jumble of boulders, which lead to the base of the wall. Now traverse right, and enter Goddard's Gully, which is a rock scramble, passing a sheep-fold built into the crag as the gully narrows and is finally blocked by a wall of rock. Now take to the steep right-hand slope, without the benefit of a path, for 15min, until you reach the rim of the gully, and can see the vast expanse of the flat limestone pavement to the north-east. *1h 45min*

Across The Limestone To The Main Summit

You now have about 30min of very rough walking, with, at first, no apparent objective to aim for. A bearing of approximately north-east (30°) is the best advice. At present there are some dead trees roughly on the line of your route, which are helpful as markers. Eventually, and thankfully, Denia appears to the north, and the cross on the northern summit of the mountain to the east. Finally, you reach a cairn on the ridge track, and turn right for the main summit. It is prudent to look around and fix the position of the cairn in your mind, as well as taking a bearing to help you traverse the limestone on your return route.

2h 15min

To The Main Summit

There is little need for route-finding now, as you move east on a good track, and views open up to the south of Jesus Pobre and Gata de Gorgos, whilst to the south-east Peñon d'Ifach and Olta appear near Calpe. In a very few minutes, you breast a small rocky ridge, to see the southern summit ahead. From here, you can also identify the ascent by picking out a large pine tree near a cave, which you will reach in an hour. Beyond the cave, the track leads upwards over some slabs to the broad summit plateau, with its massive cross. The plinth of the cross, once 3m high, contained a penitents' offertory box, but has now been demolished by vandals. However, beautiful views open up in every direction. Below you is Cabo St Antonio, with its light-house, with the south-east arête in the foreground. This is the route up the mountain from Plana de Just. Note the Val de Laguart, with its high villages to the west, and see if you can pick out the island of Ibiza to the north-east, visible on a clear day. *3h 30min*

To The Northern Summit

Those with experience of rock scrambling may enjoy a diversion, to visit

Montgo, main summit from the north. Photo: Llona Martin

Montgo's other peak, with its metal cross, which commemorates an aircraft disaster. There is a path up on to the rocky ridge just as you leave the summit plateau, but for most of the way you will be on a delightful rocky arête. It will take about an hour to reach the cross, and enjoy some different views down towards Denia. Your Peñance is, however, to descend to the main track by way of steep broken limestone. Allow an extra $1^1/_2$h for this diversion.

The Descent

Retrace your route along the ridge track as far as the cairn. *5h*

Now continue your route across the limestone pavement to the south-west. It is useful to aim for a small urbanisation on the hillside behind Jesus Pobre, with two prominent hills on its right-hand side. In poor visibility, it may be more prudent to continue along the ridge track to the Peña del Aguila on a clear route, which takes you back to the starting place in about 3h. Eventually, the red cliffs of Montgo's south flank appear, and when you can identify Gable Wall, reverse the route down once more into the rocky gully, and regain the marked path. Watch out for the marked boulder at which you turn left, to head for the base of some cliffs, through pines and flat slabs. *5h 40min*

Montgo - the summit from the west

At the base of the cliffs, move right under Crested Crag, where you gain a rough shelf with a water deposito dated precisely 11th July 1969. *6h*

Down To Jesus Pobre

A well-engineered Mozarabic trail now zig-zags down through the pines, and in 1h you regain the main track. At present, a number of fallen trees have obstructed the path. Continue now to reverse the ascent route back to Jesus Pobre, and some well-earned refreshment. *7h 30min*

ROUTE 28: SIERRAS DE CORTINA E(A) 7km 2½h

What we generally refer to as the Sierras de Cortina is a miniature range of mountains which stretch from Puig Campana (1406m) to the coast at Benidorm. They rise only to 500m and are dwarfed by their neighbour, the second highest peak in Alicante province, but despite their modest height display true mountain form and are worthy of any mountaineer's attention. They have a distinct advantage over other, higher peaks in that they are near the coast and a good number of excellent restaurants. There are in fact five summits. You can walk along the one which carries the name Cortina on the maps. Next there are Tapiada (556m) and Amanellas (520m), a real little Matterhorn, then two unnamed summits right up against the flank of the Puig. The stroll takes you along the long ridge of the Cortina, the nearest peak to Benidorm, and seldom are such extensive mountain views available for so little effort. The walk can even be contemplated on a hot summer's day. Allow 2 to 3h.

Getting There

You can approach the mountain from the north, where the AV1741 from La Nucia to Finestrat crosses a pass at Km.3.9, at a height of over 300m (a very crafty move!) This road is not shown on old maps but leaves the C3318 just before the Benidorm bypass. As you drive up the pass note the end of Cortina (The Prow, 440m) on your left and the other peaks on your right. Turn off left into the car park of Rancho Grande.

Making A Start - To The Ridge

Leave the car park at the Rancho Grande and follow a good, broad track upwards alongside the buildings in a south-east direction and, believe it or not, in 10min you are on the ridge at a broad col with The Prow on your left and the long ridge of Cortina stretching invitingly to the south-west. To the south the broad view is of Benidorm with its island, Sierra Helada and Peñon d'Ifach. The northern views are of mighty Puig Campana and Ponoch with Cortina's brothers and Amanellas.

The Ridge

Turn right to follow an excellent, unsurfaced road which follows the ridge to its south-west summit and no further. There are no buildings except a shepherd's shelter. The track now presents you with at least an hour's gentle stroll with hardly any ascent and with expanding views in all directions. Note that you pass above two deep rocky coombes or hollows and that below you are signs of Benidorm's new prestige golf course and urbanisation.

As you walk you gain height, and looking back, you can now see the two villages of Altea (old and new), Sierra Toix, above Calpe, and, behind the Bernia Ridge, Olta and even Col de Rates. You now have to climb a little to reach the highest point (520m). Below you on the right-

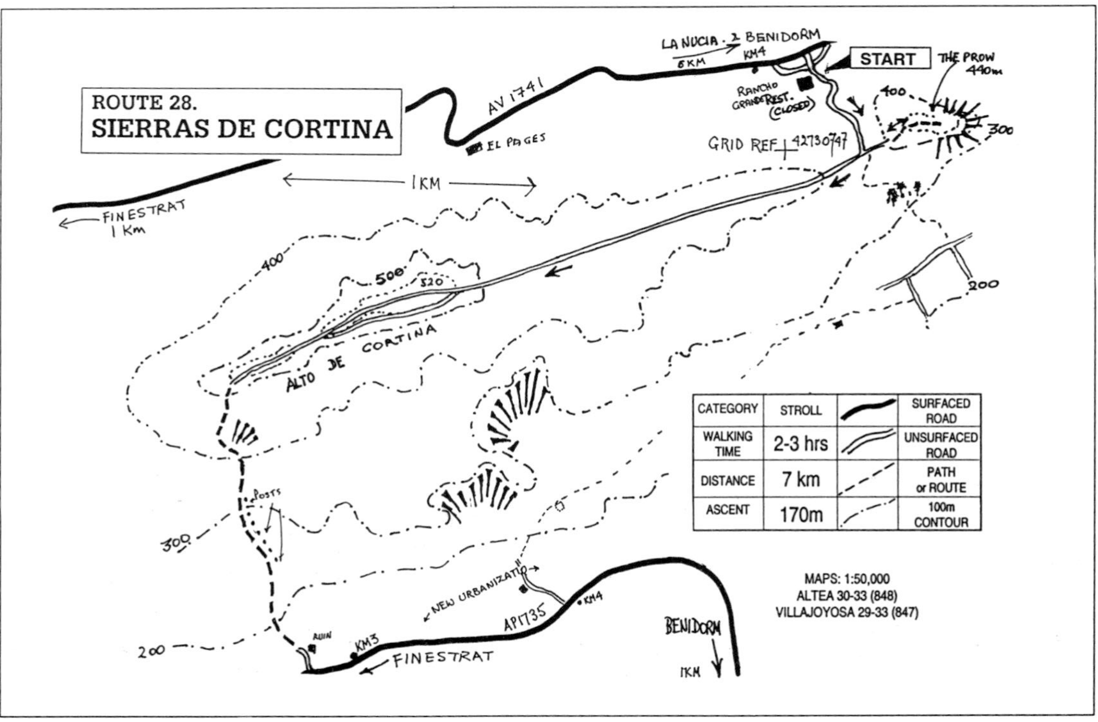
ROUTE 28.
SIERRAS DE CORTINA
LA NUCIA . 2 BENIDORM
6KM
KM4
START
THE PROW 440m
RANCHO GRANDE REST. (CLOSED)
AV 1741
EL PAGES
GRID REF 42730747
400
300
1KM
FINESTRAT 1 Km
400
500
520
ALTO DE CORTINA
200
CATEGORY
STROLL
SURFACED ROAD
WALKING TIME
2-3 hrs
UNSURFACED ROAD
DISTANCE
7 km
PATH or ROUTE
ASCENT
170m
100m CONTOUR
POSTS
300
NEW URBANIZATIO
AP1735
KM4
MAPS: 1:50,000
ALTEA 30-33 (848)
VILLAJOYOSA 29-33 (847)
200
RUIN
KM3
FINESTRAT
BENIDORM
1KM

hand side (north) can be seen El Pages restaurant and a remonta (stables) with a small bull ring with a wooden bull in the centre.

Summit Views

The little village of Finestrat has a magnificent setting with mountains all around it. Note the little church set on a red spur of rock with the Casas Colgades (hanging houses) clinging to the cliff face below. Most of your attention will, no doubt, be claimed by the shapely peak of the Puig behind the town, the only Jurassic outcrop in our area. The geological fault which causes the square notch in the south-east ridge has given rise to a number of legends concerning the giant Roldan (Roland) who occupied the mountain. (See Route 30)

Most week-ends there are climbers on the mountain and each year Finestrat is host to a Climbing Fiesta attended by climbers from all over Spain.

To the left of the Puig is another shapely mountain, El Realet, with its beautiful arête which is called locally "the shark's teeth". In the distance the radar domes help you identify the highest mountain, Aitana, whilst to the south is Cabeza d'Oro, near Busot, and on the coast Alicante, with its castle of Santa Barbara, can be seen.

To The End Of The Ridge

From the highest point you can descend a little and continue your walk for another quarter of an hour to the cairn at the end of the ridge. From there you can only descend, cross-country, to the Benidorm road (AP1735) near Km.3. It is now time for you to retrace your steps to the broad col, enjoying the views missed on the outward journey.

To The Summit Of The Prow

A rough, steep track will take you in 15min to the rocky summit of the Prow. The effort is well worthwhile as there are extensive views over the rich huerta of the Algar and Guadalest Valleys, the Bernia with Peñon d'Ifach in the distance, and the towns of Callosa, Altea, La Nucia and Polop.

Hospitality will probably await you at Rancho Grande but if not, do not despair, as 1km towards Finestrat is El Pages and in the town itself there are a number of good restaurants and bars. On the Benidorm road, just half a kilometre from the village, is the newly extended El Alcazar, which provides satisfying fare, in most pleasing surroundings, at a very modest price.

ROUTE 29: PEÑA DIVINO and ALTO DE LA PEÑA SELLA

M(B) 13½km 5½h

The attractive mountain village of Sella, 17km inland from the coast at Villajoyosa, has towering cliffs, which protect it from northerly winds. They are, in fact, the end of a long ridge which runs east to west, parallel with the highest mountain, named after the village, Alto de la Peña Sella. The ridge continues east as an attractive peak, Peña Divino. The ridge separates two lovely valleys, Barranco Tagarina and Baranco del Arc, both of which can be admired during a traverse of the ridge.

Getting There

Sella lies on the A170 which leads over the Aitana ridge at Puerto Tudons and thence to Alcolecha and Alcoy. The village is worth a visit with its well placed castle and ermita. It is extremely popular and coachloads arrive daily from the coast to visit its excellent restaurants. There are good views down onto a river, reservoir and sierra, which all carry the name Amadorio. Most of the village houses have been bought as week-end retreats.

Making A Start

Drive first along the main road, the A170, towards Alcoy then, at Km.5, turn off right onto a good, unsurfaced road with a sign Remonta Alemana leading to the Barranco Tagarina. The road is narrow, and at times rough, but at the time of writing a normal car can, with care, be driven 5km to a parking place at the head of the valley, passing the remonta on the way. Across the valley you can admire the ridge of Alto de la Peña Sella and behind you can be seen the aerials on the summit of Aitana.

To Peña Divino

Continue along the road as it climbs and crosses around the head of the barranca, passing now on the left an old finca with its era, complete with stone, on the opposite side of the road. This road continues north-east and will eventually lead to Puerto Mulero and then down into the Guadalest Valley. This is in fact the final section of the long-distance walk, Costa Blanca Mountain Way, from Villalonga to Sella. Just past the finca, on a bend, a road comes down from the right. This is both the route up to the summit of the Peña Sella and the return route. For the present your sights are set on Peña Divino and so continue upwards, passing a welcome fuente on the right. *30min*

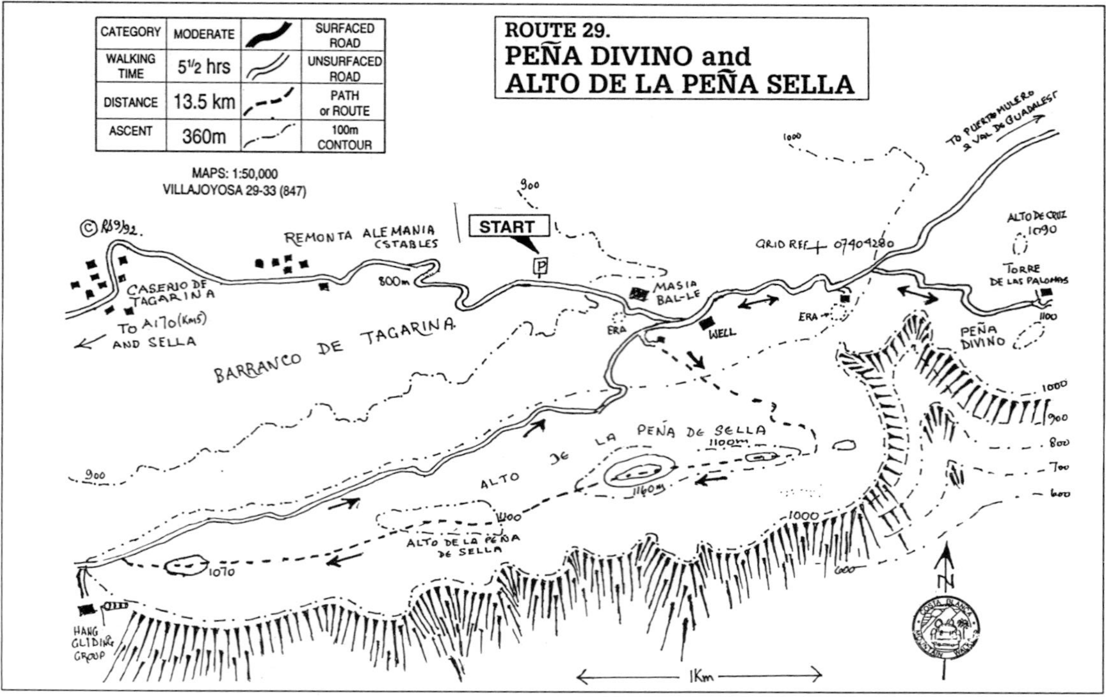
ROUTE 29.
PEÑA DIVINO and
ALTO DE LA PEÑA SELLA
CATEGORY
MODERATE
SURFACED ROAD
WALKING TIME
5½ hrs
UNSURFACED ROAD
DISTANCE
13.5 km
PATH or ROUTE
ASCENT
360m
100m CONTOUR
MAPS: 1:50,000
VILLAJOYOSA 29-33 (847)
© RB 9/92.
REMONTA ALEMANIA STABLES
START
P
800m
CASERIO DE TAGARINA
TO AITO (Kms) AND SELLA
BARRANCO DE TAGARINA
MASIA BAL-LE
ERA
WELL
ERA
GRID REF 07404280
TO PUERTO MULERO & VAL DE GUADALEST
ALTO DE CRUZ
1090
TORRE DE LAS PALOMAS
1100
PEÑA DIVINO
1000
900
800
700
600
ALTO DE LA PEÑA DE SELLA
1100m
1160m
1100
ALTO DE LA PEÑA DE SELLA
1070
1000
600
900
900
1000
HANG GLIDING GROUP
1Km
N

When you arrive at a fork in the road take the right-hand one which leads to an old finca, with its era, and dramatic views down into the cleft between the two Peñas. Now go left up a rocky path to the left of the finca and find another road. Turn right to reach another old finca, El Torre, with a tall tower of fairly recent construction. *1h 15min*

The tower is in fact, a pigeon loft with a spiral staircase to give access to the boxes. It is too remote to have been used to rear the birds and, could have been used for a local sport in which the birds have their tails plucked to ensure erratic flight, which tests the skills of the marksman. Climb up the rocks to the south and a treat awaits you, the summit of Peña Divina. You look down into the deep cleft between Peña Sella and probably marvel that bancals have been constructed in it. Probably its southern aspect and sheltered position made it suitable for cultivation, despite its situation. To the south-west can be seen the village of Sella at the end of the beautiful Barranca del Arc.

There is a road running in the bottom of this remote valley which leads over Puerto del Contadores to the Polop road near Vipas Restaurant. Beyond are the Busot mountains with shapely Cabeza D'Oro. Further south stands the rock with the castle of Santa Barbara in the centre of Alicante. To the right of this, note the Amadorio Reservoir with the Sierra Amadorio behind it. To the south-east is the jagged ridge of El Realet, called by the locals "the shark's teeth" (not a bad description), behind which stand Puig Campana (the second-highest mountain) and its companion Ponoch. Finally you can now see your route over the Peña de Sella, but a direct approach via the cleft is not to be recommended. Remember that these crags have claimed many lives, especially those who sought a short cut.

To Alto De La Peña De Sella

Follow the road from El Torre back to the forestry road over to Puerto Mulero and turn left down the valley, then just past the fuente, turn left again onto another road, but only for a very short while, taking the first available track left to a casita. Climb south-east on a good track at first, heading for a col between two of Peña Sella's summits. Finally a narrow path zig-zags upwards to gain the ridge. Views are much the same with the addition, of course, of Peña Divino. *2h 15min*

Traverse Of The Ridge

You now have the pleasant task of a 3km traverse on this easy ridge over three summits in all. On the traverse you will be able to admire the steep and rocky face of the mountain, and even pick out Monte Cabre, near

Alto de la Peña de Sella from Peña Divino. Photo: Author

Alcoy, until, in about 2h, the mountain loses its rocky crest and descends to a surfaced road. *4h*

It is worth turning left along the road to an old finca, right on the edge of the cliffs, from which intrepid "bird men" launch themselves into space at week-ends and fiestas. *4h 30min*

Back Down To The Valley

All that remains now is to descend on the good road, back to the valley, enjoying the excellent views of the Barranca Tagarina with mighty Aitana to be admired across the valley.

There is lots of hospitality available at Sella, well able to satisfy mountain appetites. *5h 30min*

ROUTE 30: PUIG CAMPANA S/Sc 14km 6h (See coverpicture)

Puig Campana, (those in the know pronounce it 'Putch'), at 1410 metres is the second highest mountain in Alicante. Second it may be in height but no other mountain, including its big brother Aitana, can hold a candle to it for sheer beauty and fine mountain form. The southwestern buttress and ridge is most distinguished, and includes the famous 'Roldan Notch', a fault which has left a square hole in the ridge. From Alicante to Campello and Villajoyosa the buttress presents a fine sight. From Benidorm it provides a dramatic back drop to the popular resort, but it is from Finestrat, the mountains' 'Zermatt' that the most intimate views can be enjoyed. The southwestern ridge is much relished by rock climbers and there are a number of routes, most of them quite hard. Each year there is a climbing fiesta hosted by local clubs and the town council. Each year too, hundreds of walkers reach the summit by means of the 'Tourist route' up the Great Gully. Many are not mountaineers but adventurers who just had to climb the Puig. A few years ago when a German mountaineer donated a handsome log book for use on the summit, it was full before the year was out.

This route follows the tourist route to the summit and then offers an alternative circuit for the dedicated and experienced mountaineer and 1,000ft scree run down the north face of the mountain. The Great Gully, in which you will spend a great deal of this walk is definitely not a walker's paradise, but the views from the summit ridge are worth the effort involved.

Getting There

Finestrat, 12km from Benidorm on the AV 1741, is the most 'Alpine' of Costa villages, built on a cliff with its 'Casas Colgadas' (hanging houses), with most intimate views of The Puig and the route up the Great Gully. The top of the cliff is crowned with an ancient Ermita and a formal garden the centrepiece of which boasts 'Finestrat, centre of the universe'. The village is well worth exploring and has lots of restaurants and bars. To the north of the village is another attraction, the Fuente Molli, with its gushing jets of pure mountain water. Drive on the AP1733 past the Fuente and continue upwards on a narrow road toward the Puig, and once over a small bridge park your transport and look for a waymarked track (red and white) which heads north towards the base of the Great Gully.

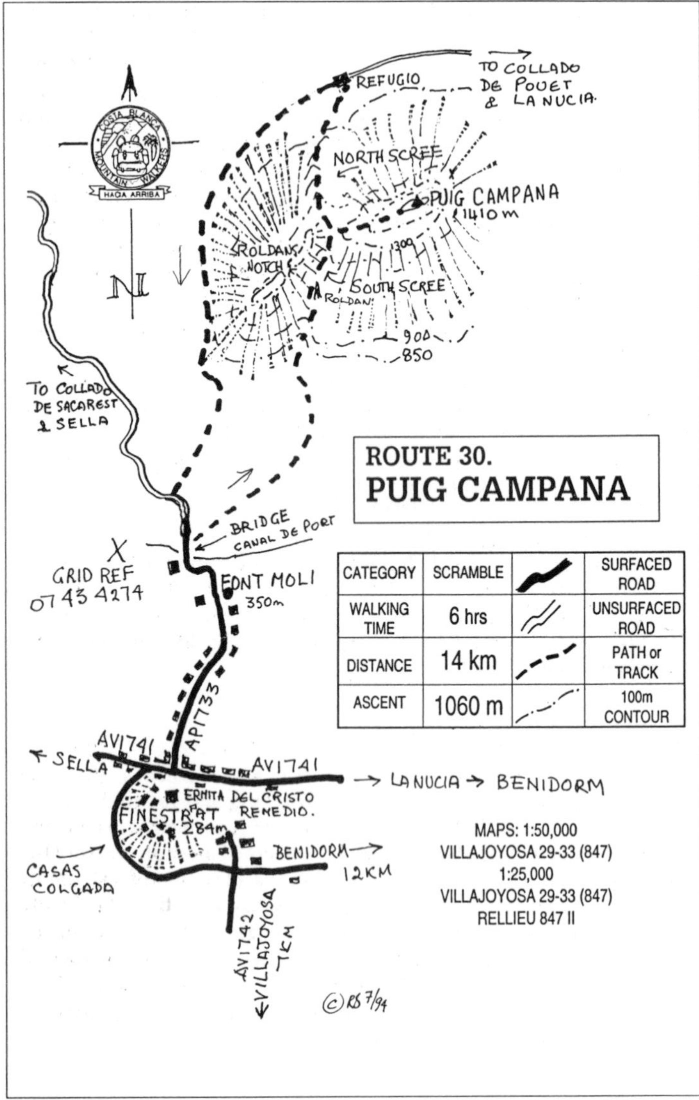

CATEGORY	SCRAMBLE		SURFACED ROAD
WALKING TIME	6 hrs		UNSURFACED ROAD
DISTANCE	14 km		PATH or TRACK
ASCENT	1060 m		100m CONTOUR

Towards Great Gully

This very well worn and clearly marked track heads just east of north towards the boulder-strewn area at the base of the Great Gully and there is little need for any directions. On arriving at the base of the gully just start climbing. *45min*

The Great Gully

Settle down now for a long hard slog up to the main col. Steady walkers might allow at least two hours for this section. There is no route to follow, but by using mountain skills and keeping to the right of the stones where you can discover little zigzags, you can find the least uncomfortable way. The gully bed is a mixture of large boulders, mixed scree and some vegetation, all of which is UNSTABLE. A ski pole is useful. Do be careful if you are a large party to stagger your routes so as to prevent a dislodged boulder causing injury to those following below.

You WILL dislodge more than a few and remember to shout "BELOW" to those on the receiving end.

On the way up spare a glance to the right where a large pinnacle is supposed to represent Roldan the Giant who lived on this mountain. There are a number of delightful folk stories about him and the notch on the southwest ridge. Roldan's daughter was abducted and the giant flew into such a rage that he kicked the ridge and sent a huge part of it into the sea. This is now Benidorm island. Hard headed and unromantic geologists disprove this, as Benidorm Island is not the same rock as the Puig. Another tale is that his wife was destined to die at sunset and the giant cut the notch to give her a few more minutes in the setting sun. *2hrs 24mins*

To the Summit

Now reap the reward for your privations in the gully and tread a lovely marked track along the ridge, east to the main summit with its cross and letter box. As might be expected the views are magnificent, only to the north is there some restriction due to Aitana and you cannot view the third highest peak Monte Cabre near Alcoy. But the rest of the panorama is enough to make your stay on the summit most memorable. There are particularly good views of Cabezo d'Oro, near Busot and Sierra de Aguilar y de la Grana at Rellieu. *3hrs*

Descents

For most folk descent is again by Great Gully, which is more hazardous and uncomfortable than the ascent. You will not cut down the time on the descent.

Descent by the North Scree

This is a very sporting alternative.

From the main col face north and you will find a well defined track leading down the face which after a few minutes turns into the only decent scree run on the Costa. When the scree runs out traverse left for a short distance to find another piste equally delightful until you are forced to breast the gorse and heather down to a good wide track which has come from the Collado de Pouet and La Nucia. If you are really lucky you should arrive at the metal Refugio (climbing hut), used by local rock climbers as a base for the northern climbs. *1hr*

Turn left, generally southwest on a good, marked track which circuits the South-western Buttress and leads you back to the surfaced road, about a kilometre from the start. *2hrs*

ROUTE 31: BARRANCO DEL INFIERNO by Roger Massingham
(See also Costa Blanca Way, Stage 2: Val d'Ebo to Fleix)

The Barranco del Infierno is a cave without a roof. Traversing it is one of the most exhilarating mountaineering experiences on the Costa Blanca. Those who have skills in caving or potholong or climbing should have no difficulty at all in getting through the gorge.

In all there are some five rope pitches or drops to descend and at least four considerable wells or swirl holes to traverse, with the odd little rock obstacle in between. None is of great difficulty to experienced rope handlers, although extreme caution must be taken due to very precarious rescue conditions. It is not wise to try this in wet weather as the gorge is prone to flash flooding.

The climb through is approximately 1.5km long, this being the throat of the gorge. In parts it is so narrow it is possible to reach out and touch both sides and in places so high and narrow you can't see the sky. As formidable as it is beautiful.

Equipment

The gorge is regularly traversed and is fully equipped with bolts. Climbing rope (at least 30m), safety line/rope (30m), Harness if possible, safety helmet, gloves (not Nylon), 6 or more karabiners, etriers, descenders or other rappelling device, caving ladder (10m) not necessary but useful, variety of slings, good climbing tape for tying off and abandoning, lots of drinking water. It goes without saying that personal safety equipment, stout boots, first aid, torch, clothes etc., should be present in your day sack.

Time

The approach to the descent is from Val d'Ebo. Follow the track along the river bed for about 5km. You will arrive at the neck in about an hour or so. The start of the climb is fairly obvious. Give a comfortable 4-5h to complete the climbing part and, if you go out through Fleix, another 2h or so to climb out. These times are only approximate; depending on the size and ability of the party these could be considerably altered. The above estimate is based on a first trip through for a party of four adults, in fairly good shape, and with one experienced climber leading. The grade of climbing skill required is about a good V.Diff.

Pitch 1 A short 4m drop. *Belay:* bolt(s) on the face.

Pitch 2 A short 4m drop slightly more exposed and overhanging than the first. *Belay:* bolt(s) on the face.

Pitch 3 A shallow well with an 8m wall with 5 bolt holes on the right wall. Here, especially in wet conditions, you must do an aid traverse using etriers, etc. Once round and on the lip of the well you will find a bolt to secure a caving ladder for the rest of the party to ascend (could be very time consuming for all the party to traverse). A short rope from the same bolt is needed to drop down off the lip onto the other side.

Pitch 4 A 10m overhanging drop into a well and because of a difficult edge, start-off is easier done with a caving ladder. *Belay:* Bolts on the face. **Once down this pitch you are committed to complete the climb as return is quite impossible.**

Pitch 5 A bit of a tricky traverse along the right side of a stagnant pool(4m) finishing on a precarious narrow ledge (room for two only) which gives onto pitch 6. *Protection:* bolts on the face.

Pitch 6 A 6m ladder or rappel drop. *Belay:* bolt(s) on the face.

Pitch 7 A 4m traverse on the left wall of a stagnant well. The wall initially had bore holes with pegs in to walk across; use these as best you can as hand holes. Quite intricate moves involved here; rock dancers will enjoy the moves; the not so agile will get a wet boot. *Protection:* bolts on face.

Pitch 8 A short drop of 2m off which you lower yourself or jump down.

Pitch 9 The final and longest traverse, being some 30m, and the most exposed. Below is a deep well; a shepherd who ventured alone here fell in, and unable to climb the smooth sides, drowned. A slightly difficult start to the climb on the left wall leads onto a series of iron pegs and a fixed rope (not to be counted on) on which to swing along. This ends on another small ledge, enough for two people, where a bolt belay should be used to rope the rest of the party round the well and down the next and last pitch.

Pitch 10 As you bring someone round the wall to your stance it is advisable to keep them roped up to manoeuvre the very intricate move onto the last wall. This is a 10m drop furnished with iron rungs to climb down. The difficulty here is that the rungs are not entirely visible from the top. To help gain the first rung you have to lower yourself down a smooth wall. A bolt is placed above where you can fix a sling to hang on to.The last climber must take great care here. Indeed the last one down or across each pitch should be top roped. This is where the climbing tape is necessary in order to tie a piece off to come down on, and so abandon.

Pitch 11 A free ground level traverse on the right round a boulder; no danger here, it just saves getting your boots wet. And you're out!

A word of warning again. There have been numerous rescues in this gorge, and a few fatal accidents. The last rescue was in 1990, helicopters were brought in to get some youths to safety. The majority of these incidents were caused through inexperience and being ill equipped. It is a fairly easy climb even for the very inexperienced, providing there is a competent and experienced climber/leader.

PART 3:
Costa Blanca Mountain Way

INTRODUCTION

The Way

The Way was proposed in 1990 as a contribution to mark the Fifth Anniversary of the Costa Blanca Mountain Walkers, and a small working party was formed. By May 1991, the route was settled, and by the end of the year it had been walked, and this guide completed.

The Way is strictly a walkers' route, and only on Caballo Verde Ridge and on Aitana is any route-finding required, and these sections are waymarked. Most of the route uses unsurfaced forestry roads, or provincial surfaced roads, constructed to allow the country people reliable access to the high pastures and crops. I make no apology for this, as not only is traffic almost non-existent but the roads follow the ancient mule tracks, and the views are more enjoyable when you don't have to watch where you are putting your feet all the time.

Since the inauguration, in 1991, the way has proved popular with walkers, back-packers and a lone cyclist. Some did the crossing as day walks over an extended period whilst others walked on consecutive days. Two pensioners completed the five sections in four days. The cyclist only left his wheels for the Caballo Verde Ridge and the final ascent of Aitana.

Completion of the first five sections entitles the walker to be entered on the roll of Companeros (See Appendix). Regular updates of the route and news of new Companeros appear in the newsletters of the Costa Blanca Mountain Walkers or can be obtained from the Registrar.

Why Walk It?

There is great satisfaction in plotting a line across a map, and even greater satisfaction in actually walking it. There is intense pleasure in looking at your route afterwards, and reliving your great experience. I shall never forget the experience when I walked right across an OS 1in map for the first time. Day walks are the norm for most of us, so the chance to "keep on walking" has its own magic for all mountaineers.

This route not only crosses a number of maps, but the whole of the Las Marinas mountains, plus a few kilometres in La Safor (Valencia), from north to south. In more than 100km it is intended to introduce the walker to the varied scenery of the area.

You start in the lush huerta of the Rio Serpis, vast well-watered orchards, spreading out to the sea. You pass your first ancient castle at Villalonga, and then through the cherry orchards to your first peak, Almisira. North of Almisira is a vast open panorama reminiscent of Scotland as you head for the deep gorge of the Val de Infierno. Descending the gorge and ascending to Fleix in Val Laguart, you use the ancient Mozarabic trail, Camio del Jubias, passing the typical lavadero or village wash-house to reach Fleix. Above the village are the towering crags of Peña Roch, and the Caballo Verde Ridge, scene of the "Moor's last stand" in the seventeenth century.

Next you descend into the Val de Pop (the valley of the Rio Jalon). Lower down, the valley spreads out into a wide fertile basin totally protected on all sides by mountains, and famous for its wine, fruit and almonds. You cross the dry bed of the Rio Jalon, and climb through the Val Galistero by the Fig Tree Path over the high plateau of Val de Alt on a new forestry road, passing a notable ancient finca, with its oven and era (threshing floor). The Val de Alt is a typical high plateau, farmed from Castell de Castells, and you see ahead the long ridge of Aixorta, rising to the high peaks of Serrella, with the beautiful natural rock arch of Atancos on their north face. You cross this ridge at its weakest point, which is, however, protected by probably the most picturesque of the castles, perched on a crag commanding the pass.

From the pass, you look down on to unquestionably the most popular and scenic of the valleys, Guadalest, with its numerous castles. Above the waters of the reservoir rises your final objective, Aitana itself. The last day is reserved for the ascent of the highest mountain in the province, with views now over the whole route of the walk, to Alcoy, Alicante and beyond. Descending to Font Moli for the final night, you can examine an ancient nevera, or ice pit.

In these five glorious days, you will not only have stored up a lot of cherished memories, but will have gained a thorough appreciation of the beauties of the mountains of Las Marinas and of the Costa Blanca.

How To Walk It?

The ultimate way to enjoy this walk is, I feel, to be alone, but if I had to have a companion, I cannot think of a more idyllic expedition than with a mule. To walk the way with a mule is traditionally to go at a modest pace, and in the manner for which most of the trails were constructed centuries ago, and without the burden of a rucksack. True, the conversation would be a very one-sided, but such a companion would immediately put you in tune with the countryside and the local people. To be practical, though, there a number of ways in which to organise your crossing of the Way.

The Way is 135km long and fairly steep and rough in parts. Walkers should be accustomed to such conditions and because it is likely to be dry and hot should carry adequate water - at least a litre. Accommodation is available at each stage but if there are friends who do not wish to do the walk it is a good idea to have a back up team with car - apart from the obvious safety aspects it can make a wider choice of accommodation available.

The duties of the support party can vary from merely logging the progress of the walkers for safety purposes, to transporting their gear, and even setting up camp, producing a meal, or making sure that the beds are aired in the overnight accommodation!

Some support teams will want to meet up with their walkers at every opportunity, and some members will even want to walk back along the route to meet them (thus logging their progress as having walked that part of the Way twice!). Others will arrange to meet their party only for the mid-day break, and at the end of the day.

The support vehicle can carry spare food and water, plus a full first aid kit, and it is recommended that they carry at least one sleeping bag.

Lucky is the walker who has a support party equipped with a four-wheel drive vehicle (and, of course, a competent driver). Over half of the Way can be traversed by such a vehicle, BUT remember that in bad weather, whole sections of the forestry road are liable to disappear, and the rest become quagmires. The modest guide (See Support Party Notes p212) is aimed at those who love their cars, and is restricted to decent surfaced roads, and is intended to make the task of the support party a little easier, by supplying routes, times and mileages, also including the *known* accommodation available.

There can be no doubt at all that an attractive way to do these walks is as a back-packer with a small tent (shades of outward bound!). The route for back-packers will be shorter, as they do not have to pass through all the villages seeking accommodation, and there are plenty of wonderful spots in which to camp. The back-packers' route will only pass through the villages of Forna, Fleix, Beniarda and Benifato. There will be no chance to replenish supplies on days 2 and 3 without leaving the route. The next way is to back-pack with a support party who will meet the walkers at mid-day, and pitch camp for them at night, but the most civilised way to do the walk is by using overnight accommodation and a support party.

For those with insufficient time, or stamina, there is no reason why the Way cannot be enjoyed a section, or even part of a section, at a time.

There is only one requirement to qualify as a Companero de la Via de la Montanosa de la Costa Blanca: to walk the first five sections and enjoy it. The way is suitable for mountain bikes, but I would not like to carry the machine over the Caballo Verde Ridge. Horse riders will be able to use about 75% of the way. The standard times are, I feel, modest, and allow for the walker to enjoy the experience. I await with interest the first 24-hour crossing, no doubt by a fell runner, but the three who backpacked said that they would do it again, and enjoy the scenery rather than set a record.

El Lavadero

COSTA BLANCA MOUNTAIN WAY
TIMETABLE AND DISTANCES

SECTIONS	km	hrs & mins	TOTAL km	TOTAL hrs & mins	Ascent (m)
STAGE 1					
Villalonga to Forna	8	3.30	8	3.30	
Forna to Adsubia	4	1	12	4.30	
Adsubia to Castillo de Gallinera	4.5	2	16.5	6.30	
Castillo de Gallinera to Almisira	3.5	1.30	20	8	
Almisira to Val d'Ebo	9	3	29	11	1100
STAGE 2					
Val d'Ebo to Pla de Mollo	3.75	1	3.75	1	
Pla de Mollo to Rio Ebo	6.75	3	10.5	4	
Rio Ebo to Fleix	1.5	1	12	5	
To Barranco del Infierno	5	2	17	7	
To Isbert's Folly	5	2	22	9	439
STAGE 3					
Fleix to East Col	3	1	3	1	
East Col to Collado de Garga	6	2.30	9	3.30	
Collado de Garga to Km.4.5	5	2	14	5.30	
Km.4.5 to Corral del Somo	11	4	25	9.30	
Corral del Somo to Castell de Castells	4	1	29	10.30	824
STAGE 4					
Castell de Castells to Serrella Castle	7.75	2.15	7.75	2.25	
1h allowed at Castle					
Serrella Castle to Beniarda	8.25	3.10	16	5.35	
Beniarda to Abdet	5	1.30	21	7.05	
Abdet to Confrides	4	.55	25	8	884
STAGE 5					
Confrides to Fuente Arbol	6	1.30	6	1.30	
Fuente Arbol to Partagas	4	1.20	10	2.50	
Partagas to Summit of Aitana	1	.50	11	3.40	
Aitana to Font Moli	10	3.20	21	7	772
STAGE 6 (OPTIONAL)					
Font Moli to Puerta Mulero	6	2.30	6	2.30	
Puerta Mulero to Sella	14	4	20	6.30	640

Costa Blanca Way 115.5km. With Barranco de Ebo 135.5km
Whole 6 sections 135.5km. With Barranco de Ebo 155.5km
Ascent C.B.M.W. 4019m. 6 sections 4659m

The Route

STAGE 1: VILLALONGA TO VAL D'EBO

Overall Time:	12h	*Walking Time:*	11h
Distance:	29km	*Ascent:*	1100m

Getting There

The Way officially starts at Villalonga Castle, which is about 2km south-east of the town itself. There is now no accommodation in the town, but there is a vast amount available in the seaside town of Gandia, 12km to the north. From Gandia, travel south on the CN332 in the direction of Alicante, and 1km out of town, turn off right (west) on to the VP1012, near to the village of Bellrequart. In 8km, enter the town of Villalonga, go down the main street heading north-east, and head for the local brickworks, which has a tall chimney in line with the castle itself. Passing the brickworks on the right, look for a good unsurfaced road going off to the right (red marker), and after 1/2km, an aqueduct marks the start of the walk.

Villalonga (long village) is of Roman origin, established by "Colonia"; retired soldiers who remained in the Colony to farm. Their villas were set in a line, probably along a water supply. The castle is of Moorish origin, but by the year 1240, was in the possession of King Jaime I of Aragon.

To The Castle

Walk over the aqueduct (south-east) along a concrete road, passing a gate and very high terrace walls on the right-hand side along a dry stream bed, to join a well-marked track which climbs out of the barranco up the northern slopes of the castle ridge. The last section, to gain access to the extensive ruins, is much eroded, and a bit of a scramble, but at least, nowadays, you do not have to face the missiles of the castle defenders. *1/2km - 20min*

There are excellent views to the north, with the large town of Gandia on the coast (north-east), and the Sierra de Falconera behind it. North-west is the Sierra de Ador, and west the Serpis Valley, leading to Alcoy, with Sierra de Azafor (south-west). Due south are the slopes of Sierra de Gallinera, which you have to cross on your first leg towards Forna.

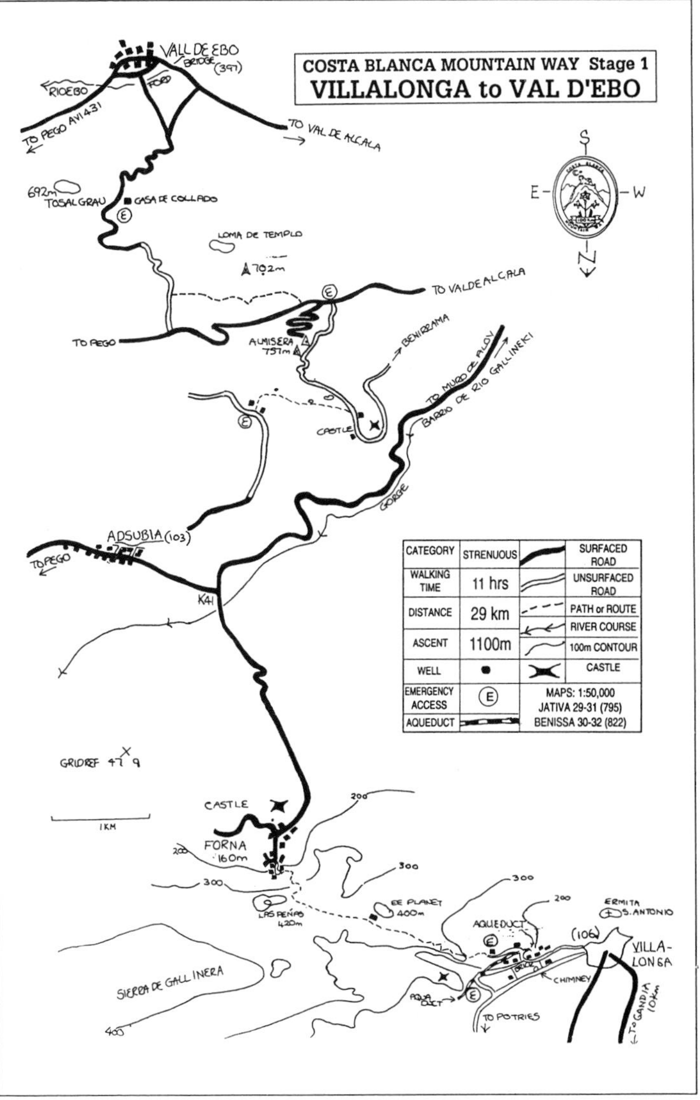
COSTA BLANCA MOUNTAIN WAY Stage 1
VILLALONGA to VAL D'EBO
VALL DE EBO
BRIDGE (397)
FORD
RIOEBO
TO PEGO AV1431
TO VAL DE ALCALA
692m
TOSAL GRAU
CASA DE COLLADO
LOMA DE TEMPLO
702m
TO VALDEALCALA
TO PEGO
ALMISERA
757m
BENIRRAMA
TO MURO DE ALCOY
BARRIO DE RIO GALLINERA
CASTLE
GORGE
ADSUBIA (103)
TO PEGO
K41
CATEGORY
STRENUOUS
SURFACED ROAD
WALKING TIME
11 hrs
UNSURFACED ROAD
DISTANCE
29 km
PATH or ROUTE
RIVER COURSE
ASCENT
1100m
100m CONTOUR
WELL
CASTLE
EMERGENCY ACCESS
MAPS: 1:50,000
JATIVA 29-31 (795)
BENISSA 30-32 (822)
AQUEDUCT
S
E
W
N
1KM
CASTLE
FORNA
160m
200
300
LAS PEÑAS
420m
EE PLANET
400m
AQUEDUCT
ERMITA S. ANTONIO
(106)
VILLA-LONGA
CHIMNEY
AQUA DUCT
TO POTRIES
TO GANDIA 10km
SIERRA DE GALLINERA
400

Descent

Leave the castle, and retrace your ascent route as far as the aqueduct, and turn left on to a broad unsurfaced road. *1km - 1h*

This road goes west-south-west following the aqueduct until another road forks right to bring you to a more substantial road near Casa de la Belatera Lolita, just above the brickworks. *1h 30min*

The Ascent Of Sierra De Gallinera

Turn left up a concrete road, passing villas on the left and orange groves on the right-hand side, until the surface ends at a new villa, and you take a very rough rocky track which climbs upwards to the south-east. Sadly, this is the venue for Sunday motor-cycle trial riding by the local lads, so the track is much eroded in places. Soon the track becomes more reasonable, as you climb a parallel ridge to the one on which the castle stands across the Barranco de Castillo. You now reach the more level area between the two valleys, and say goodbye to the northern mountains as you reach a small casita with views to the south. *4½km - 2h 20min*

Your views are now of the rocky ridge of Sierra de Segaria, with the headland of Llorensa, near Moraira, in the far distance. Almisira, with its TV transmitters, where you can have your lunch break, is to the south-west, with the quarries on the northern flanks of the Sierra Negra.

The track leads towards Almisira for a while, then, after contouring round a broad valley, you change direction east, to descend a steep gully leading to Forna. Montgo now appears on the coast behind the Segaria ridge. *2h 50min*

Forna

Pass through this pretty little village, through the square with a bar and the Restaurant Nautilus, passing the church, going south on a good surfaced road. Pass a ruined calvary on the right, to reach a little rise with a crossroads. In 10min the road on the left (east) leads to the ruins of the ancient castle, which is in reasonably good repair. A hundred kilometres above sea-level, and quite extensive, it is Moorish in origin, belonging at one time to Al Azadrach, the Moorish king. In 1262, records show that it belonged to Don Bernardo de Guillen, whose six sons were known as the Caballeros del Penacho Negro (Knights of the Black Plume). Notable features of the castle are the entrance, fortified walls and four towers facing north. You will need a torch for a full exploration. Strangely, the castle survived the great earthquake of 1644, which destroyed other castles in the Gallinera Valley, including Gallinera which you will pass later in the day. *8km - 3½h*

To Adsubia

The road undulates and twists in between the hills, and you get a good view of your next goal, the summit of Almisira, with its antennae on top. In 15min you pass a quarry on the left and, in half an hour, an extensive farm on the right. In 50min cross the Rio Gallinera, with no surface water in the summer but quite beautiful in winter. You now get your first view of the Castillo de Gallinera, on a rocky spur below Almisira. Turn left (east) on the main road, and take care to walk facing the traffic, as there are many heavy lorries using the road due to the quarries in the area. Drop down now to the larger village of Adsubia. The new restaurant, La Moleta, is on the right of the road, and will one day have accommodation. The present proprietor will, however, put you in touch with villagers who will rent you a room for the night. This could be useful if you have had to make a late start from Villalonga.

12km - 4½h

To Castillo De Gallinera

Pass through the village square, and at the fountain, turn right, passing the church (on right) up towards a cross, where you bear left to walk through lush orange groves in the Barranca de Michel for 40min. You are heading for a col to the north of Almisira, and in 25min bear left at a junction, climbing and zig-zagging up a little, with a casita on the left. You can now see the col just to the right of the quarry on the flank of Almisira. The road is now unsurfaced, and you pass another casita on the right, and a road goes down to the left, which you ignore. As you climb more zig-zags, take time to admire the view behind you, of Adsubia, Pego, the coast, and the craggy ridge of Segaria. Ahead, above you, is a little white casita, which is on your route. Just before you reach the power lines going up to the summit of Almisira, turn right up a short road to the casita, and pass in front of it to find a mule track going north-east. In 10min the track divides (the upper path leads to a good well) and you go down for another 10min to reach a large fallen pine tree, which was once a good marker (red markers). *15½km - 5½h*

Looking south-west, you can pick out your next objectives. The first is a ruined building on the skyline, with crags on the left. The second is a white building between the ruins and the castle. (Red markers on this section to the castle.)

Leave the lone pine and keep level on a good path, to climb up to the ruins on a small, level area. Now climb a little on a good path under some rocks to reach the unsurfaced road coming up from Beniarrama towards Almisira close to the castle. *16½km - 6½h*

Castillo De Gallinera

This is a beautiful castle, strategically situated to guard the entrance to the valley. Although destroyed in the earthquake of 1644, there is still much to see, including a water cistern, and the views are very rewarding. Unfortunately, it is privately owned, and in 1990, the owner installed a new gateway, and it cannot be visited without permission. So far, we have been unable to trace the key-holder. Moorish in origin, the castle was conquered in 1259 by Jaime I, who gave it to his son in 1322. The approaches (from the south) are marked in red, but are much overgrown.

To Almisira

Turn south on the good unsurfaced road which has come up from the village of Beniarrama, and start to climb towards Almisira. The road, which now moves south-west under the cliffs of the mountain, soon starts to deteriorate into a rough track. It is hard to imagine cars using this road only eight years ago, such is the devastation caused by winter rains, showing nature's contempt for the puny works of man! On this stretch, you will be treated to extensive views of the whole of the Gallinera Valley, with its many scattered villages. It is famous for fruit growing, especially cherries, which flourish here. Bordering the valley on the southern side is the ridge of Forada, beyond which can be seen Alicante province's third-highest peak, Mont Cabrer, and next to it (north) the beautiful Benicadell. As you gain height, the Castillo de Gallinera looks like something out of a fairy tale, by far the most beautiful viewpoint from which to take photographs. Just off to the right above the village of Beniarrama are the cliffs of Alto de Chap, a sporting scramble.

Above you, the cliffs of Almisira close in, and behind you are extensive views of the coast - Gandia and eventually Cullera appear to the north-east. As you gain a small rise, Sierra de la Carrasca, beyond the Val d'Ebo, appears to the south, and you pass a ruined finca on the left to reach the road which runs along this high plateau. This is a remote, high wilderness, reminiscent of Wester Ross and Sutherland, with no buildings, and frequented only by foresters and shepherds.

19km - 7½h

To The Summit

Turn left (east) along the road, and in 5min reach the Pla de Almisira, and turn up the service road to the summit, which is reached in 20min.

20km - 8h

Vistas Unlimited

On this, your first summit, you can spend a happy time plotting the various mountain ranges, etc., which can now be identified. Notable amongst them are, to the south Penon Roch and the Caballo Verde Ridge (Section 3), Castillo de Serrella, the highest point on Section 4, and finally Aitana ridge with Pena Mulero. Note the prominent road which leads down from Aitana summit (Section 5). The summit of Aitana, however, remains tantalisingly hidden by the intervening ridge of Carrasca, behind the Val d'Ebo which itself is hidden in its deep valley.

To the north, beyond Villalonga, can be seen the serried ridges of the Sierras of Azafor, Gallinera and Almirante.

The Castle

Much is known of the history of the extensive castle which once crowned this strategic mountain, but only a few stones remain. Moorish in origin, its governor was Abdalla Marhop. In 1243, it fell to Nicolas Scals. It was the scene of the signing of the important Treaty of Almisira, between the Moors and the Christians. The Castle probably suffered from the earthquake of 1644, but it is more likely that what little remained was scattered when the road to the Transmitting Station was constructed. A forestry lookout cabin has been newly installed on the summit, and is manned during high fire-risk periods. Just below the cabin, on the north side, is a small section of wall with a cement coping. Local people whom I asked disagreed about its origins, some saying that the wall was one of the remains of the Moorish Castle, others claiming that it is even more ancient, and was of the Iberian period (the search for authentic details of Spanish castles is very frustrating!)

To Val d'Ebo

Leave the summit and descend once more to the Pla de Almisira, crossing the road, and heading on a good track through some pine trees, towards another transmitter on a small hill to the south. You head left (east) of the hill on a good marked track which contours its flanks. Below, you can see Pego, and the straight road leading to Vergel, the coast beyond, and Segaria ridge to the south-east, with Montgo in the distance. At a fork go left, and now watch out for my markers, as the trail forks off left down some zig-zags, and passes under some small flat slabs to gain a broad ridge. From here, the track is at times indistinct, and red markers have been placed. Be prepared for the line of the path to zig-zag to lose height now and then, but generally keep heading east on the broad ridge until you can see an unsurfaced road ahead, join it near a ruin, and turn right (south).

Passing a casita on the left, top a little rise to see Tosal Grau ahead. You will cross a col to the right (west) of its summit. Look out for a well with water on the left, then start to climb again. You now have to drop to negotiate the head of a barranca, after which the road gains a surface (for how long, I know not, as the wild plants are growing through it already!). Start climbing, passing some caves on the right, and gain the col at Casa de Collado (now being rebuilt) with its excellent well. Look back and say farewell to the northern mountains, and start the descent to Val d'Ebo. *25km - 10h*

As you cross the col, you can see the village below you, with the bulk of the Sierra de la Carrasca as a backdrop to the south. We get this view earlier now, due to the ravages of a recent forest fire (August 1991). Relish now thoughts of dinner and a good night's rest as you stroll the remaining 3km down the well-engineered road through orchards of apples, pears and cherries, to turn left at a junction, cross over the ford, and into the village with its bars and restaurants. *29km - 11h*

Val d'Ebo is isolated but also cosmopolitan, as for generations young men have sought employment in France, and at times the numbers of French-registered cars outnumber the Spanish ones. The Hostal has been closed, but the present patron of the Bar la Plaza, Juan Frau, has offered to find accommodation in the village for walkers who can dine at his bar. The bar is in the main square (557 11 91).

Alternative accommodation is to be found in Pego, 13km away.

STAGE 2: VAL D'EBO TO FLEIX

Walking Time:	to Fleix 5h, with diversions	9h
Distance:	to Fleix 12km, both diversions	22km
Ascent:		439m

On this stage you do not climb a mountain but descend into the deep gorge of the River Ebo. The modest mileage allows time to explore the valley of the Ebo, and visit the Barranco del Infierno. The Barranco itself is strictly for rock-climbers, and I am indebted to Roger Massingham's climbing guide to this thrilling expedition. (See p.174)

To Pla De Mollo

Leave Val d'Ebo, and go down Avenida Marina Alta (east) towards the river, and just before the bridge, turn off right along a surfaced road which gives access to an unsurfaced one, which follows the south bank

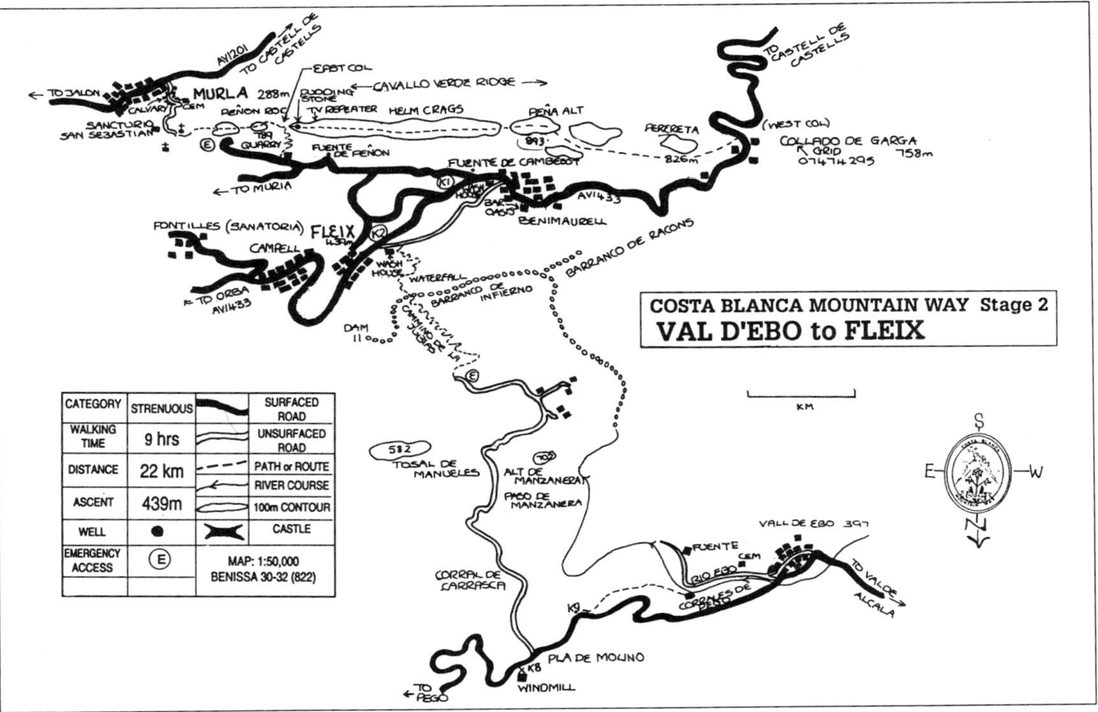
COSTA BLANCA MOUNTAIN WAY Stage 2
VAL D'EBO to FLEIX
KM
S
E
W
N
TO JALON
MURLA 288m
CALVARY
CEM
SANCTURIO SAN SEBASTIAN
AV1201
TO CASTELL DE CASTELLS
EAST COL
PUDDING STONE
CAVALLO VERDE RIDGE
PEÑON ROC
TV REPEATER
HELM CRAGS
PEÑA ALT
893
789
QUARRY
FUENTE DE PEÑON
TO MURIA
FUENTE DE CAMBEROT
K1
WASH HOUSE
BAR OASIS
BENIMAURELL
AV1433
PERERETA
826m
(WEST COL)
COLLADO DE GARGA 758m
GRID 07474295
TO CASTELL DE CASTELLS
FONTILLES (SANATORIA)
FLEIX 439m
K2
CAMPELL
TO ORBA
AV1433
WASH HOUSE
WATERFALL
BARRANCO DE INFIERNO
BARRANCO DE RACONS
CAMMINO DE LA JUBIAS
DAM
582
TOSAL DE MANUELES
702
ALT DE MANZANERA
PASO DE MANZANERA
CORRAL DE CARRASCA
FUENTE
CEM
RIO EBO
VALL DE EBO 397
CORRALES DE PEDRO
TO VALDE ALCALA
K9
PLA DE MOLINO
K8
WINDMILL
TO PEGO
CATEGORY
STRENUOUS
WALKING TIME
9 hrs
DISTANCE
22 km
ASCENT
439m
WELL
EMERGENCY ACCESS
SURFACED ROAD
UNSURFACED ROAD
PATH or ROUTE
RIVER COURSE
100m CONTOUR
CASTLE
MAP: 1:50,000
BENISSA 30-32 (822)

of the normally dry Rio Ebo. Pass the cemetery and a ford across the river, and in a few minutes, another, shallower ford. If the river is in flood, you may have to use this ford to cross it, and walk through apple orchards on the north bank towards Corrales de Pego, an extensive ruined finca, which is your first objective. Normally, you gain access to it from the road via the dry bed of the river. *1½km - 30min*

Seek out an old Mozarabic trail behind the ruins of the finca, which climbs up the south side of a ravine, with the road on the other side. Soon the road can be seen ahead, and you reach it just below Km.9. Turn right, and walk up the road to reach the pass, Pla de Mollo (480m), with its old windmill, converted into a private house. On the way you get good views of Val d'Ebo and the cliffs of the Barranco del Infierno.

3¾km - 1h

To Paso De Las Manzaneras

At Km.8, turn off right (south-east) towards the ridge of the Sierra de Mediodia. Ahead are the peaks of Monte Negre (649m) and Manzanera (702m) with the jagged rocks of El Castillo in the foreground. You will get a brief glimpse of the sea on your left-hand side and, to the right, in the far distance, the peaks of Monte Cabrer and Benicadell.

Keep left at a junction. *5km - 1½h*

On your right, pass an extensive finca with a good well, Corral de Carrasca. *6km - 2h*

Look back over your shoulder for a last glimpse of Almisira (the lunch stop on the last stage) with Forada Ridge.

Climb up now to the modest pass of Manzanera. To the west are the Sierras de Carrasca, and below, in a depression, are a few farms on the lip of the gorge. Descend from the pass to a junction with an extensive ruin, where a good track goes down into the gorge. Keep straight on.

7km - 2h 20min

On the next section, you get good views of the gorge to your right, then the southern views of the Sierra Solana, and the houses of Campell on the south side of the river valley above the gorge. The long wall across the hillside is the boundary of Fontilles, a leper colony, and Orba Castle can be seen. The twin peaks of Peña Roch at the eastern end of the Caballo Verde Ridge next appear and, finally, the church and the village of Fleix, your objective, which is on the lip of the gorge in the Val Laguart. Rushes growing by the path indicate a stream, and your good road starts to degenerate as the stream invades it, and you arrive at a flat area with a good well with five troughs, much used by shepherds. This is the Pozo de las Jubias. *8km - 2½h*

Down The Camino De Las Jubias

The Mozarabic trail starts within a few metres of the well, under a wall, but is at present obscured by a lush growth of vegetation encouraged by the stream, which has completely taken over the path. Thankfully, within a few minutes, the stream loses interest, and leaves the trail, which you will follow down to the bed of the Rio Ebo.

These ancient ways were most soundly constructed, and extremely well-engineered. Do not be tempted to take short cuts because to follow these trails as they skilfully negotiate the most severe gradients is one of the great pleasures of this area. At the moment, you cannot see where the trail is going but, once you have passed a squarish boulder, you start to follow the western edge of a deep rocky ravine, and then, suddenly, the southern view opens out, to reveal once more the deep valley of the Rio Ebo. This is not all. On the far side of the valley, on the lip of the gorge, is the little village of Fleix, and above it is the Caballo Verde Ridge, your first objective on the next stage. Note a complementary Mozarabic trail winding up from the valley floor - your twin - and half way up the route is the waterfall Cascade de Llet Tallat (Sour Milk Ghyll), which you will pass on the ascent to Fleix. In summer, the waterfall is often dry, but after heavy rain, or in winter, it is a delight to see. Now, you lose height, and can see to the north-west sheer cliffs, which are the "jaws" of the Barranco del Infierno, and the stony bed of the river, which you reach. To cross the river is usually possible, even in winter, but in extreme conditions you may have to get your feet wet.

Take a break, and perhaps have lunch before deciding what to do next as Fleix is only just beyond the top of the waterfall, one hour and 300m of ascent away. *10½km - 4h*

Possible Diversions

Barranco Del Infierno (north-west)

If weather conditions permit, a very rough walk north along the river bed will bring you in an hour to the narrowing walls of the Barranco, and the caves and rock scrambles which lead to the climbing pitches, which have some fixed ironwork of extremely dubious security. Very impressive, even in its lower stages. *5km -2h*

Isbert's Folly (south-east)

After heavy rain, you will be confronted with a lake, which will prevent this diversion. Whoever Isbert was, he certainly got it wrong! At the end of this diversion is an extremely narrow cleft in the crags, into which was built a concrete dam, which does hold water when the "Gota Fria" comes. The snag is that whilst this does flood the valley right up to the river crossing where you are lunching within a few days the precious water has percolated through subterranean channels, and the valley is dry once more! This inundation, however, encourages a lush growth of grass, which in its turn, attracts not only shepherds with sheep and goats, but also herdsmen with bulls! To visit the dam, follow the river bed, or the paths on its banks, as it twists and turns between red-coloured crags with some interesting caves, and in about an hour you come to a broad area where the reservoir *should* have been. Now look to the right for the cleft in the crags and the old dam. *5km - 2h*

Up To Fleix Via The Waterfall

Start to ascend (all the way on the Mozarabic trail), first under some cliffs on the east side, then in 20min cross the barranca and the stream directly under the waterfall (or, in summer, the alleged waterfall) to the other side of the valley. Ascend to a cave, pass through it, then recross the stream, and in 15min pass the village wash-house (lavadero) of Fleix, and emerge on to the road at Km.2, just 2min from the Bar Nostros, where a warm welcome awaits you. This is a simple village "pub", with very basic decor.

You are now in the Val Laguart, a collection of three villages, and at Fontilles there is a Leper Sanatorium (now, thankfully, mostly engaged in research). Accommodation is difficult to find, and more reliable hospitality is available 6km down the valley at Orba, where there are two hostels, and more facilities. *Direct 12km - 5h*

Barranco Del Infierno 22km - 9h

STAGE 3: FLEIX TO CASTELL DE CASTELLS

Overall Time:	14h	*Walking Time:*	$10^{1/2}$h
Distance:	29km	*Ascent:*	824m

This is a very long hard day, suitable for enthusiasts in training, and for masochists. We pass through some sensational scenery, and traverse a lovely 6km ridge, with historical connections, ending the day at a remote mountain village.

For those not in the above categories, the walk can, if required, be shortened:

(a) By shortening Stage 2, by forgoing visits to Isbert's Folly and Val de Infierno, to allow for a traverse of the Caballo Verde Ridge as part of Stage 2, thus shortening Stage 3 by walking up the road direct to Collado de Garga.

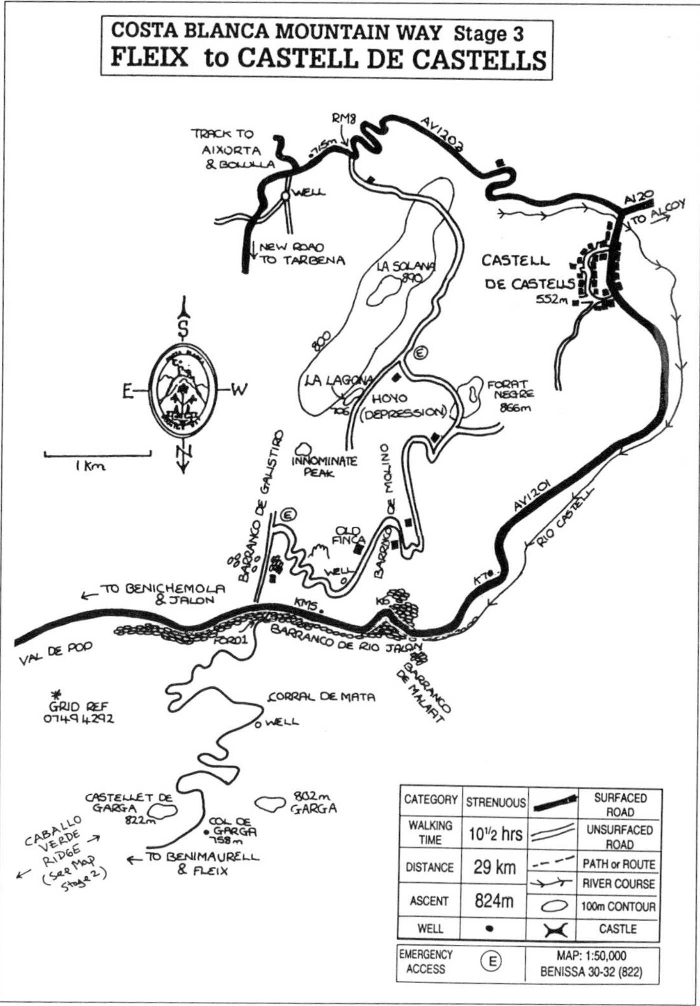

(b) By ending the walk at Corral de Somo, and accepting a lift into Castell de Castells, thus saving 3km and 1h.

The Caballo Verde Ridge is no Striding Edge but it is composed of broken limestone, and is treacherous in wet weather, difficult to navigate in bad visibility, and NOT TO BE ATTEMPTED IN DARKNESS. The many grykes (fissures) are not known as ankle snappers for nothing! The rest of the route is on good surfaced or forestry roads, and will accommodate sturdy vehicles. On the Fig Tree section, however, the Barranco Molino section is steep and loose, and even local farmers' vehicles have trouble in wet conditions.

To The Western Col

Start the walk from the church at Fleix, and go up a concrete road passing a telephone kiosk and the fuente on your left. The route is generally south as you pass a casita (Tosalet), and admire the views ahead of the Peñon Roch and the Caballo Verde Ridge, with Helm Crags half-way along it. Climbing through orchards of cherries and apples, you can see the first objective, the col beneath Peñon Roch. In a few minutes, ignore a road off to the right, and in 12min reach a level road and turn left (east), passing the Fuente Peña, with its analyst's report on the mineral qualities of the water.

Below you is the Val Laguart and the village of Campell. Across the valley rises Sierra Mediodia, and to the east the jagged ridge of Segaria and the mighty bulk of Montgo. Ignore a road on the left going down to Murla. Pass an old finca on the left, and reach Casita del Cerezas on the right with its pretty garden. At the end of a wall (marker) turn off right (south) for the col. To the left, under the crags of Peñon Roch, you can see a quarry, which is where the surfaced roads ends. You will pass a new red-roofed casita, which can be seen below the col. *1½km - 30min*

The unsurfaced road ends after a few metres, and you climb a rather overgrown Mozarabic trail, to emerge at the new casita (markers), and turn left (east) through the vegetable garden towards Molar Rock.

2km - 40min

Now turn south up towards the col. There is no good path - go up through the terraces, making for the right-hand side of the slope to the col. Within 10min a tempting path appears, but only follow it until bare slabs appear, as the path will lead into a jungle of wild briars! Now take to the slabs, and climb direct to the col. *3km - 1h*

You now have views to the south down into the Jalon Valley (Val de Pop), and the village of Benichembla. To the east can be seen the beautiful buildings of Fontilles, the Leper Colony, where so much important research has taken place, and has resulted in the virtual elimination of the disease in the western world. To the south-east, Col de Rates with Rates Peak above it, and the small white restaurant are now visible. Walk up a little, and you can see the first section of the ridge with Pudding Stone and, in the far distance, Peña Alta, the highest point (842m).

To the south, Cocoll, Sierras de Aixorta and Serrella appear, and we can pick out the Barranco de Gallistero, with the forestry road climbing over to Forat Negre - your afternoon walk. To the east-south-east are the rounded summits of Silla de Cao and Tosal de Navarro, between which runs the Greenwich Meridian. In the far distance behind Rates is the jagged ridge of the Ferrer.

Peñon Roch (793m)

This craggy summit (actually, there are two) marks the eastern end of the Caballo Verde Ridge and on its highest summit there once stood a Moorish castle. Nothing now remains except a few dressed stones and tiles scattered over the slopes, but things were much different in the seventeenth century, as this ridge marks the Moors' last stand in Valencia. In 1609 a great battle occurred on this ridge as the troops of the Spanish king subdued the last remnants of the Moorish occupation. (See Route 17)

Ascent Of The Peñon (Diversion)

To reach the summit of the Peñon is a rock scramble, and to cross the two summits, follow a rocky arête and ridge down to the Ermita San Sebastian, and then via a Calvary to the village of Murla, a very rough expedition, with no paths, but very rewarding. Allow $2^{1}/_{2}$h to Murla. There are orange markers on the ascent and descent of the summits ONLY. *For those experienced in rock-climbing ONLY,* start on the south side of the summit crags by crossing a maze of large boulders, well vegetated with spiky plants. If this does not put you off, perhaps the 4m wall will! The obstacle, however, has its weakness, and is the last obstacle before traversing carefully upwards towards a small belvedere. From here, strike straight up to the summit on broken ground. The small holes made by treasure-seekers, and a few broken pots and tiles, indicate that you are nearing the summit. To descend, go down a short rock climb (easy) on the north side, which is a little exposed, and traverse up to the eastern summit. From here, keep to the ridge as far as possible, passing Dog Rock on the left whilst descending slabs, to gain the short but delightful Murla Arête, then make for the metal cross above the village, descending through old terraces to the Ermita, then down to Murla on a good track.

The Ridge Walk

Start your traverse of the ridge by passing the Pudding Stone on the north side. There are no markers on the ridge itself, as there is no path, and the best advice is to keep to the rocks whenever possible. At times, however, small sections of what would pass as a footpath do appear. These have probably been trodden out by hunters. Where you do have to leave the crest to avoid pinnacles, etc., it is *usually* easier on the southern side of the ridge. In 10min you reach a TV repeater cabin which was blown over in the winter gales of 1989 and has never been repaired, and then you reach a small cairn. *3½km - 1h 10min*

Overhang Rock and Helm Crags can be seen below you, which is avoided by dropping down slightly on the south side. Below Helm Crags on the northern side is a cave, and you pass a tiny rock shelter and a cairn, before reaching the pinnacles at the western end of the crags. *4½km - 1h 50min*

Between you and the rocky crest of Peña Alta are two intermediate summits and in half an hour you can see Intermediate Summit, and a substantial cairn, from which can be seen your final objective, Aitana (1558m), with its array of antennae, away to the south-west, and with diligence you can see the Castillo de Serrella, your first objective on the next stage. *5¼km - 2h 20min*

Now head for a small rock shelter on Intermediate Summit. *5.8km - 2h 50min*

It is now necessary to move slightly to the right across some terraces to rejoin the ridge up to the summit of Peña Alta (842m), following a number of very small cairns. Below, to the north-west, you can see Perereta (826m), with its stone cross and, next to it, Castellet de Garga (822m), beyond which is the col guarded by Garga (802m). *6.6km - 3h 5min*

Below, under Perereta, is a ruined finca, which is your next objective, and which is reached by descending the easy slopes of Peña Alta. The crosses mounted on crags overlooking mountain villages are to ward off both evil spirits and lightning. Obviously the villagers of Benimaurell still favour this form of protection, as the young men of the village, no doubt persuaded by the old folk, rebuilt this cross in 1952 after the old one collapsed. *7½km - 3h 15min*

On reaching the ruins of the finca, find a footpath which contours under Perereta to the col between this mountain and the Castellet de Garga. From here, a path leads south, to the road, about 1km below the col. The way, which is now waymarked red/orange, leads on a good path to the Collado de Garga, by way of a short section of the original

Mozarabic trail, passing an old nevera on the left. *9km - 3h 50min*

The col is occupied by a number of shepherds' stone huts, and usually smells strongly of goats. After admiring the view, it is probably better to drop down to the oak grove for a break. All the wells are locked to preserve the water for the animals. From the col you can see your next objective, the river culvert across the Rio Jalon on the A1210, and you can appreciate the views of the Barranco Gallistero and the Fig Tree Route across to Forat Negre, your afternoon walk.

To The Rio Jalon

As a contrast to the last four hours of rough walking, you now have 5km to walk and 500m to descend on an excellently engineered, surfaced road, which leaves you free to admire the ever-changing views as you zig-zag down. In half an hour, pass an oak grove on the left, a shady resting place and, at 3km (45min) you pass through a small collection of houses, Corral de la Mata, with a new house on the left. Just past this is a ruin with a well with water in it. Pass a house, La Hermitage, on the left, then a restaurant called Chez Pierre et Christina, where meals can only be obtained by advance telephone booking. You now cross the dry river bed to the main road and Barranco Gallistero. *5km - 2h*

Where the Barranco Gallistero joins the Rio Jalon, you start the next stage of your walk. Here, a few years ago, stood a grove of old and fruitful fig trees. Sadly, the construction work has taken its toll, and only one wounded specimen survives. With your back to the road, look up a broad valley (east of south). To the left is the bulk of Cocoll (1047m). Immediately ahead is a broad track and an unnamed peak (part of La Laguna) on the right. The summit ridge ends in a rock gully, and between these points can be seen the new forestry track zig-zagging up over the ridge.

To The Barranco de Molinero

Follow the track up the Barranco de Gallistero alongside the dry river bed, passing a casita on the right, and a fuente on the left, and in 15min reach a junction. Take the right-hand fork, which leaves the valley, and starts to climb in well-engineered zig-zags to the right-hand flank of Innominate Peak. As you gain height, look back to see the Caballo Verde Ridge appear to the north, and finally arrive at Innominate Crags, where you find an old finca. Carry on round the edge of the ridge, where there is a fuente.

After a short climb, around another bend, is an old, quite extensive finca, with a well, oven and era (threshing floor), a wonderful spot to rest for a while, with commanding views. *2km - 45min*

To the north-east is Peñon Roch, the end of the Caballo Verde Ridge, and Montgo is visible. Leave the old finca moving south-west, and press on down a little, into the Barranco de Molinero.

Below, you can see the substantial new road bridge over the Rio Jalon; seeing the river in its normally dry state, it seems hard to justify such a bridge, but, when winter comes with its storms, it certainly proves to be of great benefit to the people of Castell de Castells and beyond. It seems a long way down to the head of this barranco, and a long climb (now north-west) up to regain the height lost, but soon, turn south-west again to reach another ruined finca, and a deep roadside well on the left. *4km - 1h 45min*

Just past the ruins a road leads off left. You keep straight on.

Above to the right is the summit of Forat Negre (866m). Reach a high plateau with a depression below on the left, which has some dew-ponds; it has in the past been cultivated. The road now rises a little, and ahead you can see new views and a ruined casita on the left of the road, and another road striking off south under La Solana (890m). Reach the ruins, then turn off right (south-west) on the road which will lead to Corral del Somo. *7km - 3h 15min*

To Corral Del Somo

As the road climbs steadily, you get a brief glimpse of Castell de Castells below on the right. Take the opportunity on this section to look back in appreciation of the day's route, as Caballo Verde disappears from view and, on gaining a small rise, you are treated to magnificent views of Aitana and the Castillo de Serrella. Between Aitana and Alfaro in the far distance is Monte Cabrer (1389m), the third-highest peak in the province. Ahead, the ridges of Sierra Aixorta appear and, amongst the pinnacles on its northern slopes, is the beautiful natural rock arch of Arc del Atancos. *11km - 4h*

Descend now, passing a new villa, to the surfaced road at Corral del Somo. This fertile plateau, with plenty of water, is now farmed from Castell de Castells. Back-packers can now seek out a camping site for the night. For the rest it only remains to amble down the road, and in 4km you will reach your resting place for the night. *4km - 1h*

STAGE 4: CASTELL DE CASTELLS TO CONFRIDES

Overall Time:	(allowing 1h for castle) 9h 40min
Walking Time:	8h
Distance:	25km
Ascent:	To Castle 498m To Confrides 386m

No rocky ridges today, all good forestry and country roads through beautiful mountain scenery, crossing the Sierra Serrella, and reaching the highest part of the walk so far at Serrella Castle (1050m), then descending into the picturesque Guadalest Valley, with its reservoir, and accompanied by the sound of rushing water (a rare experience on the Costa), ascending to Abdet and Confrides for the night. Sturdy vehicles, horse riders and mountain bikes may also use this whole route.

Making A Start

Leave Castell de Castells by the A120 which leads west to Fachega and Alcoy, and as you climb, you will see above you to the south your first objective, the castle, and below it is a horizontal scar on the hillside, which is a forestry road. Beyond Km.3, seek out a broad forestry road, which leads off left upwards towards your goal.

3½km - 1h

To The Castle

As you climb, note a broad, wooded gully ahead, with a road zig-zagging upwards to a ridge. This is your route to the Serrella Ridge. Above to the right is the bulk of Mala del Llop, the most eastern of the Serrella peaks, rising to 1361m. In 5min you drop down to go around the head of a small barranca, and in another ¼h, enter the forest, and immediately turn off right on to another road, to climb upwards.

5½km - 1h 25min

For the next half-hour, the only views will be to the north as you put your "nose to the mountain", but all this will be worthwhile when you reach the ridge, and the views to the south are revealed.

6½km - 1h 50min

To the east rises the dramatic crag on which the castle stands. To the west is Mala del Llop. Below, to the south, is the beautiful Guadalest Valley, with the reservoir and all the scattered villages (except for Abdet, which remains hidden). The three castles of Guadalest and the castle of Confrides also come into view as you walk along a good road, east towards the castle col. To the south, above the valley, is the long

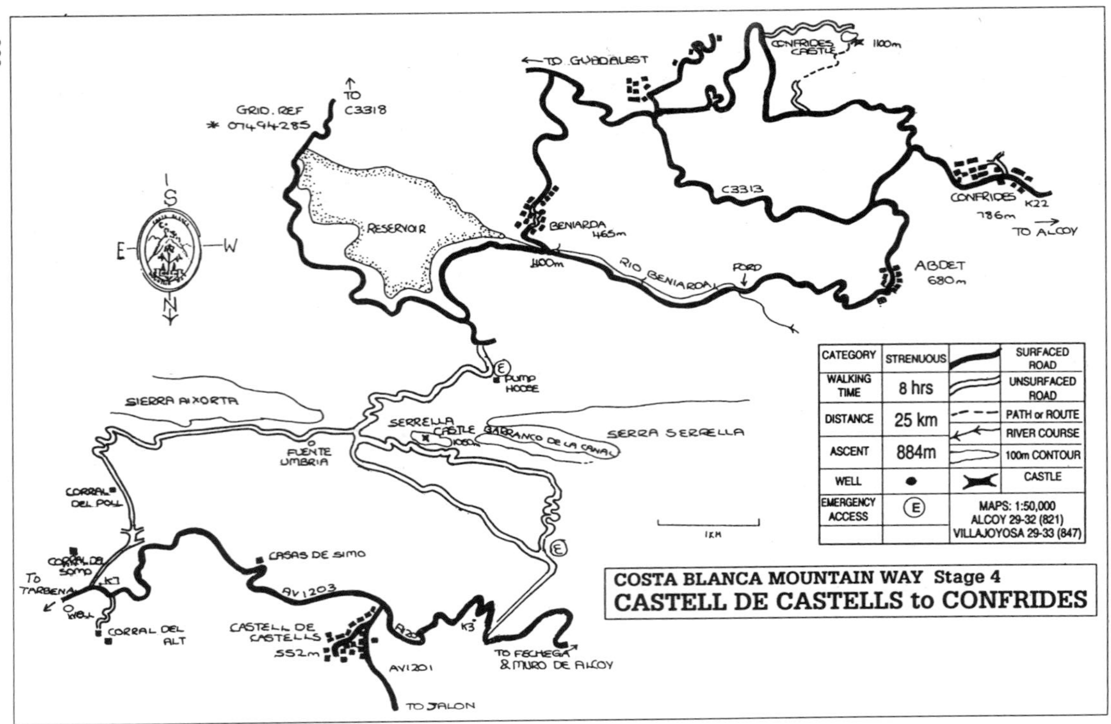
COSTA BLANCA MOUNTAIN WAY Stage 4
CASTELL DE CASTELLS to CONFRIDES
CATEGORY
STRENUOUS
WALKING TIME
8 hrs
DISTANCE
25 km
ASCENT
884m
WELL
EMERGENCY ACCESS
SURFACED ROAD
UNSURFACED ROAD
PATH or ROUTE
RIVER COURSE
100m CONTOUR
CASTLE
MAPS: 1:50,000
ALCOY 29-32 (821)
VILLAJOYOSA 29-33 (847)
1KM
TO GUADALEST
CONFRIDES CASTLE
1100m
TO C3318
GRID. REF
* 07494285
C3313
CONFRIDES
786m
K22
TO ALCOY
RESERVOIR
BENIARDA
465m
400m
RIO BENIARDA
FORD
ABDET
680m
S
E
W
N
PUMP HOUSE
SIERRA AIXORTA
SERRELLA
CASTLE
1060m
BARRANCO DE LA CANAL
SERRA SERRELLA
FUENTE UMBRIA
CORRAL DEL POU
CORRAL DE SOMO
TO TARBENA
K1
WELL
CORRAL DEL ALT
CASAS DE SIMO
AV1203
CASTELL DE CASTELLS
552m
K2
K3
AV1201
TO FACHECA & MURO DE ALCOY
TO JALON

Aitana Ridge on which, above Benimantell, is Peña Mulero. A road descends from a col on the right of Peña Mulero, which you will use to descend from the summit at the end of the next stage. The array of antennae mark the summit of Aitana (1558m). Last to come into view is Confrides at the head of the valley, with its castle on a detached pinnacle on a spur of Aitana.

The route ahead (west) to the Collado de Castillo can clearly be seen. First, descend for 15min then climb steep zig-zags to reach the col right under the castle in half an hour. *7¾km - 2h 25min*

Ascent To The Castle Ruins

Try to make this a long halt to allow for the ascent of the castle. To get to the top will only take a few minutes. Strike up to the right (north) on an indistinct path to pass to the right of a large stone water cistern. Despite the passage of many centuries, it still holds water, and toads breed in it. Still moving to the right along a shelf, at a broken arch start to zig-zag upwards to gain the rocky ridge. Now move left along the ridge to enter the extensive ruins. As might be expected, the all-round views from such a strategic situation are sensational; to the east, the sea, Sierra Helada, Ponoch and the second-highest peak in the province, Puig Campana (1410m). To the west, the "glacier" of the Serrella or Barranca de Canal dominates the view. (1h allowed in timing.)

Descent To The Puerta De Castillo

Leaving Collado de Castillo, the view ahead is dominated by Sierra Aixorta, as you descend a steep road under the northern crags of the castle. When you reach a lone pine tree on a bend, look down to say farewell to Castell de Castells. Ahead, on the northern flank of Aixorta, you will see a tree-lined road leading to Fuente Umbria. This is the back-packers' route from Corral de Somo, which will shortly join your track on the col. To the left, you get your last views of Cocoll and Forat Negre. In the far distance, the Bernia and Ferrer ranges peep over the intervening ridges, as you reach a crossroads and turn right (south). In a few minutes, as if by magic, the Aitana range appears, and you look down once again on Guadalest. *9km - 3h 45min*

Down To The Reservoir And Beniarda

Descend now on a broad road under the southern crags of the castle as the dam at the eastern end of the reservoir appears below. In half an hour you pass a large crag on the left, and are treated to excellent views right up the "glacier". In 20min, just after passing an old finca on the left, you join a surfaced road at the pumping station and follow it to the main road below. *13½km - 5h 10min*

During this descent, you will have the best views of the Aitana range. Peña Roc is at the eastern end, with Peña Mulero and Peña Alba, and finally the summit of Aitana itself. On the northern flank, note the Partagas fissures and cliffs, beloved of pot-holers. Just below the summit antennae are some rock formations which many people mistake for a castle. The actual ruins of Confrides Castle are on a jagged crag detached from the mountain. You now get your first view of the rocky pinnacles of Pla de la Casa (1379m), another of the Serrella's main four peaks to the west. Finally, you can see the three fortified crags which protect Guadalest.

Turn right (west) on to a surfaced but narrow road along the side of the reservoir, and in a few minutes, your next objective, the remote village of Abdet, comes into view ahead. On the left, above, is the picturesque village of Beniarda (with a municipal swimming pool if you need one, and a good restaurant). As soon as the bridge crossing the Rio Beniarda is reached, you have a very rare treat in this drought-ridden area - THE SOUND OF RUNNING WATER!

16km - 5h 35min

Climbing Up To Confrides

Here, crystal water plunges down in a pretty little waterfall to join the stream which tumbles and dances between well-worn boulders all the year round. Follow this road all the way to Abdet, first alongside the stream, then crossing it at a large culvert.

18km - 6h 25min

There is the last steep pull up to Abdet, where there are three bars and two restaurants. On the way, the main bulk of Serrella's twin summits dominate the view ahead. *21km - 7h 5min*

All that remains now is to walk along the AV1035 up out of the village to join the main road (C3313) in 1½km, then turn right (west) towards Confrides. Ignore the access road up into the village, keeping on the main road, as the Fonda, El Pirineo, is at the other end of the village on the right-hand side of the road. *25km - 8h*

Fiesta

24th to 27th August.

Bus Service

Once per day to Alicante

STAGE 5: CONFRIDES TO FONT MOLI VIA AITANA

Overall Time:	$7^{1}/_{2}$h	*Distance:*	21km
Walking Time:	7h	*Ascent:*	772m

This is the last day of the Costa Blanca Mountain Way, and a lovely day it is, not too demanding, through beautiful scenery to reach the crowning glory of Alicante Province, Aitana (1558m), then an amble down to a Hostal nestling on the slopes of the mountain, which specialises in Valencian cooking.

To Fuente Arbols

Leave the Hostal, cross the road, and go up the main street of the village, Calle St Antonio, passing the fuente on the left, and take the first narrow street on the right, which goes up through the houses to reach an unsurfaced road. In 5min, fork right on to a concrete path with a mesh fence on the right-hand side, and pass the gate of El Pouet San Ignacio. Ahead you can see Confrides Castle on a jagged spur of Aitana. Over to the left, yesterday's route over the Serrella Pass can be seen. Bear right at a junction, and ignore a track to the right, settling down to some well-spaced zig-zags as you start on a western tack to gain height. Behind, the end of the Bernia Ridge has a look of the Matterhorn seen from this angle. *2km - 25min*

Now the antennae on the summit of Aitana are in view ahead. Below, to the right, will appear the road climbing up towards Puerto Confrides and Alcoy. Serrella's two summits appear with Pla de la Casa behind them. The road contours round a barranca. You pass a small casita, and Monte Cabrer appears in the distant west.

Down below is an old ruined finca with an era. As you breast a rise, there are more little casitas near Casas de Aitana. Still moving west, you see the western buttress of Aitana, and swing left (east) parallel to the ridge. All the summit is now visible, and across the level cultivated area with its casitas can be seen another track climbing towards Aitana. This is the next section of the route.

The road now levels out, and below can be seen the hamlet of Casas de Aitana, and the Fuente Arbols (Fuente Aitana on the map), and in 15min, at a large walnut tree, turn right on to a road leading to the fuente, with its tables and benches. This is a popular place for Spaniards to hold paella picnics at week-ends and fiestas, and for walkers to camp in the summer. The trough of the fuente is often full of cans of beer and bottles of wine, keeping cool whilst a barbecue is being prepared on the stone shelves. *6km - $1^{1}/_{2}$h*

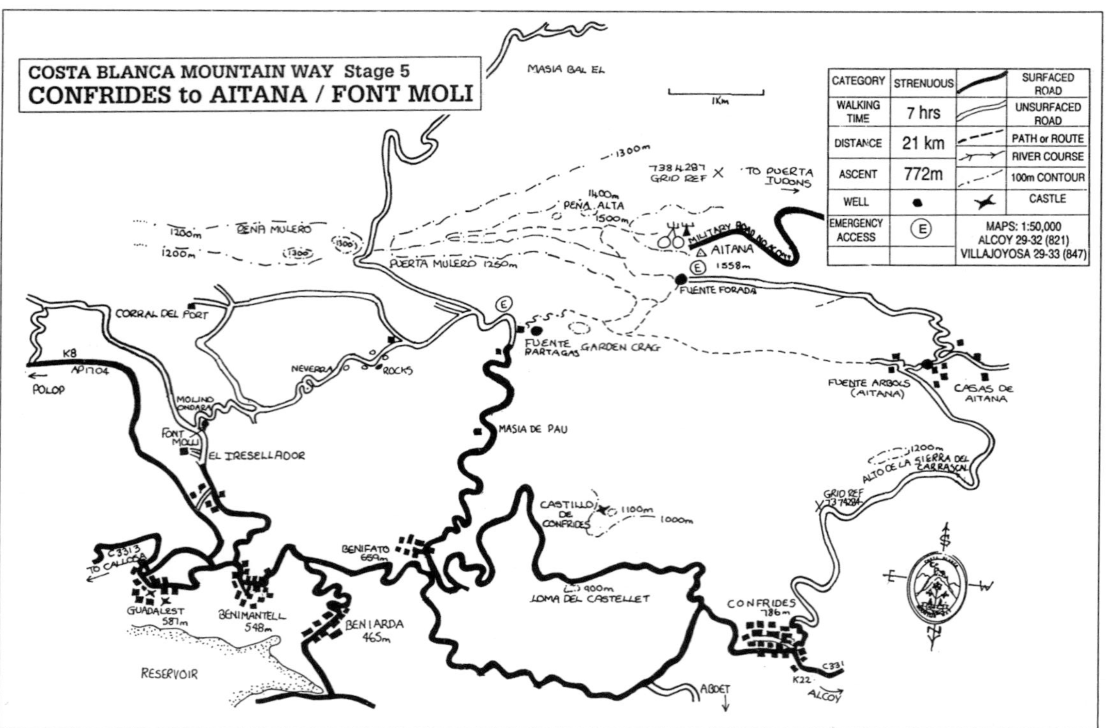
COSTA BLANCA MOUNTAIN WAY Stage 5
CONFRIDES to AITANA / FONT MOLI
CATEGORY
STRENUOUS
SURFACED ROAD
WALKING TIME
7 hrs
UNSURFACED ROAD
DISTANCE
21 km
PATH or ROUTE
RIVER COURSE
ASCENT
772m
100m CONTOUR
WELL
CASTLE
EMERGENCY ACCESS
E
MAPS: 1:50,000
ALCOY 29-32 (821)
VILLAJOYOSA 29-33 (847)
1Km
MASIA BAL EL
1300m
738 4287 GRID REF
TO PUERTA IUDONS
1400m
PEÑA ALTA
1500m
MILITARY ROAD NO ACCESS
AITANA
1558m
FUENTE FORADA
1200m
PEÑA MULERO
1300
1200m
PUERTA MULERO 1250m
CORRAL DEL PORT
E
FUENTE PARTAGAS
GARDEN CRAG
K8
AP1704
POLOP
NEVERRA
ROCKS
MOLINO ONDARA
FONT MOLI
EL TRESELLADOR
MASIA DE PAU
FUENTE ARBOLS (AITANA)
CASAS DE AITANA
1200m
ALTO DE LA SIERRA DEL CARRASCAL
GRID REF
CASTILLO DE CONFRIDES
1100m
1000m
C3313
TO CALLOSA
BENIFATO 659m
900m
LOMA DEL CASTELLET
GUADALEST 587m
BENIMANTELL 548m
BENIARDA 465m
CONFRIDES 786m
C331
K22
ALCOY
RESERVOIR
ABDET
E
W

To Fuente Forata

Leave the fuente, taking the forestry road which climbs up towards Aitana (south), and zig-zags steeply gaining height, then turns east below the northern crags. Climb steadily, ignoring two tracks which lead downhill on the left. Note the large split boulder on the right, and the missing section of it below on the left. On this section, you pass four neveras (ice-pits), so keep a look out for them.

The road finally makes one or two zig-zags to gain more height, and in half an hour you will be directly under the main masts of the transmitters. You may be tempted to go up directly to the summit, but even if there is a viable route, there is no saying what the effect would be on the military guards as your head appeared at the perimeter fence! *8km - 2h 25min*

Look over your shoulder (north-west) to see Benicadell appear, and ahead, the Bernia Ridge, Montgo, Col de Rates, Segaria and Llorensa on the coast near Moraira.

In 10min, you are directly under the radar domes, and the track drops a little to a flat area with the third nevera and the fuente with its trough. On this section you get your first view of the Forat - a hole in the rocks high up ahead of you. *9½km - 2h 40min*

To Fat Man's Agony

Go up right of the nevera on broken ground and scree without a regular path. Head for a cleft crag, which you pass on the right-hand side (east). The fourth nevera is below the crag. *10km - 2h 50min*

The track moves slowly upwards towards another small col, but soon has to cross some scree, and you can now actually touch the crags. Ahead is a jumble of rocks filling a gully. A prominent yew tree will be seen high up and a gap in the rocks to the left of it. This is "Fat Man's Agony". and the route. Behind you, high up on the ridge, is a small rock Forat.

Scramble up the rocks, pass left under the tree, go through the gap, and you have crossed one of the Simas de Partagas. Turn left as you leave the gap, and traverse until you meet a path near some painted rocks - souvenirs of past speleological explorations. Look back into the fissures, they are very impressive. At these painted rocks, turn right (due west) and climb along the edge of the fissures to reach the broad summit of Aitana, the highest point (not quite 1558m, but near enough), which is accessible to the public in the whole province. *11km - 3h 40min*

Wonderful Views

From the summit can be seen the second- and third-highest peaks in the province, Puig Campana (1410m) looking south-east, and Mont Cabrer (1389m) to the north-west. Further access to the west is prohibited, so views in the direction of Alcoy are limited. In all other directions, however, the vistas seem endless. It is not often that you can pick out the square tower of Cocentaina Castle (north-north-west) from these walks. Confrides, Serrella and Guadalest Castles are also visible to the north-east. The ice-pit, or nevera, was a necessity in ancient times, for keeping meat fresh. Below on the northern flanks, see how many of these circular pits you can spot. You will visit one on your descent. You have now successfully completed the Costa Blanca Mountain Way.

Descents

If you have become hooked on "Fat Man's Agony", then, by all means, reverse the ascent route. Campers may wish to return to Fuente Partagas for the night. A recommended alternative is to follow the ridge down and over Peña Alta to Paso Mulero.

To Paso Mulero Via Peña Alta

Return first to the painted rocks, and follow a reasonable path going up east, keeping to the left of a large fissure. *11½km - 3h 55min*

The traverse along the edge of the escarpment east towards the sea provides exceptional views along the ridge to Peña Roc at its end, with Ponoch and Puig Campana in the distance. Eventually, the coastal mountains of Sierra Helada (near Benidorm) and Peñon d'Ifach and Toix (near Calpe) will come into view. Below you on the north side are glorious views of the Guadalest Valley, and you may be able to pick out your route down to Font Moli. Behind you to the west, you get fine views of the massive fissures and land slips which form Aitana's northern face. To the south there are views of the barrancas which lead down to Sella (Stage 6). There is no reliable path over the five buttresses, which we have to traverse to gain the pass. Try to keep as near to the edge of the escarpment as prudence permits, not only to admire the views, but there is usually less vegetation on the bare rocks of the lip. You will soon get tantalising views of the forestry road coming up to the pass from Sella (Stage 6), but the pass itself remains hidden until the very last moment, as you negotiate the last steep slope to the forestry road. *15km - 5h 15min*

To Fuente Partagas

Turn left, and start a long descent west, with Confrides Castle and Partagas ahead of you. You pass under some pinnacles, and when they give way to gentler slopes (in about 15min), look ahead and upwards about 200m from the road to locate a large nevera, which is well worth a visit. At the end of this straight section are a number of zig-zags leading to Fuente Partagas. At the second one are two small roads leading off to the right. Take the first of these, which heads east parallel to the ridge of Peña Alta. *16½km - 5h 45min*

To Font Moli

First avoid a track going right, then avoid two others which go down left (red markers), and you will reach, in 20min a small cultivated hollow with a small shelter on your left, and the road drops towards a ruined finca. *17½km - 6h 10min*

Ahead, behind the ruins, are some crags, and the route descends just to the right of them. Turn left at the old ruined finca, and go down to and pass between some picturesque rocky pinnacles and, as you emerge from them, note a last nevera on the left-hand side, then continue on to reach a concrete road. *20km - 6h 40min*

Turn left down this road, and in 10min approach the hamlet of Font Moli, with the Font below on the left. Either descend by the small track direct to the Font, or follow the surfaced road down to it.

20½km - 6h 50min

Now, follow the road, which goes west, passing a large house on the right, with a sun-dial on its wall, and a small lavadero (wash-house) under a tree on the left, and in 10min, turn right up the drive to the Pension El Trestellador, where a warm welcome awaits you at the end of a wonderful day on Alicante Province's highest mountain. *21km - 7h*

STAGE 6: FONT MOLI TO SELLA (optional)

Overall Time:	7h	*Distance:*	20km
Walking Time:	6½h	*Ascent:*	640m
		(via Peña Mulero)	

This section is an optional finish to the Costa Blanca Mountain Way, which allows those with sufficient time and energy to finish the walk further south at Sella, from where there is a bus service to Alicante. For those who do not wish to retrace the route up to Paso Mulero via Partagas, an alternative is provided, which will allow a visit to Peña Mulero.

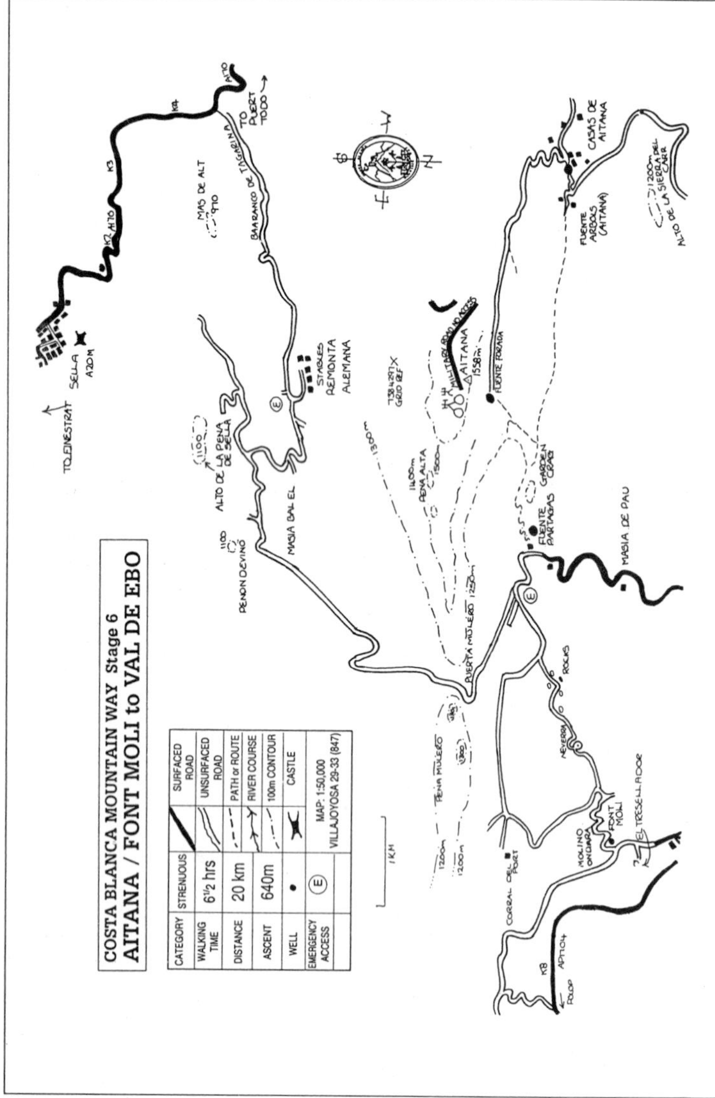
COSTA BLANCA MOUNTAIN WAY Stage 6
AITANA / FONT MOLI to VAL DE EBO
CATEGORY
STRENUOUS
WALKING TIME
6½ hrs
DISTANCE
20 km
ASCENT
640m
WELL
EMERGENCY ACCESS
SURFACED ROAD
UNSURFACED ROAD
PATH or ROUTE
RIVER COURSE
100m CONTOUR
CASTLE
MAP: 1:50,000
VILLAJOYOSA 29-33 (847)
1KM
TO FINESTRAT
SELLA
A20M
K2
A170
K3
K4
A170
TO PUERT TODO
MAS DE ALT
970
BAARANCO DE TAGARINA
1100
ALTO DE LA PENA DE SELLA
1100
PENON DEVINO
MASIA BAL EL
STABLES
REMONTA
ALEMANA
1300m
738429 GRID REF
1400m
PENA ALTA
1500m
MILITARY ROAD NO ACCESS
AITANA
1558m
FUENTE FORADA
1200m
PENA MULERO
1200m
PUERTA MULERO 1250m
CORRAL DEL PORT
FUENTE PARTAGAS
GARDEN CRAG
K8
AP1104
POLOP
NEVERRA
ROCKS
MOLINO ONDARA
FONT MOLI
EL TRESELLADOR
MASIA DE PAU
FUENTE ARBOLS (AITANA)
CASAS DE AITANA
1200m
ALTO DE LA SIERRA DEL CARR

Direct Route (6km - 2h)

From The Font Moli To The Nevera

Either climb up a path to the left of the Font, or walk round by the road, which leads behind the Font, in a generally north-westerly direction, but only for a few minutes. On a concrete section of the road, at a sharp left-hand bend, look for a red arrow on the road surface, indicating the route to the Peña Mulero. IGNORE THIS SIGN, but look to the right, and you will see a good track, with a red marker on the wall. The track continues through almond terraces with views of Confrides Castle and Aitana. After a few minutes, note a well-preserved nevera (ice-pit) on the right-hand side of the track. Above you and ahead are some very attractive rock pinnacles, and your path winds and climbs through them, eventually reaching the ruins of a large finca. *30min*

To The Partagas

Behind the finca ruins, there is a good broad track which continues in a generally south-westerly direction, towards a small col, from which good views can be had of the summit of Aitana, with its array of aerial and the two radar domes. Below the summit, note the impressive crags of Las Simas de Partagas. Pass a small cultivated hollow with a tiny shelter, and a ruined finca comes into view on the skyline on the right. You are now nearing the end of your western "tack", and on your left can be seen your next section, the road leading east up along the flank of the mountain, towards the col (Paso Mulero). In another 15min, join the unsurfaced road coming up from the Fuente Partagas and Benifato. *1h*

To The Col

Stop here for a rest, and take in the majestic scenery, then settle down to a half-hour steady climb on a well-engineered forestry road up the col between Peña Alta and Peña Mulero. As you gain height, your views are extended as more and more mountains come into sight, including Montgo, near Javea.

After half an hour, and one tight hair-pin bend, you are on the broad col. *1½h*

To Paso Mulero Via Peña Mulero *6km - 2½h*

Leave the Font Moli, and follow the road which you used to descend on Stage 5 until, on a bend with a concrete surface, the track to the Partagas forks right. You keep straight on upwards. Views are of the Bernia Ridge, and the coastal mountains of Toix and Peñon d'Ifach at Calpe. Peña Mulero, a large buttress, can be seen ahead, and you will reach the ridge to the east of its summit. Ignore a track on the right, and one which leads off north-west to the Partagas. You keep generally to a south-easterly course towards the eastern edge of the ridge, where you can see a narrow path leading across scree towards a rock gateway. This is the route. *2km - 40min*

You are helped on this section by red square markers nailed to the trees, which are boundary markers. At a crossroads, keep to the right and, later, when the road forks, also keep to the right. Views now of Llorensa and Montgo. Eventually leave the track in an almond grove, to take to a narrow path which can be seen making for the ridge. In 5min the path crosses scree, and emerges on to the ridge by means of a rock gateway (red markers on rock). *3km - 1h*

Views to the south are revealed of the Barranco de Arcos which leads down to Sella, Puig Campana and El Realet (the beautiful sharp ridge). Turn right (west) to seek out a fairly good path which keeps to the northern edge of the escarpment where possible to avoid the vegetation. On this section look to the north just right of Serrella Castle (on its blade of rock) for a view again of Almisira. This is the last view of the mountain: the mountain which you scaled on the first stage. In 20min, find a depression with a "pot-hole", a good place to shelter from the wind, and as you gain height you will see Albir Lighthouse at the northern end of Sierra Helada appear to the south-east, and you get your first views of the summit buttress of Peña Mulero. The broad summit is marked by a number of cairns, and you can see, to the south, the city of Alicante with its castle of Santa Barbara, with the mountains of Murcia beyond. To the west are Monte Cabrer and Peña Alta.

4km - 2h

Down To Paso Mulero

This is the last summit on the Costa Blanca Mountain Way, and the start of the final descent to Sella. Drop down to the west, without the benefit of a path, to the pass. New mountains appear below, Alta de Sella and Peña Divino, as well as the reservoir of Amadorio near Villajoyosa.

6km - 2½h

Down Into The Barranco De Tagarina

There is a long walk down to the main road on a good forestry road. As you descend, there is only one possible place to take a wrong turning. In 45min, a road goes off left. Take the right-hand one, and immediately pass a large well-preserved finca on the right, with an era and its stone still in place. Above are the summit installations of Aitana, as you cross the head of the barranca, and the road improves a little. *10km - 4h*

In 1km, you pass through a cluster of casitas, and Remonta Alemana (German riding stables), and in another hour, reach the main road near Km.5. *15km - 5h*

If your support party is waiting, you can, I am sure, indulge yourself by accepting a lift after over 100kms of walking. Purists, of course, will insist on walking the last 5kms down through a gorge to the pretty village of Sella, with its ancient castle, with an hermita built into it. Sadly, most of the village houses have become weekend homes for Spaniards and foreigners, but the village bars and restaurants are geared to providing meals and refreshments for holidaymakers from the coast. There are only two buses each day to Villajoyosa (at present 9.30am and 5pm). There is no accommodation in the village. So. There are no more mountains to climb, only a return to the coast, "civilisation", and, I hope, happy with the memories of a long walk, with all its varied scenery and experiences. *20kms - 6½h*

Peña Mulero and the road to Sella from Peña Alta, with Bernia behind

Support Party Notes

For those not following the walk but who wish to keep in touch here are useful notes about walks, accommodation etc.

Stage 1: Villalonga to Val D'Ebo

To Villalonga (Valencia Province)
This large town (pop.3696) is a good plàce to stock up with supplies before the walk, and is 12km due south of the larger town and holiday resort of Gandia.

Leave the CN332 about 1km south of Gandia, and take the VP1012 near the village of Bellrequart, and in 8km enter the town of Villalonga.

Villalonga To Forna *Walking time 3h Driving time 1h*
Return to the CN332, and turn south-east for Oliva, and a turn-off right (south) on to the C3318 to Pego (pop.9415). In Pego, follow signs C3311 to Cocentaina via Adsubia (pop.557), 1km west of Adsubia, turn right (north-west) on to the AV1004, and in 4km reach Forna. In the village there is a restaurant, the Nautilus. *Total driving 30km*

Forna To Adsubia *Walking time 1h*
Accommodation is at the Restaurant La Moleta (557 13 09). They will have four rooms someday! This stage will make a suitable short walk for those who started late, and need a modest first day.

Forna To Pla De Almisira *Walking time 4½h*
Return via the C3313 to Pego, and make for the Pla de la Font, and the Paseo Cervantes, which is a shady park near the football ground in the south-west of the old town. From here a narrow undistinguished and unsigned road leads off left, heading for Val d'Alcala, passing the Ermita St Joachim, crossing Barranco de la Canal, and winds its tortuous way up to the Pla de Almisira. In 7km at a col, the service road to the summit transmitters goes off right to the top of the mountain (757m). In an emergency, a car can be driven along the walkers' route until it becomes a footpath. A car can also be driven up to the Castillo de Gallinera from Beniarrama. *Walking distance 15km*

Pla De Almisira To Val D'Ebo *Walking time 2½h*
Most cars will, in dry conditions, be able to negotiate the walkers' route

as only 1½km of it is unsurfaced.

Retrace your route east for 2km, and at a small casita (waymarking), turn off south on a good broad track for 1½km, until the surfaced section starts, which leads to Val d'Ebo. *Driving distance 5km*

For those with delicate cars, or in bad conditions, retrace the route to Pego (10km), and leave the town by the C3318 going south, until, at Km.1, turn right (south-west) on to the AV1431, and in 12km reach Val d'Ebo (pop 368).

There are three bars in the village, and some rudimentary accommodation is available in private houses. Juan Frau at Bar de Plaza is your contact.

Alternative accommodation is in Pego (hostal), Vergel (pensions - Km.176 on the CN332 is a hostal with 19 rooms), Gandia (many hotels and pensions), and Oliva (pensions on the CN332).

Stage 2: Val D'Ebo To Fleix *Walking time 5h*

The walking route will take an hour to get to the top of the col (Pla de Molinos) (Km.8), so you may pass your walkers on the route to Fleix. Retrace yesterday's route from Val d'Ebo - east along the AV1431 to regain the C3318, turning right (south) for 9½km to Orba, where you turn west (right) on the AV1432 (joins the AV1433), signed Val de Laguart and Fontilles, for 6.8km to Fleix.

Val de Laguart is a collection of four small villages, of which Fleix is the administrative centre. The walkers' route will join the main road near Km.2 just to the west of the village, coming up past the lavadero to head for the depths of the Val de Infierno. The only access point is to follow the walkers' route for 8km to Paso de Manzanera which can be reached with care by normal cars.

Alternative Accommodation At Orba: Hostal Quixote, Hostal Arcades.

Stage 3: Fleix To Castell de Castells

(1) Fleix To Garga *Walking time 4h*

Follow the AV1433 west up the valley (2km) to Benimaurell, skirt the centre on the northern side by following the signs for the Bar Oasis, and keep going upwards (west) on a narrow road. In 2½km you reach the Col de Garga. The walking route joins the road here near a small casita (waymarkings). *4½km*

Access by surfaced road to the quarry is by following the walkers' route from the Church Square at Fleix, or from Fuente Cambesot at (Km.1) just outside Benimaurell.

(2) Col De Garga To Val De Pop *Walking time 2h*

The walkers' route follows the road down into the valley for 5½km, where it joins the AV1201, Jalon to Castell de Castells road.

(3) Val De Pop To Castell De Castells *Walking time 5h*

Follow the AV1201 for 6km, go through the village and, at its western end, where the bridge crosses the river, turn left (south-east) along a narrow road for 4km to Corral de Alt to meet the walkers, who will come over the hill to the north, passing an isolated casita. Castell de Castells (pop 562) has bars, restaurants, and a hostal with accommodation for eight persons. The present owners are English - Eric and Jan Wright, Calle San Vincente 18 (551 82 54).

All of this section is on forestry roads, so in good conditions there is access for normal cars. From Innominate Crags, the gradients are steep with loose surface in the Barranco del Molino section.

Stage 4: Castell De Castells To Confrides *Walking time 8h*

Today's route is all on forestry roads, so it may be possible for those with four-wheel drive vehicles to follow the walkers.

Normal Route

(1) Castell De Castells To Beniarda *Walking time 5h 10min*

Leave Castell de Castells, and turn up the minor road from the river bridge, to climb in 4km to Corral del Somo, and continue east on the AV1203 to Tarbena. In a further 7km, turn right on to the C3318 near Km.30, and drive south to Callosa d'Ensarria. In the town centre, turn right with signs Guadalest on the C3313, and at Km.14, turn right (north) down a minor road to the village of Beniarda. You have now to negotiate very narrow streets, passing through the main square, and *under* the pretty shrine to San Francisco, and in a further kilometre reach the valley bottom, and a bridge over the river. Turn right along a surfaced but narrow road for 3km, and the walkers' route comes down a surfaced road from the north (left), where an inlet of the reservoir indicates a valley, Barranca de Cuevas. *Note:* This road is subject to devastation every year during the "Gota Fria", and land-slips bury and carry away part of it! There are bars and a good restaurant in Beniarda. *45km*

(2) Beniarda To Confrides *Walking time 2h 50min*

Return to the C3313, and turn right (west) to reach Confrides in 7km. The hostal, El Pirineo, is at the west end of the village, on the right, on the main road. There are numerous restaurants in the village. *If preferred,* normal cars can follow the walkers' route via Abdet to Confrides which has now been surfaced.

From the south in emergency normal cars can be taken to the pumping station on a narrow surfaced road. Beyond this, gradients are very severe, the surface often loose, and subject to land-slip in winter or bad weather.

From the north some normal cars have been seen driving up to the castle, but it is really for four-wheel drive vehicles, although in good conditions a normal car should get you to the forest below the zig-zags.

Accommodation: Fonda El Pirineo.

Stage 5: Confrides To Font Moli *Walking time 7h*

Leave Confrides, and go east on the C3313, through Benimantell, and as you leave the village, nearing Km.13, turn right (south) on to a very steep and narrow road signposted Restaurant el Trestellador. In 1km reach the Hostal/Rest El Trestellador, which is marked on the map as Molino de Ondara. Font Moli is the spring nearby, by way of which the walkers will arrive at the end of the day.

Hostall: El Trestellador

IN EMERGENCY.

(1) A normal car can easily reach the Fuente Arboles in good conditions and, with care, the Fuente Forat, by following the walkers' route.

(2) A normal car can also get to Fuente Partagas, by leaving the C3313 near Km.15, and turning off south on an unclassified road to Benifato. At the entrance to the village, turn off right (House - La Foya), and follow a narrow country road for 3km to the fuente. Four-wheel drive vehicles can easily go further to Puerta Mulero, and so can normal cars in good conditions.

Stage 6: Font Moli To Sella (optional) *Walking time 5h*

Font Moli (Benimaurell)

The walkers' route is on good forestry roads all the way to Sella, so is passable by four-wheel drive vehicles. Be warned of Jeep Safaris who also use this route.

Normal Route

Return to the C3313, and turn west through Confrides, over the Puerta de Confrides (Km.26) and on the descent, turn off left (Km.31) near Benasau. Go south over Puerta Tudons, and drop down to Sella (pop.419) on the A170. *42km*

IN EMERGENCY

From Km.5 follow the walkers' route to the German riding stables. Four-wheel drive vehicles can go up to Puerta Mulero.

BACK-PACKERS' VARIATIONS

The camping back-packers, being self-sufficient, and not needing to seek accommodation at the end of the day, have the freedom to really enjoy the route without having to worry about reaching a village for the night. They can also use one or two variations to the route, which are now described:

Stage 3

Can be ended at Corral del Somo, where there is a good well, and plenty of scope for a camp-site.

Stage 4 (a)

Can be started from Corral del Somo, joining the normal route at Serrella Castle. (b) If there is no objection to using a road, there is a direct route with 550m of ascent to Fuente Partagas, where there is excellent camping.

Stage 5

From Fuente Partagas there is a good route up to "Fat Man's Agony" where the normal route is joined.

Stage 4 (a) **Corral Del Somo To Serrella Castle** *5km - 300m ascent - 2h*

Red markers show where the track leaves the main road on the south side, (AV1203 Corral to Tarbena, Km.7.5) 5km from the river bridge at Castell de Castells. Follow a broad track generally south, and in 10min go across a crossroads heading straight for Aixorta and a prominent crag. High above can be seen a forestry road which is your objective. Pass the ruins of an old finca with a well on the left, and zig-zag down a little to join a broad forestry road (15min) near a casita on the left. Ignore a road on the right-hand side, and pass another casita on the left, before turning off right at another junction. There are good views ahead of the Sierra Ferrer, Passo Tancat and Rates, as your road merges with another coming up from the valley. The Bernia Ridge can be seen to the north-west.

Climb gently through pines, and bear right at a junction (50min) to drop slightly, going west to reach Fuente Umbria (on the right). Continue towards your first objective, Serrella Castle, which is visible ahead, and join the walkers' route at Puerta de Castillo.

Stage 4 (b) **Beniarda Bridge To Fuente Partagas** *10km - 2½h*

This is a direct and unremitting climb on a minor road to an excellent camping area. The variation extends this stage by 2km but shortens the ascent of Aitans by over an hour. You pass through the picturesque village of Beniarda, where there are shops and a good restaurant. It is a totally different sort of walk from the normal route, which ascends the valley by easy stages.

Leave the normal route and walk up the narrow surfaced road to the south. It climbs steeply out of the valley, passing a fuente on the right, and the municipal swimming pool on the left. Excellent views of the reservoir and Guadalest and, as you pass through an archway, look back to see the shrine on San Francisco. Go through the main square with the church and a fountain, to an upper square near the school, where there is a bar. Now you must use the road, passing a good restaurant on the right, and in 1km you reach the main C3313 road, on which you turn right. This road can be very busy at times, so make sure you walk on the LEFT, facing the traffic. In 1km pass another good restaurant on the left, and just round the bend, go off left (south), to climb to the village of Benifato. You are now on a country road again, free of traffic. As you are about to enter the village, turn off right at a house (La Foya) on to an access road which twists and turns for 3km to reach the Fuente Partagas, where you can camp for the night under the protection of the crags. The views over the Guadalest Valley and the day's route over Serrella are outstanding. The road continues upwards to Puerta Mulero, and after 15min, there is a deep ice-pit on the south side, about 100m from the road.

Towards The Partagas Rocks

Behind the Fuente Partagas can be seen the solid wall of double cliffs which are the Partagas, and it is necessary to first outflank them by turning them on their eastern end. To do this, strike up west-south-west keeping a prominent crag (Garden Crag) on your right, towards a small col, then seek out an indistinct path with zig-zags upwards in the same direction, until the masts on the summit of Aitana are visible. Look back now, and see that the impressive Garden Crag is, in fact, cultivated nearly to the summit, and you have glorious views of the coast, Peñon d'Ifach, the Bernia and Mala del Llop, with Confrides Castle just below the ridge. Carry on heading for the summit masts for a while, passing a deposito and a spring, until you reach a large flat area, which gives onto a broad shelf running almost parallel with the main ridge. You can now see all the summit installations.

To "Fat Man's Agony"

Change direction to south-east to follow below the Partagas cliffs away from the summit. You have outflanked the lower cliffs, and have to cross another band to join the main ridge of Aitana itself. Rejoin the walkers' route to "Fat Man's Agony".

BARRANCO GALLYSTERO AT THE START OF THE FIG TREE WALK TO THE FORAT NEGRE

Appendix

COSTA BLANCA MOUNTAIN WALKERS

"An informal group of those happy people who enjoy taking strenuous exercise in the magnificent Sierras of the Levant, formed to provide companionship on the mountains, sharing enjoyment and knowledge of the high places of the Costa Blanca".

What was true in May 1987, when the Group was formed on the summit of the Peñon d'Ifach, is still true today. We have always resisted the temptation to form a "Club", and remain still extremely informal. There is no membership, therefore no membership fee. The modest expenses of organising the Group are provided for by members donating 200 pesetas (twice per year), for which they receive a full programme of walks, and a comprehensive newsletter, which keeps them in touch with Group activities. All other publications or badges, etc., are the responsibility of individual members, who voluntarily accept this work, subject only to two criteria: (a) that the items be supplied at cost to members, and (b) that no charge falls on the Group.

The Group comprises about 50 regular residents of the Costa Blanca, supplemented by an increasing number of "Winterers" and, of course, holiday-makers.

Every season, from the beginning of October to the end of May, the 20 Leaders of the Group (Cuerpo del Guias) take over 2000 walkers into the mountains and, what is more important, bring them back again, tired, but elated. We basically still remain an English-speaking Group but, at the last count, 21 nationalities were identified. In 1993, we welcomed our first Spanish Leader, with the distinguished name of Cristobal Colon (Christopher Columbus).

We maintain friendly relations with all other walking groups on the Costa Blanca, especially the Spanish Mountaineering Clubs at Alcoy, Altea, and Calpe.

In 1992, the Group celebrated its Fifth Anniversary in grand style, again on the summit of the Peñon d'Ifach. Founder members were invested with special souvenir medals, and the chairman was pleased to present certificates to those who had completed the Costa Blanca Mountain Way. This 100-150km long-distance walk, right across our walking area, Las Marinas, was instituted especially to celebrate our Fifth Anniversary.

In our Fifth Anniversary year, we were flattered and gratified to find that *Lookout Magazine* (the premier English-language magazine in Spain) had chosen our Group out of 80 others, to feature on the cover and in the main article as "an example of a new type of Club and a new type of resident, a Group of active people who desire to know Spain better".

Walking is probably the most popular recreation on the Costa Blanca, and mountain walking is the quintessence of this pastime. Although we are the oldest-established walking group in this area, there are now many more informal groups, some founded by our own members, who were dissatisfied with only one walk in the mountains per week. Some publish their programmes in the local papers, as we do.

The walking season starts at the end of September, and usually over 50 walks are provided before the season ends with our AGM on the last Wednesday in May. During the summer months, Leaders meet once each month for lunch, sometimes including a short stroll, and those members who are still in Spain are more than welcome to join them.

The Publications Secretary of the Group provides members with guide-sheets, and a comprehensive Walking Guide to the Costa Blanca Mountain Way, and to the new Gallinera Way.

Anyone who completes the first 5 sections of the Costa Blanca Way is entitled to become a Compañero. Certificates and badges are available at a modest charge, on submission of a suitable log. Information is available from the Secretary, Mary Gowland, La Armonia, Partida Benarrosa, Alcalali, Alicante, fax or tel 648 2241.

Citrus Fruits